# OUT OF AFRICA

# OUT OF AFRICA

## Sub-Saharan Traditional Arts

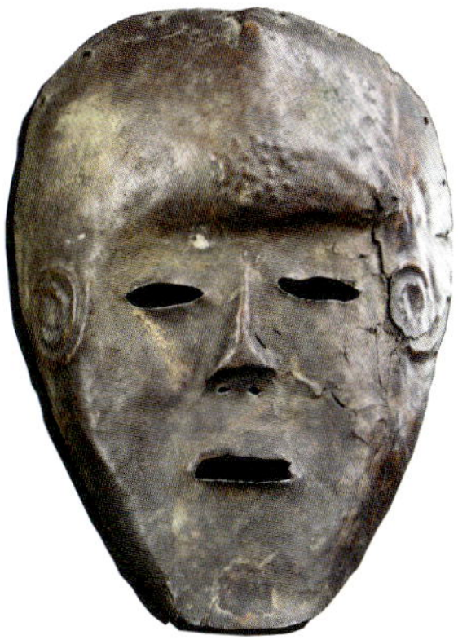

ROY SIEBER

Niangi Batulukisi

Karen Abney Korn

Meredith Palumbo

THE DAYTON ART INSTITUTE

EXHIBITION SCHEDULE
*OUT OF AFRICA: Sub-Saharan Traditional Arts*
*December 16, 2000 - March 4, 2001*

This exhibition is made possible through the generous support of our Presenting Sponsor Fifth Third Bank, as well as the gifts of The Robert S. and Grayce B. Kerr Foundation and Dianne Komminsk.



Published in 2000 by The Dayton Art Institute
456 Belmonte Park North, Dayton, Ohio 45405

Library of Congress Control Number: 00-135136
ISBN: 0-937809-22-5

EXHIBITION CURATOR
Dr. Roy Sieber
*Rudy Professor Emeritus, Indiana University*

EXHIBITION ENTRIES
Dr. Niangi Batulukisi
*Assistant Curator, African Art, The Dayton Art Institute*
Karen Abney Korn
Meredith Palumbo
Martin Pleiss

CATALOGUE DESIGN
Jennifer Perry

EDITORS
Heather Galecka
Ena Murphy
Roy Sieber

MAP OF AFRICA
Charles Meur

PHOTOGRAPHY
Rollyn Puterbaugh

PRINTER
Brown & Kroger Printing Company, USA

Cover: *Mask*, Kongo-Dinga peoples, Democratic Republic of the Congo or Angola, copper, h: 11 inches. Dianne Komminsk Collection

Back Cover: *Figure (dege)*, Dogon peoples, Mali, wood, h: 32 inches. Vincent and Elana Bolling Collection

# CONTENTS

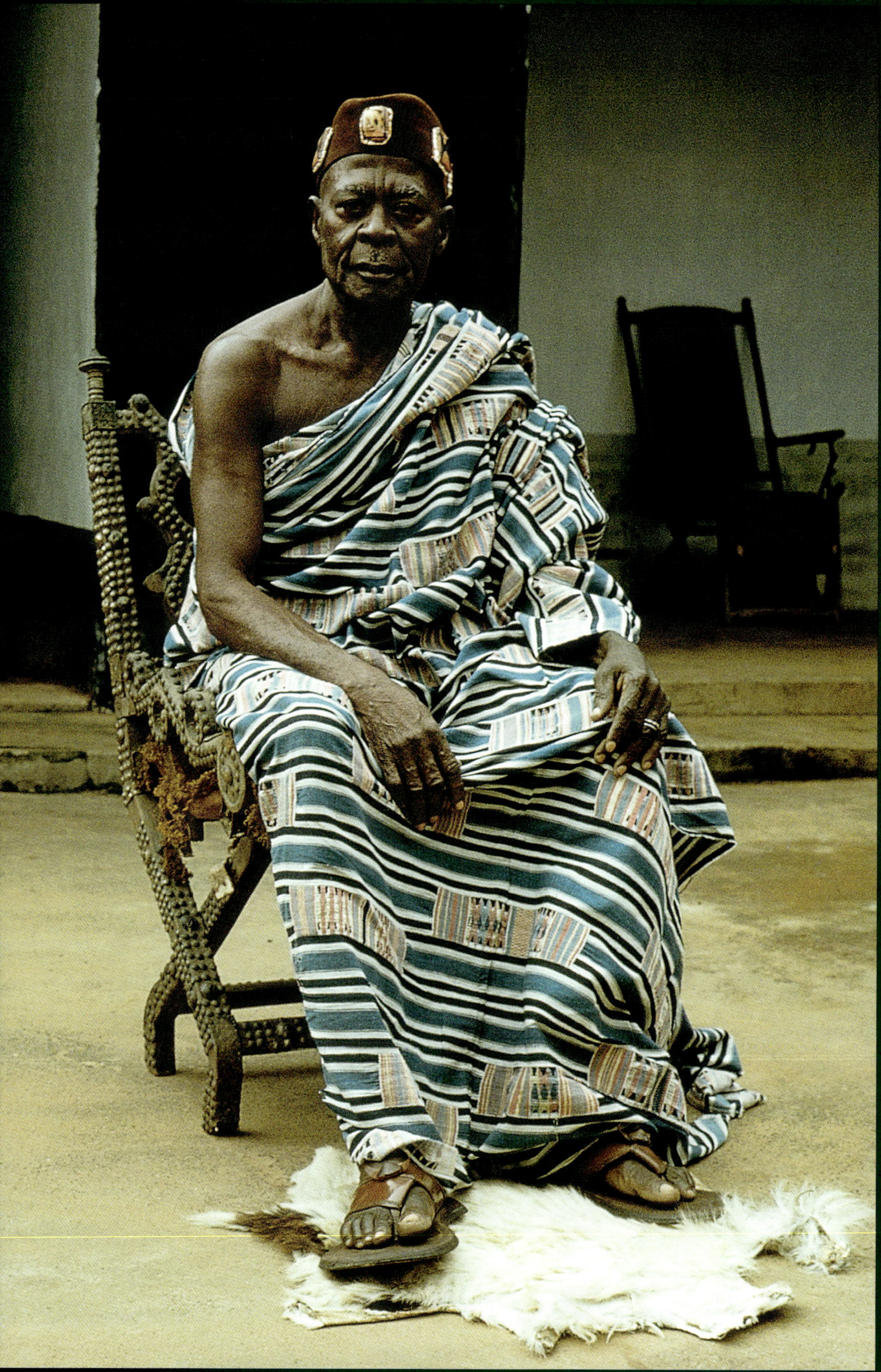

**Nana Kwaku Kumniapa III**

Wrempehene of Kwahu, Kwahu peoples, Twenedurase, Ghana,
Photograph: Roy Sieber, August 1964

*The chief is seated on a prestige chair (akonkromfi) and wearing the kente cloth given to his ancestor, Nana Kumniapa Panin I, by the Asante King (Asantahene), Kofi Kakari, for gallantry during the 1868-71 Krepi war against the Ewes.*

# FOREWORD

*OUT OF AFRICA: Sub-Saharan Traditional Arts* is a testimony to both the beauty and power of African art and to the collectors who have assembled such treasures. This exhibition celebrates a long-standing passion in our community for the art from sub-Saharan Africa. This exhibition also commemorates a resurgence in The Dayton Art Institute's attention to African art as a major focal point for its collection and institutional resources. During the past few years the museum has reinstalled its permanent collection of African art in significantly expanded quarters, added several new key acquisitions through gifts and purchases (thanks in large part to the generosity of Dianne Komminsk, a museum friend and trustee) and curated this landmark exhibition. More important has been the recent creation of a curatorial post dedicated to African art. Made possible through a generous gift from Vincent and Elana Bolling—long-standing supporters, collectors and former trustees of the museum—this is the Art Institute's first curatorial post dedicated solely to the art of Africa and one of only a few such positions in the Midwest.

The impetus for this exhibition can be directly attributed to the creativity and enthusiasm of several of the collectors themselves. A few years ago, in the excitement surrounding the acquisition of a marvelous Hemba sculpture, the idea of a show from area collections was born. LaVerne Shone, a charmingly persuasive collector and former trustee, soon discussed this idea with fellow collectors and friends Dianne Komminsk and Elana Bolling. From there, the idea was met with enthusiastic support from all who listened. Almost overnight a casual conversation gave rise to an exciting exhibition concept that has now come to fruition.

The choice of a curator to organize this exhibition was simple and straightforward. No one but Dr. Roy Sieber would do. "Papa" Sieber to many of his close friends in Dayton, gladly and fortuitously accepted the challenge despite his usual daunting and overwhelming schedule of obligations. So much for retirement.

The passion for collecting African art in this community runs deep, but it is a relatively new phenomenon. Although Mrs. Carnell and other founders of the Art Institute voraciously collected art from around the world, they paid little attention to art from Africa. It was not until the arrival of Tom Colt as director of the museum in 1957 that an interest in the wonderful and varied traditions of African art was demonstrated. Several collectors, all of whom have generously agreed to lend their works to the museum for this exhibition, quickly shared Tom's passion. By the late 1960s, the museum itself began to actively collect in this area. The acquisition of the Bena Lulua sculpture from the Congo in 1970 coincided with the first major special exhibition of African art at the museum, *Masterpieces of Art from Black Africa.* Tom and his wife, Priscilla, an expert in African art, ignited a flurry of acquisitions that included gifts from Vincent and Elana Bolling (*Twin (Ibeji) Figures*, Yoruba peoples, Nigeria, 1975.63a and 1975.63b), David King (*Cap mask in the form of a buffalo head*, Mama peoples, Nigeria, (1975.53), and Allan Gerdau (*Female Spirit Figure*, Baule peoples, Ivory Coast, 1975.59) as well as several significant purchases including the *Kongo peoples male fetish figure from the Congo* (1978.111) that had previously been exhibited in *Art from Zaire: 100 Masterworks from the National Collection* (1975). Tom and Priscilla Colt also contributed a number of African works shortly after Tom's retirement from his post at the Art Institute. In 1985, in memory of Tom Colt, who died that year, the museum acquired the magnificent *Lobala slit gong drum from the Congo* (1985.39). The work was purchased through the generous gifts of Tom's friends and supporters, many of whom shared his passion for African art.

More than a dozen years would pass before the museum would again acquire a major work of African art. In 1998, shortly after the museum reopening following its massive expansion and renovation, the Art Institute purchased a magnificent *Hemba peoples standing male figure* (1998.19), a stunning *Bozo peoples antelope head puppet* (1998.94) and a *Yoruba peoples headdress* (1998.95). These works were complemented by a significant gift from Dianne Komminsk who contributed a group of 11 works of African art including a powerful *Luba peoples throne stool in the form of a caryatid female figure* (1999.20), a *Luba peoples mask* (1999.19) and a graceful *Hemba peoples bow stand* crafted from iron and wood (1999.26). This wonderful gift was quickly followed with funds given to the museum by Dianne Komminsk to purchase an impressive and complete *Kuosi Society elephant costume* (1999.76) from Cameroon. This latter work is now a focal point to the entrance of the Gallery of African Art.

I would be remiss for failing to mention the role played by Marc Léo Felix in the creation of many of these collections, including that of the Art Institute. Throughout the past three or more decades, Marc Léo Felix, a dealer, author and connoisseur, has traveled from his base in Brussels to show us the finest examples of African art. His network of friends and collectors has aided us tremendously in this exhibition.

Today, at the dawn of the 21st century, the museum stands poised to further the study and appreciation of African art. This major exhibition, a new curatorial post devoted exclusively to this art form, and a corps of active and enthusiastic collectors provides great promise for the future.

*OUT OF AFRICA* is dedicated to the spirit of collecting, to African art and especially to the passion of the collectors who have made this wonderful endeavor possible.

Alexander Lee Nyerges
Director and CEO
THE DAYTON ART INSTITUTE

# ACKNOWLEDGMENTS

First and foremost The Dayton Art Institute would like to thank the collectors who made this exhibition possible. Their connoisseurship and passion for African art was the impetus for *OUT OF AFRICA*: Dianne Komminsk, Art Shone, LaVerne Shone, Irv and Tracy Bieser, Jr., Willis Bing and Audrey Davis, Vince and Elana Bolling, The Dayton Society of Natural History/Boonshoft Museum of Discovery, Bonnie Bozorgi, Dr. and Mrs. William E. Rogers, Don and Sue Dugan and Pam Houk. This exhibition is also made possible through the generous support of our Presenting Sponsor Fifth Third Bank, as well as the gifts of The Robert S. and Grayce B. Kerr Foundation and Dianne Komminsk.

*OUT OF AFRICA* pays tribute not only to the power and beauty of sub-Saharan African art but also to the abundance of fine works found in the Dayton area. This exhibition showcases the lenders' impressive collections and their generous willingness to share personal treasures with the community. The Dayton Art Institute would like to express its gratitude especially to Dianne Komminsk, whose generosity provided for this beautiful catalogue and LaVerne Shone, who enthusiastically assisted with the planning of the exhibition, catalogue and its photography.

Dr. Roy Sieber, Rudy Professor of Fine Arts Emeritus at Indiana University (Bloomington) and noted African art scholar, served as the guest curator for *OUT OF AFRICA*. His profound knowledge and great vision as one of the pioneers in African art historical studies was paramount to this endeavor. His colleagues, Karen Abney Korn, who assisted with formulating the checklist, interviewing the collectors, catalogue photography and various other tasks and Meredith Palumbo, who worked closely with Dr. Sieber on the catalogue, were integral to the success of this project. Dr. Sieber also wishes to thank Kent Davis, Jay Heilman, William Itter, Charles D. Miller III, Budd Stalnaker and Sophia Sieber. In addition, Dr. Niangi Batulukisi, The Dayton Art Institute's new assistant curator of African art, provided essential support and contributed to the catalogue text.

*OUT OF AFRICA* would not have been possible without the Art Institute's able, talented staff. Helen Pinkney, curator of textiles, with the assistance of Suman Shenoi, worked tirelessly on the textiles. With great precision, Mary Ellen Goeke and Betsy Wilson assisted with the exhibition's logistics. Having carefully designed the installation, Martin Pleiss, along with the help of Todd Hall and Sally Kurtz, prepared and installed the exhibition. The catalogue is the result of Jennifer Perry's fine design, Charles Meur's mapping skills, Heather Galecka's editing, Rollyn Puterbaugh's photography and Sara Spidel's coordination. Roberta Simon, assistant to the director and Dominique Vasseur, former senior curator, provided both vision and hard labor in the conception and realization of *OUT OF AFRICA*. Finally, the Art Institute extends its gratitude to curatorial assistant to the director Ena Murphy. Ena provided much-needed continuity and coordination as the project coordinator. This exhibition stands as a worthy enterprise—both in its presentation of marvelous objects from significant world cultures and as the fine achievement of the collectors, scholars and museum staff who realized it.

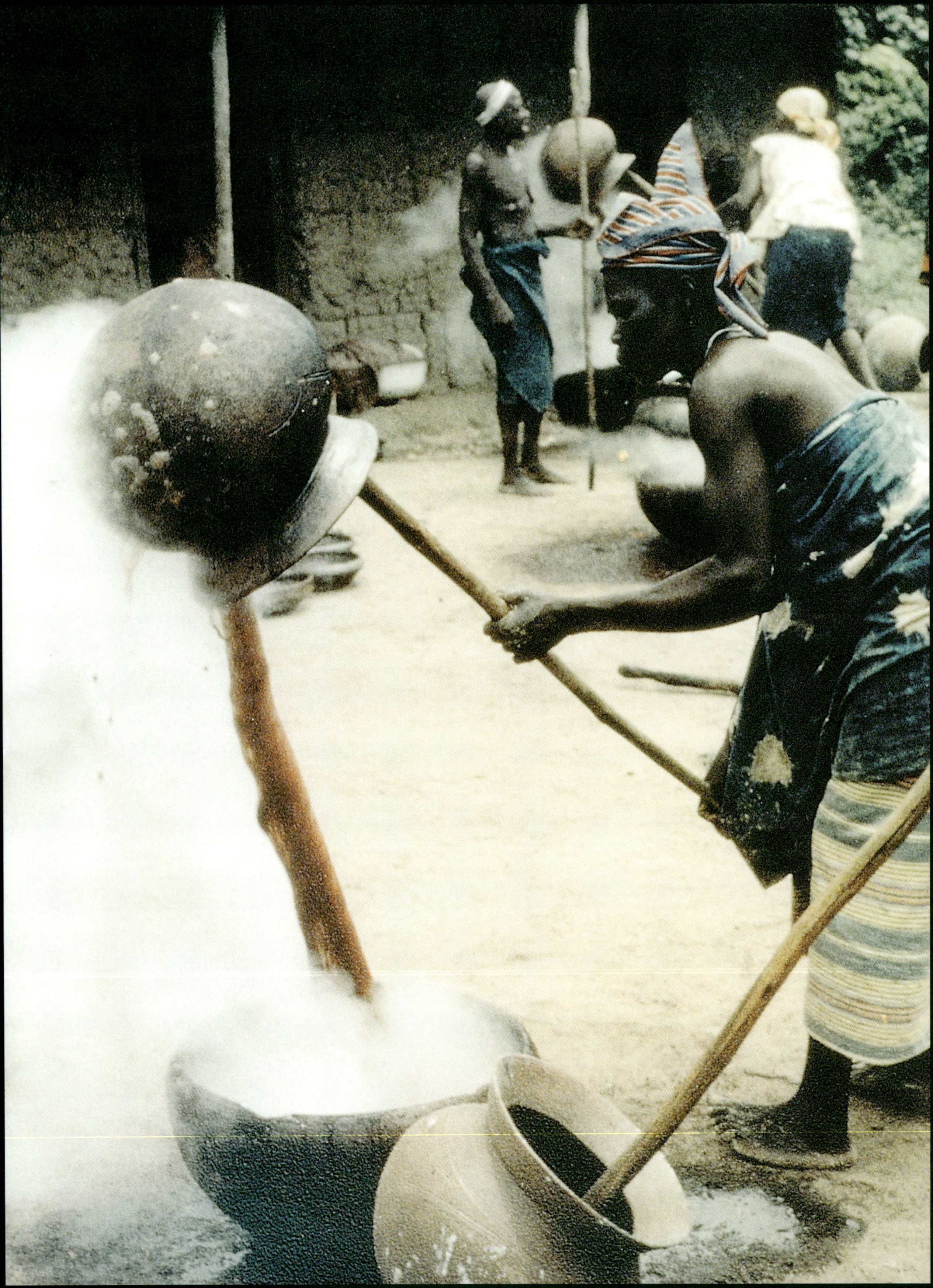

**Woman potter**
Mo peoples, Branam, Ghana,
Photograph: Roy Sieber, April 1967

*While still too hot to handle, vessels are lifted from the surface firing area with a long pole and dipped into a vegetable sealant. The pots are very resistant to thermal shock and make ideal vessels for cooking over an open flame.*

# INTRODUCTION

African art is many-splendored. In cultures that were not dependent on mass production, objects that expressed religious beliefs, demonstrated leadership or were for everyday use were created one-by-one as needed. Although aesthetic judgments were certainly present, contextual and utilitarian considerations took precedence.

Africans did not share the concept of "art" separated from "real life." In fact, art was integrated into African ritual and secular life to a far greater degree than Westerners do. At the same time that the works were respected and their creators known and often celebrated, the attitude toward the objects was remarkably unprecious. Most of the works were of fragile materials and did not survive fire, insects or weather. They were considered life enhancing, functional objects, used until they were gone, then replaced. The flow from creativity to utility to loss and to replacement was normal. Consequently most objects in this exhibition date from the late 19th or early 20th century unless otherwise indicated. As a result, we have neither history of styles of earlier artists nor of masterpieces preserved. Each generation had to create its world of objects anew, recreating earlier forms and types as best remembered. Indeed each object in this exhibition has been wrestled from its context, its life cycle and would long since have disappeared.

Masks were used in the initiation of young men and women into adulthood, or as part of the equipment of societies or cults. Figures may have celebrated ancestors, served as protection against malign forces or ensured the continuity of the group through human or agricultural fertility. In short, all ritual works were protective and were believed to guarantee a better life and a more secure world.

At the same time, many objects considered decorative or utilitarian could reflect the status of the owner. Some were works of intensely personal significance such as Asante stools that housed the soul of the owner, Luba ivory amulets in human form that honored ancestors or mask-like amulets that announced a man's membership into adult Dan society. Although practical, furniture, ceramics, currency, weapons and elements of dress were also statements about the place and role of the owner in the culture.

Out of necessity each family produced its own food through subsistence farming often supplemented by hunting, fishing and husbandry. As a result, the contributions to the society by leaders, priests, diviners, musicians, potters, weavers, sculptors and blacksmiths were not their sole responsibility. Nearly every work of art was made by a part-time specialist working on commission from a local patron. Male and female artists worked in different media: men were wood and ivory carvers, weavers, blacksmiths and the masters of the lost-wax technique of copper alloy castings; women were weavers (on a different type of loom from that of men), textile dyers and accomplished ceramists.

The works were created in an astonishing variety of materials, including, but not limited to, wood, ivory, clay, cotton, wool, barkcloth, leather, feathers, beads, shells, iron and copper.

It was a world that in many ways was self-sufficient; one that has, however, changed significantly. The political control of colonial powers and the zeal of missionaries undermined older political, economic, educational and religious foundations. Not that earlier there had never been changes. History is, of course, a constant flow of change. Yet the changes wrought by Europeans over the past few centuries along the coasts and the advance of Islam from the north and east has been greater, more massive, indeed more destructive to older belief systems than any we have reason to believe happened in the preceding millennia.

Roy Sieber
GUEST CURATOR

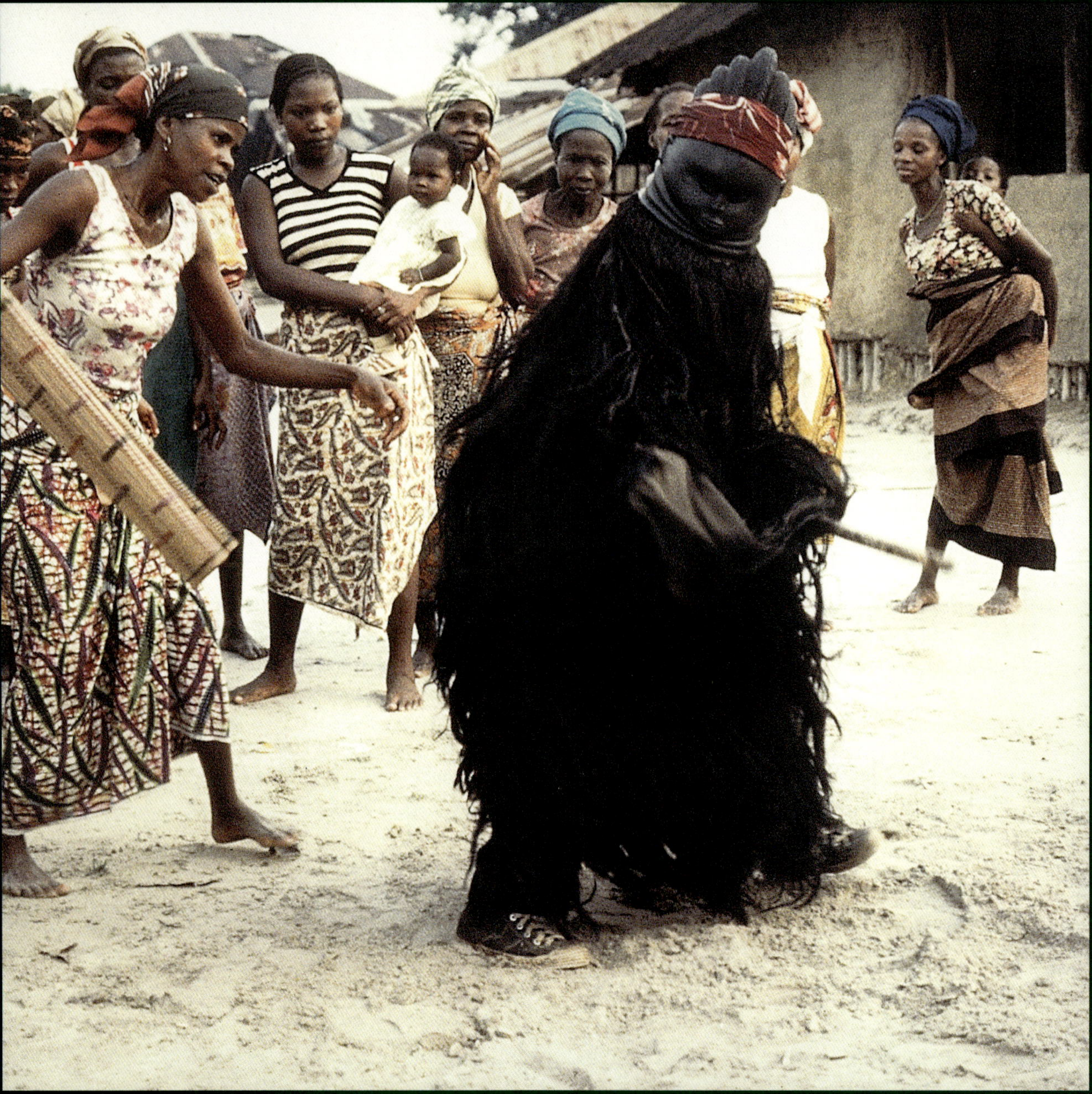

## Nowei masquerader
Dwazahan village, Ma Bahn subgroup, Bassa peoples, Liberia
Photograph: Charles D. Miller, III, 1984

*This Nowei is the senior masquerader of three masked dancers at the opening day of the Sande women's society seven-year cycle of ceremonies. Because she speaks in a secret language a translator accompanies her. As an outside overseer, she supervises all activities during several weeks of the local Bundu initiation activities to ensure that they are properly conducted.*

# LENDERS

The Dayton Art Institute thanks the lenders to this exhibition for their generosity:

Mr. and Mrs. Irvin G. Bieser, Jr.
Vincent and Elana Bolling
Bonnie H. Bozorgi
Willis Bing and Audrey Davis
The Dayton Society of Natural History/Boonshoft Museum of Discovery
Donald and Sue Dugan
Pamela P. Houk
Dianne Komminsk
Dr. and Mrs. William E. Rogers
Arthur Shone
LaVerne Shone

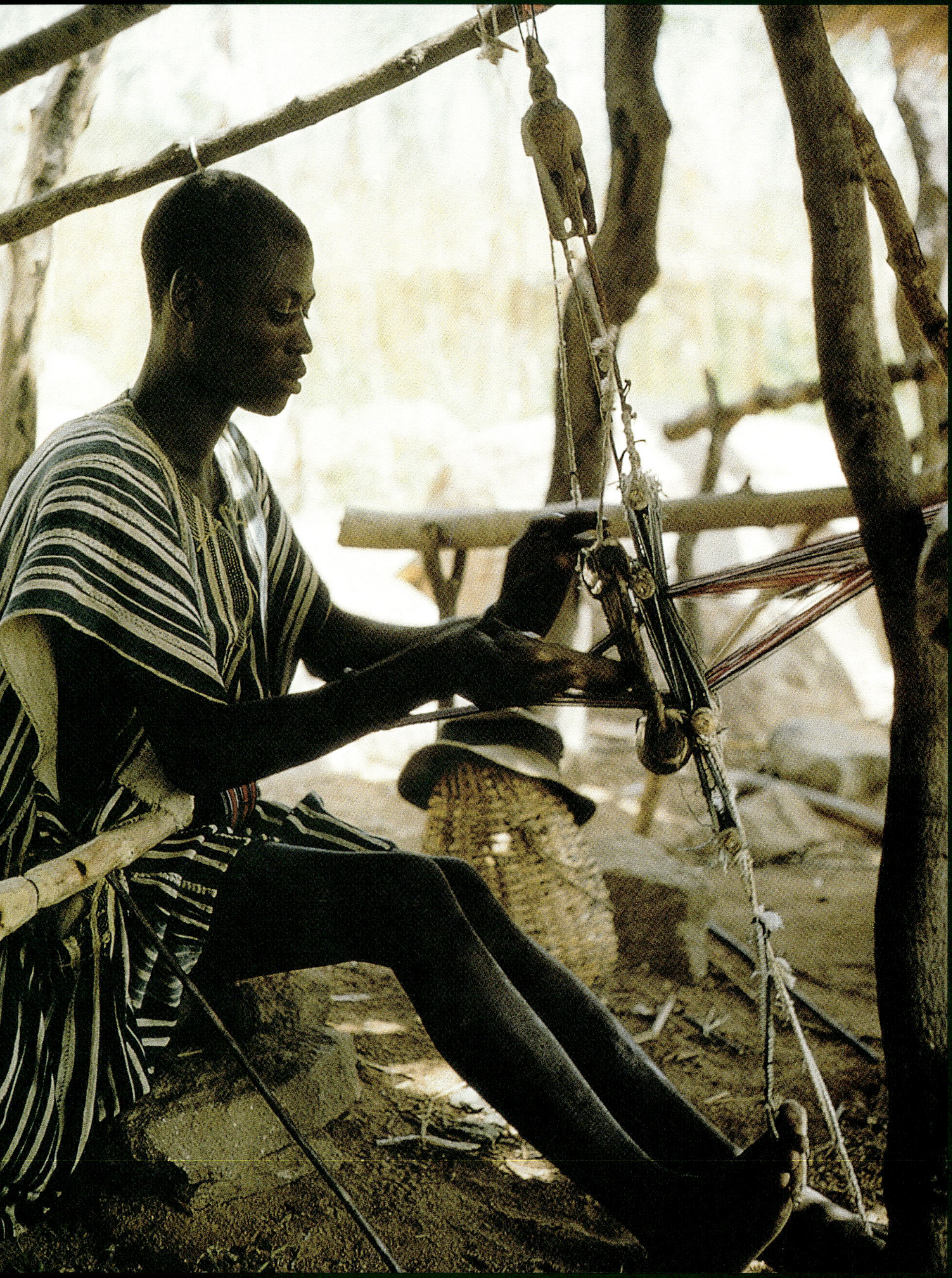

## Male weaver

Frafra peoples, Zoko village, Northern Ghana,
Photograph: Roy Sieber, November 1964

*In west Africa men typically weave on a horizontal loom with two heddles strung over a pulley. Each heddle, made up of rods, reeds or cords carries and separates half the total number of warp threads. Alternately raised and lowered by foot pedals, they create sheds in the warp for the weft threads. The long warp threads crossed by short weft threads result in a long narrow strip of cloth. The strip is rolled into a wheel that may serve as currency or be cut into segments that are sewn together to create a cloth six or more strips wide to serve as a blanket, a wrap or be made into clothing.*

# LENDERS' STATEMENTS

Collecting art is a pleasurable activity, and at times, an obsession. There are nearly as many reasons for collecting African art as there are collectors. Karen Abney Korn has interviewed the eleven private lenders as well as the former curator of the Boonshoft Museum of Discovery.

Each was asked to select a favorite work to accompany his or her statement. For some this proved difficult; how does one choose among many favorites? Yet, eventually each did settle on one work, and those choices are as varied and revealing as are the statements.

I wish to thank the lenders, collectively and individually, for their patience (forbearance might be a better word) with me and for agreeing to lend their treasures to this exhibition that focuses on the older sacred and secular arts of sub-Saharan Africa.

Roy Sieber

# IRVIN BIESER, JR.

I began collecting African art in 1967 and collected until around 1970 while I was in the Peace Corps in Liberia. I have continued a bit, but I did the bulk of my collecting during those three years. At the time, I had had little exposure to African art. My parents were avid art collectors, but they did not collect African art. When I was in school at Harvard, I had taken two art history courses and the only real reference to African art was through Picasso and others who drew inspiration from the formal qualities of African sculpture.

While in Africa, I met people who sold art, not those who produced it. These sellers, called "Charlies," were people who traveled to other regions and returned with art objects to sell. They were usually Muslim and had an Islamic name, but we all called them by number. The "Charlies" would come to my door almost every night after they learned that I was interested in collecting. They would lay out all of their pieces on the floor and describe each one. The prices were inconsistent. I started with sculptures and masks, and then became interested in other things as well, such as textiles and contemporary painting.

Through trial and error and by talking with other collectors, I learned about collecting. A good friend of mine had more experience with collecting and gave me little tips about the importance of patina in understanding fakery. While I made a few mistakes, I eventually purchased some good pieces. As it is for most people, time and money were the primary limits on my collecting. I was operating on a subsistence Peace Corps salary at the time, so sometimes I had to dip into my savings. However, it was a different era then as far as prices go and I was one step closer to the source.

It has always been important for me to have something real—an object is one that is produced without a thought of copying another tradition. Something real is created for immediate use and incorporates somebody's immediate understanding or perception of the world. If a carver tries to copy a mask that comes from a fine tradition but that tradition and the people who produced and used these masks are gone, I may appreciate his work or craftsmanship, but I can't think of these objects as "real."

I returned to Liberia in 1997 to serve as a monitor in the electoral process and learned how much things had changed from the 1960s. I came to understand that you just can't recreate all of those sources in a matter of a four- or five-day visit. I would agree with the general consensus that the majority of world-class pieces of African art are out of Africa at this point. Occasionally something good still comes out, but the production of objects for the marketplace is so common that 99 out of 100 things you see now have been recently created.

I think that some of my most wonderful experiences with collecting African art occurred when I was obtaining a piece from the source. Being able to talk with someone and buy a piece right there in the village was great. There were things, however, that I purchased without being sure of the quality. The most horrible result of these circumstances is when you drop or chip a piece causing it to crack and there is brand new wood inside. There are also some things you buy by chance or circumstance that you don't think much about until you later realize they are real gems.

The experience of collecting is distinctly different from other forms of consuming, such as shopping. I do not enjoy shopping, but love collecting. When collecting, you embark on a quest for a beautiful treasure which brings you in contact with interesting people and exciting places. It can be compared to trout fishing: It isn't the fishing that is so great an experience, but rather that it takes you to some of the most beautiful places in the world.

I love living with all of the art I collect. I enjoy being surrounded by beauty and by objects that make a house unique or distinctive in a way that reflects my interests and experiences. I simply enjoy getting away from the typical.

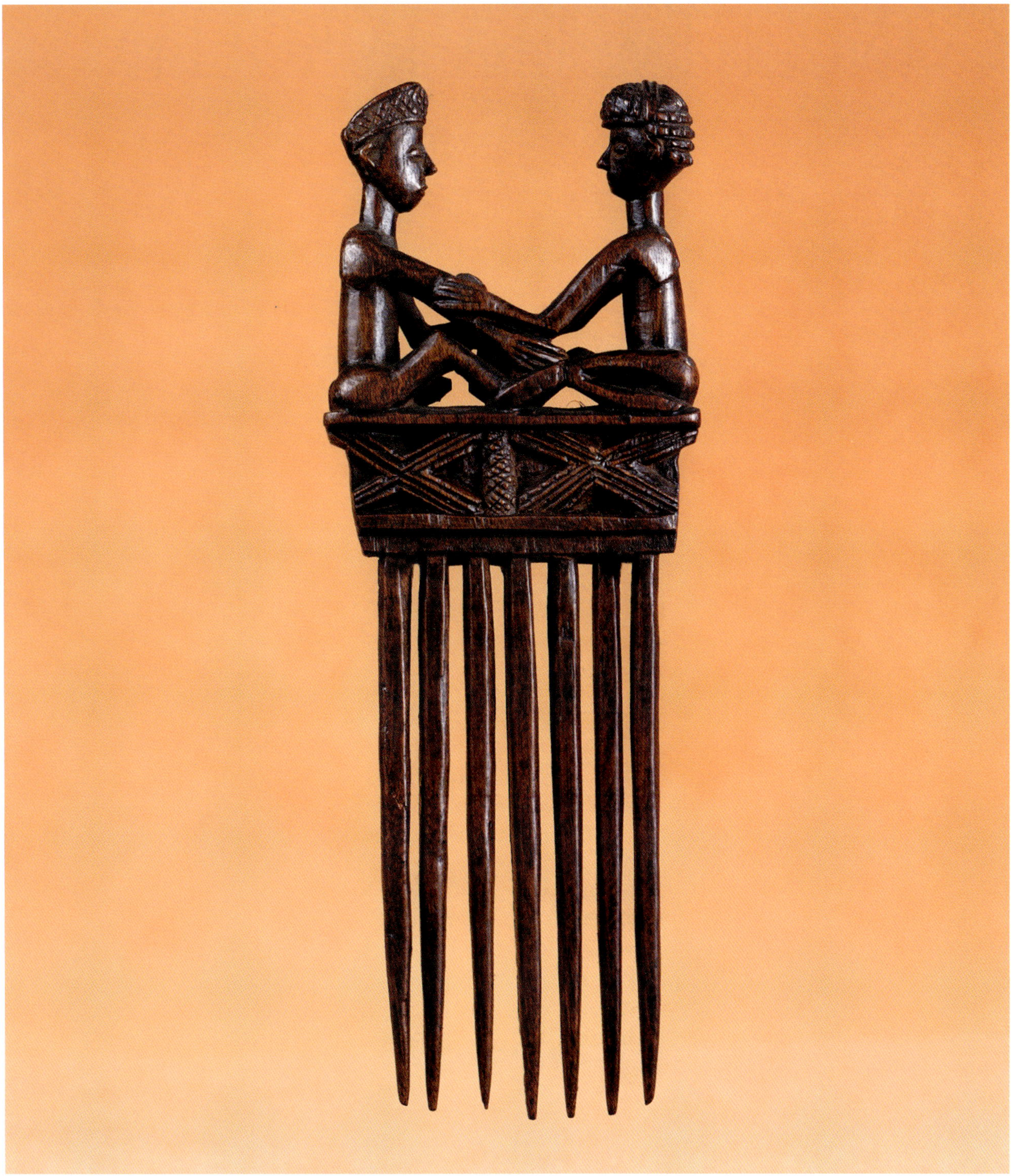

## Comb (cisakulu)

Chokwe or Lunda peoples, Democratic Republic of the Congo, wood, h: 7 inches
Mr. and Mrs. Irvin G. Bieser, Jr. Collection

*Both a useful hairdressing tool and an elegant ornament, finely carved combs are reserved for dignitaries. They combine function and aesthetic refinement (utotombo) and exhibit the acute Chokwe sense of decoration.*

# VINCENT & ELANA BOLLING

We began our interest in African art following The Dayton Art Institute's purchase of the fabulous Bena Lalua figure in the museum's Permanent Collection. When Tom Colt, who was the director at the time, "unveiled" the new purchase at a board meeting, we were emotionally taken with it. Afterward, we spoke with some friends, who also loved the piece, about their response to it and together we began our quest for knowledge of and exposure to African art.

Aside from this one other couple, we were quite alone in our passion. Over time, we became very good friends with Tom Colt and really valued his insight and ideas on art, but we did not always agree with him. For example, one of our favorite pieces in our collection is the Dogon figure. One day, we were having a drink with Tom Colt and he looked at this piece and said, "Well, I *think* that is art." We said, "What do you mean? Of course it is." After all, this man purchased that fantastic sculpture for the museum. He replied that his criteria for something being art was that it was man-made. He felt that the termite destruction and the weathering that had helped to form this piece made it suspect as an art object. For us, what makes this piece so spectacular is the way that a human hand worked in concert with nature to produce something so beautiful.

We began collecting through a dealer in New York. Later, we developed a relationship with a dealer who came to Dayton on a regular basis. Knowledge is funny in this field, and we try to collect pieces that are truly museum quality ones, but to know for certain is difficult. In collecting, it is difficult to know all that you need to choose a good piece. Therefore, we tend to trust our instincts and have to love it to want to live with it.

We purchase items that we both like, which causes us to sometimes not purchase something one of us loves that the other simply cannot respond to. Our approach differs somewhat. Vince likes to collect pieces based on the emotional impact without concerning himself with ethnographic information. He believes that his attraction is so subjective that describing what attracts him is difficult. It is better to ask someone who has watched him collect what he likes best. Elana, while passionate about her emotional attraction to a piece, is always intrigued by the contextual and ethnographic information provided by the dealer. She enjoys learning about the objects prior to and following the purchase.

The abstraction of certain pieces reminds one of Picasso. These were the kind of formal aspects that were compelling to both of us when we first began our interest in African art. No matter how much you understand about the art, if the objects do not speak to you, you should simply direct your interest elsewhere. It is the kind of art that really hits you in the gut much in the way that music does; it is visceral. It evokes so many different feelings. However, we always say that we have to want to live with a piece. There have been pieces that have evoked strong responses in both of us, yet we were not interested in living with them.

Collecting art for investment purposes does not interest either of us. However, we both value authenticity in that a piece must be what it purports to be. It has to be legitimate. Yet, forgers are to be respected because the work they do to forge a piece of artwork is phenomenal. We remember sitting on Roy Sieber's floor in his living room while he looked at a Kota piece that a friend was going to purchase. Roy pondered the piece and said, "You know, it is just too perfect. There is something about it that makes me think that it can't be real." If it is worth 20¢ or one million dollars, we don't care. We just want it to be what the dealer says it is.

Our second home is decorated much differently than our one in Dayton. It is a mix of contemporary art, African art and some interesting furniture. It is very open and light and much more eclectic. Here, we have a mixture of our antique French furniture, European paintings and African art. We enjoy living with the African art in both environments, and we enjoy sharing our collections with our friends and family. All of our children have developed an interest in the arts, and this pleases us greatly as parents and grandparents.

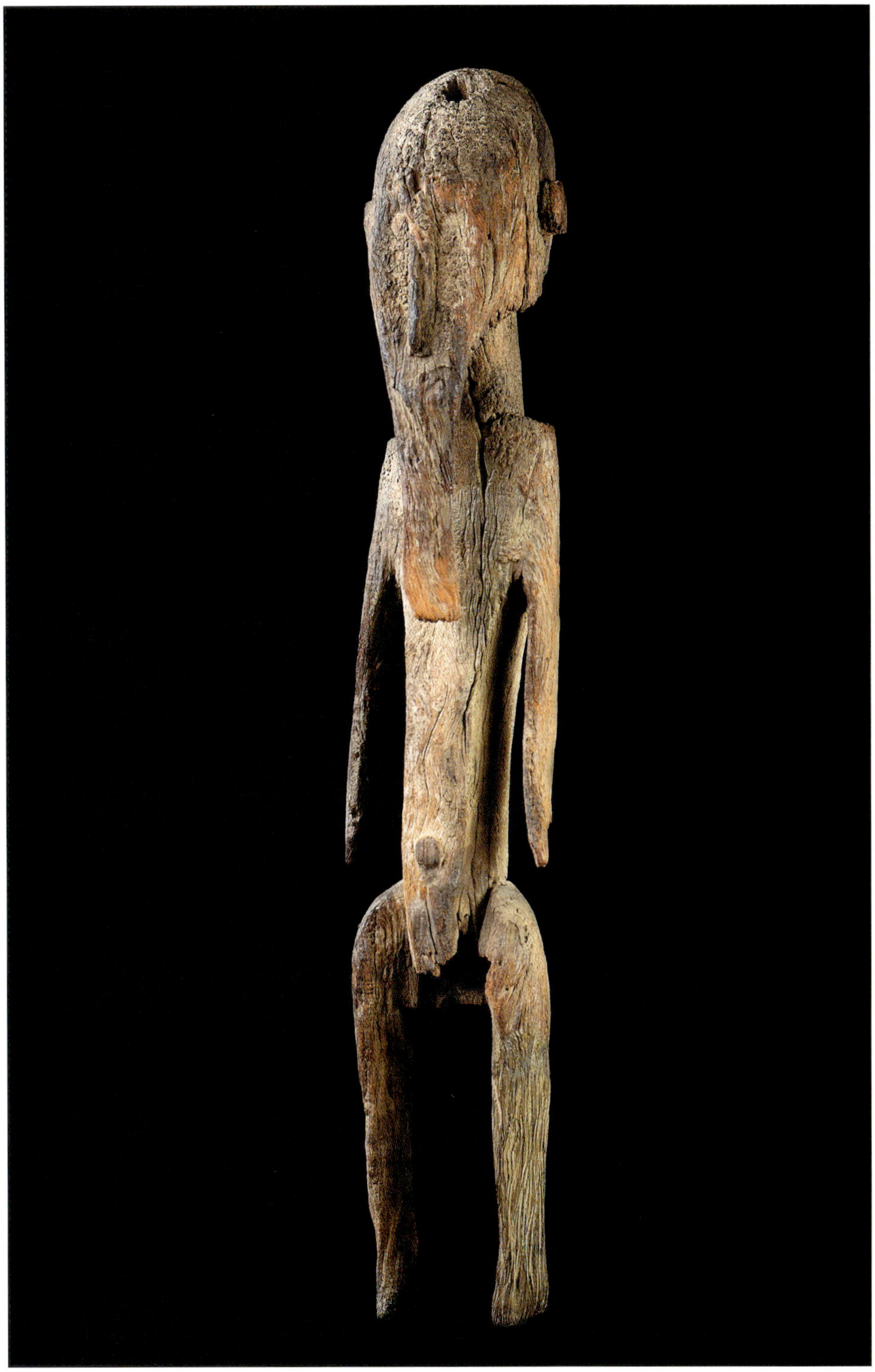

## Figure (dege)

Dogon peoples, Mali, wood, h: 32 inches
Vincent and Elana Bolling Collection

*The Dogon are noted for their amazing array of ancestor figures at the core of their religious beliefs. Some represent the primordial couple; others, depicting more recent ancestors, are the focal point of family shrines. Some have been dated earlier than the 14th century. This figure is in an unusual style and possibly is quite early, showing traces of its exposure to the elements.*

# BONNIE BOZORGI

I have been fortunate to have had the opportunity to travel a great deal, and developed an interest in art because of my travels. My first interest in collecting was in more traditional art forms, such as paintings and prints. When my ex-husband and I would travel, we would bring back antique prints as they transported well. In addition to African art, my current collecting interests include antique silver, Majolica, antique beads and tortoise shell objects.

Approximately 14 years ago, a friend of mine invited me to meet an African art dealer. I liked the objects very much, which surprised me because I did not think that I would. I took my daughter with me that first time. She was in high school, and through her education and our family's travels, had been exposed to Picasso and other Western artists who drew inspiration from African art. It was so interesting to see her respond to the objects in front of her. She pointed out a mask that she thought reminded her of Picasso's art and said that she liked it. She urged me to purchase it and asked the dealer how much it cost. Well, he replied something like "80," and she said, "Oh Mom, we have to buy it, it is only $80!" I gently said, "No, honey, I think he means $80,000!" She was floored.

So, I began by purchasing some of the little Pende ivories because I like the idea that I can actually wear them. I use my silver and antique dishes—everything that I collect. I do not typically want to collect things that I am not going to use in some way. I do not, as of now, have a very large African art collection. I would say that I am just starting.

Approximately six years ago, I traveled to Nairobi, Kenya, and went out on a safari to some game preserves. I loved it. The beautiful skies were such a deep blue set off against the shades of brown during the dry season, making all color seem very intense. I thought that perhaps I could find some art when I was over there, but the things that they sell to tourists are not of good quality, which gave me a whole new respect for dealers who track down quality pieces.

I have found that I have a wonderful eye. I say this partially in jest because inevitably the pieces that I am most interested in are the most expensive ones. If I were to come upon a windfall of money, I can think of a number of pieces I would love to acquire. I never feel like I am settling, though. I do not purchase something unless I really love it. I think that certain pieces of art or antiques call my name. When I go to an antique show, for example, I will look at something and walk on by. It will seem to call out to me, "Bonnie, come back here!" If I go back and it is still compelling me to buy it, I will if the price is right.

I have purchased most of my African objects from one dealer. However, there are a few pieces that I have purchased at antique shows that are passable but not outstanding examples. At a gallery near Hilton Head Island where I have my second home, they sell African objects as well as ones made by the Gullah people from the coastal islands where escaped slaves set up their own communities hundreds of years ago. I have become very interested in their culture and have begun to collect some art produced by a well-known African-American artist who grew up in that area.

There is something in African art to which I really respond. Somewhere in the simplicity of it, there are elements of sophistication and spirituality. However I don't like all of it. I do not respond to some of the pieces that are very fierce or ugly, but those that have a goodness to them draw a strong, positive response from me. I like the pieces with spirit and those that are utilitarian. I am attracted to the spirituality of many of the pieces, which is somewhat odd for me, as I am truly not a "religious" person. I am simply moved by a feeling that I get from some of the pieces, but cannot put this feeling into words.

My favorite piece is the Ovimbundu scepter. What appeals to me the most about this piece is that it is simply beautiful. I like the fact that one side of the top pictures a male face and the other a female one. Supposedly, chiefs used this staff to bring harmony and peace to the tribe. I thought, "Well, if it can do that for the tribe, maybe it can do that for my house!"

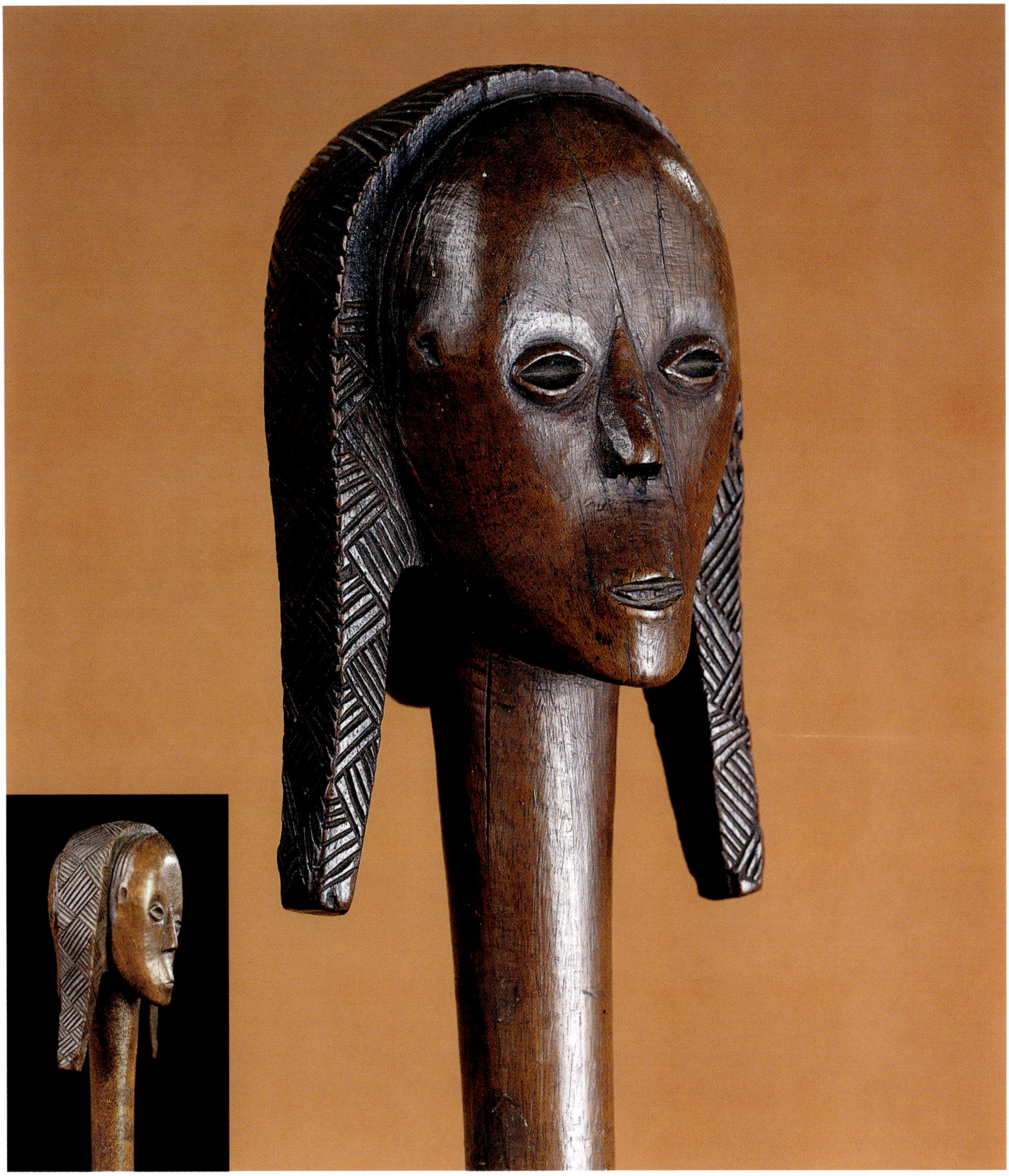

# Baton

[Detail]

Ovimbundu peoples, Angola, wood, w: 20 1/2 inches
Bonnie H. Bozorgi Collection

*Most probably a royal scepter, this baton is somewhat unusual with its male and female janus finial. Usually royal batons depict a female head with an elaborate coiffure.*

# WILLIS BING DAVIS

In both my undergraduate and graduate training as an artist and educator, I never received information about any African-American or African artists—not a name, no reference to subject matter, nor even a general explanation of the content of African or African-American art. I wanted to be as sound an educator and artist as I could, so I began my own personal research on Australian Aboriginal, African, Native American and Pre-Columbian arts. It gave me a greater understanding of what art was about. I learned that art is more than just a pretty painting on the wall or something you set on a pedestal. It reflects the spiritual, cultural and social values of people. As I looked at traditional societies, I saw that the role of the artist within these societies was similar to what I wanted to do with my personal role in life as an artist and an educator.

I began collecting sometime in the early 1970s. I had the opportunity to visit Africa on a study grant in 1973, and being poor at the time, I was cautious about what I collected. I focused on textiles because I had always had a great affinity for textiles and fiber arts. This was good because they are also much more affordable to collect. When I was teaching at DePaul University, I remember traveling down to Bloomington to hear any public lecture by Roy Sieber. I had learned early on from him that it is good to take a focal area rather than a shotgun approach to collecting.

When choosing a piece, my immediate emotional reaction motivates my purchase. I get excited when I see a piece that I really like. It may be the tactile sensation of the piece or the embellishment of the surface that I respond to. It has to do with the quality and the craftsmanship. I don't want it to be a new piece of wood that is blackened with shoe polish. A certain quality of the piece tells me it is not trying to be something other than what it actually is. I have very seldom met up with a dealer with the intention of obtaining a particular piece. If I see an object, it feels right and I like what I hear the dealer telling me about it as well as what I see, I will purchase it.

I have always wanted to surround myself with things African. I want to be able to draw from my response to these wonderful, colorful, textured objects and incorporate that response into my work. Having focused predominantly on west African art, I don't know if this has been an intellectual decision because a tremendous amount of African-American interest in African art is centered on west Africa. Historically, this is due in part to the slave trade, but it is also a much more geographically accessible area for travelers.

African art has been a tremendous resource and inspiration for my own work and has actually permeated every part of my life. It guides what I do and how I do it, including where I choose to teach. I always joke with students that while I may seem very well educated and can carry on a conversation about the merits of the work of Monet, Renoir, Cézanne and Delacroix, traditional art history left me empty. What was missing from the pages of these textbooks was *me*. I see myself as a descendent of the traditional artists of the past. With all of the forced migration, slavery, et cetera in between, I feel that I can relate to the "first man." I embrace African art as a part of my heritage and a legacy from the past, as well as appreciating it from an aesthetic point of view.

I am fortunate that my wife shares my passion for African and African-American art. It would be very hard for me if she did not. You know how we men often accuse our ladies of sneaking extra shoes into the closet! Well, I am fortunate that she understands and shares my feelings. When African dealers are in town, we invite them to dinner and over time, they have become friends of the family. She shares my view that as African-American collectors of African art, we are custodians of the culture. We view these objects as ones that are not ours forever, but rather that we are guarding them or simply possessing them for a period.

At one time, I thought a lot about the fact that some of these things may not truly be mine to possess. I still regret that the artist will never see the money I am paying to the dealer for the object. I prefer to collect objects that are no longer needed by someone for their original use. After all, I have a strong belief that it is people that are truly precious, not things.

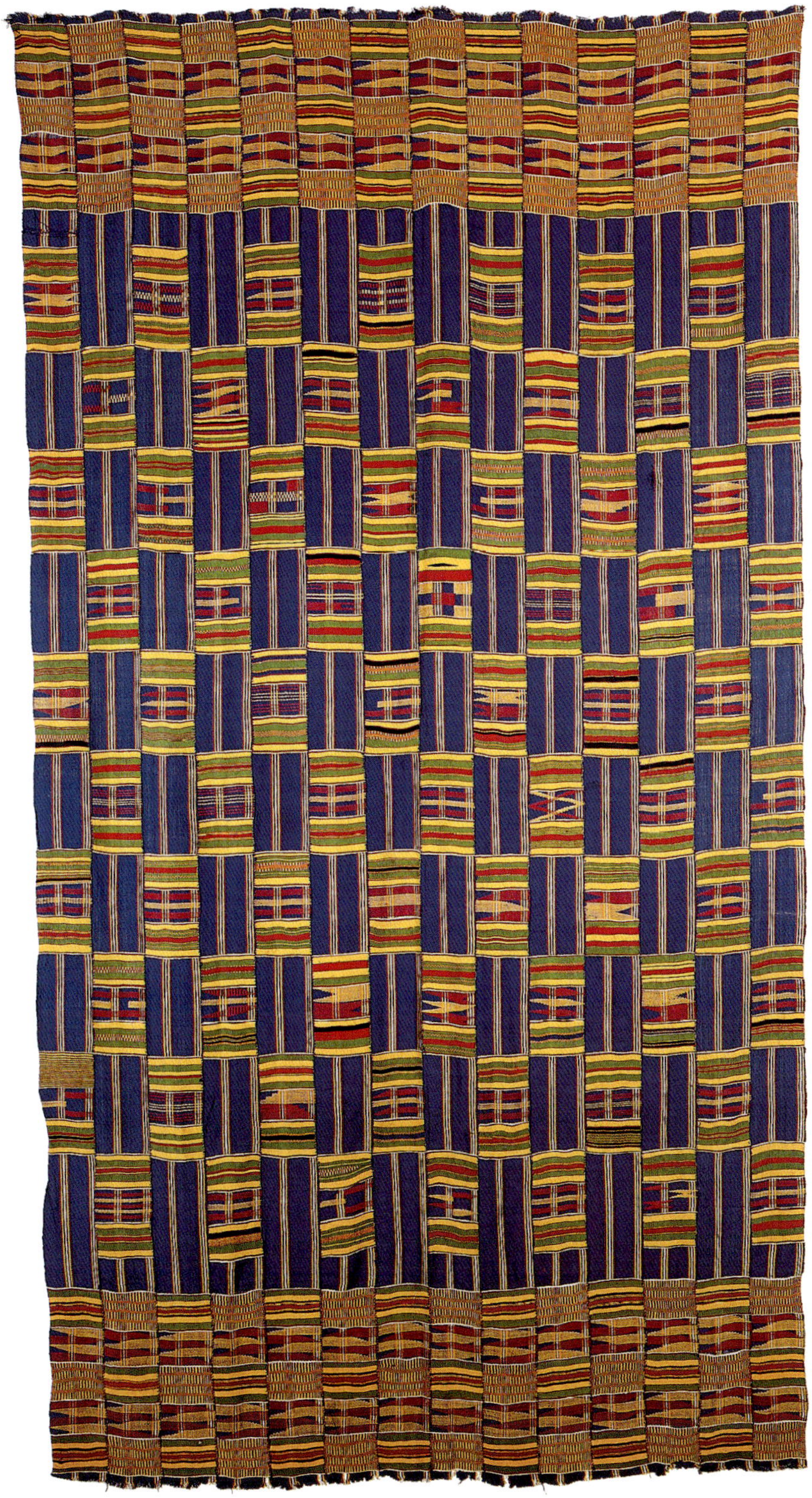

## Cloth (kente)

Asante peoples, Ghana, cotton, silk, dye, w: 89 inches
Willis Bing and Audrey Davis Collection

*Narrow band strip cloth called kente, created by Akan male weavers, has been produced since shortly after foundation of the Asante confederacy early in the 18th century. Woven of cotton, silk and more recently, rayon, in various colorful combinations, it was long the prerogative of royalty. After independence it became the national costume.*

# DAYTON SOCIETY OF NATURAL HISTORY/BOONSHOFT MUSEUM OF DISCOVERY

The Dayton Society of Natural History's Collection began in 1893, when it was part of the Dayton Public Library. Like many museums and libraries of the Victorian age, it was essentially a curio cabinet displaying the "rare and exotic" material culture of little known parts of the world. Many of the artifacts were brought back from foreign travels, while others represented local archaeological, biological and geological curiosities.

Our collections have grown considerably since these early days. While our focus is that of a regional museum, we have extensive comparative collections from many parts of the world, with Africa being but one of these areas. We collect from all parts of Africa and our collections vary from others in this show in that we are particularly interested in the cultural context of the items. While we collect the mundane artifacts of everyday life as well as those considered to be fine art, we are particularly focused on how the artifacts fit within the culture from which they come. Our primary interest is in how they were adapted to the needs of the society into which they were incorporated.

With no budget for accessions, our collection has grown through the generosity of many donors over time. As such, it reflects a variety of collecting philosophies. However, all of the pieces work together to allow us to educate the public about a variety of lifestyles within Africa. These range from hunting and gathering societies to pastoralists and farmers. While we are delighted to have specimens that have great antiquity, we are equally pleased to have new pieces that represent modern adaptations to the needs of these ever-evolving cultures.

Many of our pieces are only exhibited in the more traditional, static museum case because of their rarity or fragile state, while others are considered to be somewhat expendable because of lack of data or duplication within the collection. These objects are used for school classes, where they can be handled. This allows us to expose students to material that they have never before touched. So many of us have never tanned a skin, stretched a drumhead, carved a figure or retted fiber. In this way, process is of primary importance to our institution and we view our collection from this perspective. While we are demanding of provenance for our specimens, many of our earliest donations have little data as they were collected at a time when their scientific value was not considered.

It is with pleasure that we lend parts of our collections to other institutions so that we can educate more individuals through our holdings. Thank you for allowing us this opportunity to share our collection in your exhibition that focuses on the excellent African collections that have developed here in the Miami Valley. It is a particular treat for me to be working with Dr. Roy Sieber again, as he was one of the professors I respected most when I was a graduate student at Indiana University.

James M. Heilman III
Former Curator of Anthropology
DAYTON SOCIETY OF NATURAL HISTORY/
BOONSHOFT MUSEUM OF DISCOVERY

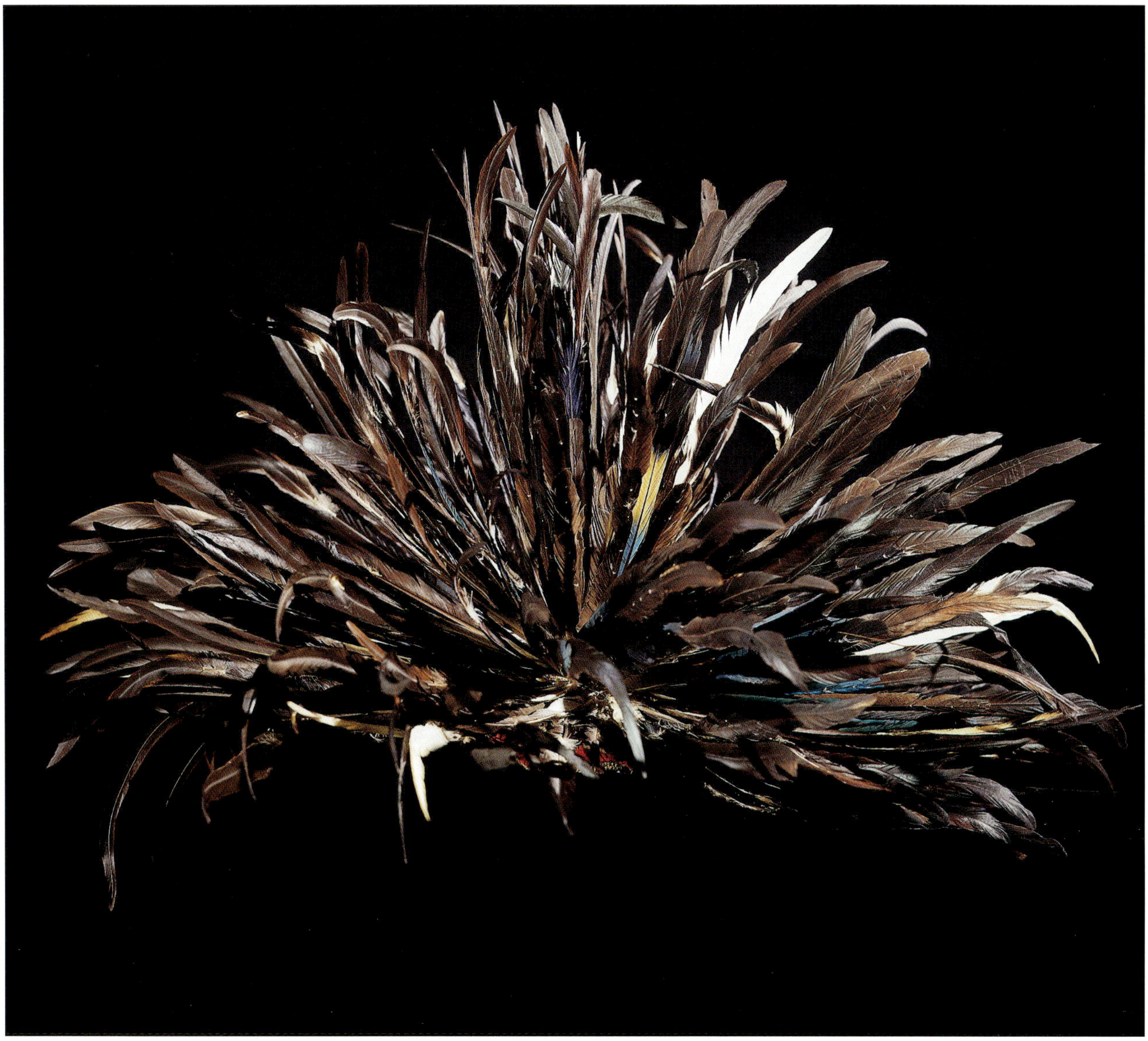

## Hat

Western Grassfields, Cameroon, feathers, fiber, w: 43 inches
Dayton Society of Natural History/Boonshoft Museum of Discovery Collection

*Elaborate bouquet-like feather hats are the exclusive privilege of Fons (chiefs) or members of the royal courts. They are worn at important ceremonies including funerals. When not worn, the fiber cap is turned inside out allowing the feathers to collapse into a tight bundle.*

# DONALD DUGAN

My wife and I began our collecting by snooping around small shops and galleries. Approximately six or seven years later, we started going through the auction houses. It is the act of the hunt and the subsequent possession that thrill me the most about collecting. With any form of tribal art, you know you have a really good piece if you never tire of looking at it.

I collect what appeals to me, but my primary fascination is with wooden things. To me the worst thing that you can do is to buy for investment purposes. The object may not be what it purports to be, and someone with a little better eye than you will know it and you will be stung with a fake. The less expensive pieces I have purchased will probably never sell for much more than I paid for them. That price, therefore, is their intrinsic value—more expensive pieces tend to appreciate in value.

Provenance is particularly important when you are buying a piece at auction because it plays a big part in establishing the value of a piece. Whenever I get the chance, I like to go back and authenticate my purchases to establish a provenance for them. I learned early on that you must also buy the books in order to authenticate the pieces. I have spent a small fortune on books to learn about my collection. When you purchase pieces from a tradition that has a classical style about it, you can authenticate it based on expense. When it is expensive, people track it. There have been times that I have seen a piece and said to myself, "Now who in the world would want to buy that?" But then after some research, I end up buying things that grow on me as a result of what I learned about them.

My wife and I have a particular conversation every now and then. We call it "starting another arm." When presented something different and exciting that we may have an interest in collecting, we always ask ourselves whether we are starting another arm of our collection. For example, when we were offered the goldweights as a purchase, we debated whether they were another "arm" of our collection. However, we decided that because they were a group of metal African objects and we already had a number of other metal pieces from Africa, they were not too out of line.

I collected my African objects early on but my interest in tribal art has changed over time. I have turned to Oceanic art as African art began to make me nervous. While doing some research on objects, I discovered that there are steel mills in Africa that create tools to make the pieces faster and to make them look older. I wouldn't necessarily call the pieces fakes or forgeries. The prices were very reasonable, but the sellers wouldn't come right out and tell you that they had just made the piece last month.

Because I like big pieces, my interest turned to Oceanic art. Some people collect miniature objects, like the goldweights, but I prefer the big pieces and I find that you get a much better price on them. I don't buy art by the yard, but I am rather an opportunist and a lot of my objects were acquired as a result of being in a group of objects, for which I could get a better buy.

There are fads in collecting. Unknowledgeable people go for things that are trendy; the market spikes up and then it crashes. I don't think that I have ever purchased something that I wished later I hadn't purchased at all. I think there have been times that I thought that perhaps I paid too much money for a piece, but I never said that I didn't want to own it. In the past, I have purchased something that was somewhat suspicious in terms of fitting a popular model. However, my taste was later vindicated because someone who knows a lot about the objects told me that the piece in question was a very good, unique example.

As far as the future of my collection, I don't have any goals with the exception of some specific, higher priced Oceanic Hems. I have gone out on a limb for such pieces in the past. While I have made some small African purchases to balance my collection, my focus has predominantly been Oceanic art. However, if I run across something and the price is right, I just might buy it!

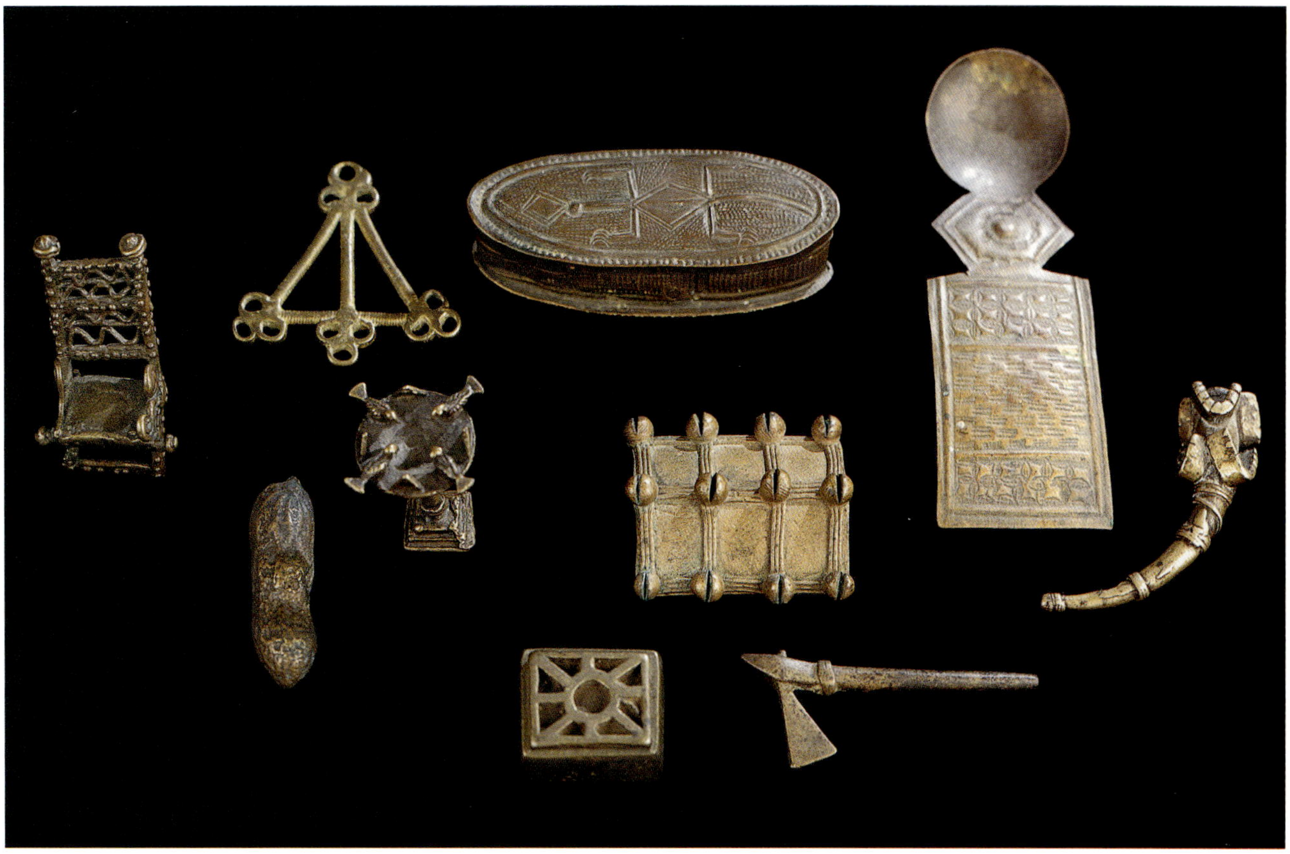

## Gold weighing equipment

Asante peoples, Ghana, copper alloy, h: 4 1/2 inches
Donald and Sue Dugan Collection

*Gold was (and is) one of the best known forms of currency in Africa. The Asante developed a complex set of measuring devices, in part probably from Islamic north African merchants. It consisted of a large number of geometric and figurative weights (often depicting parables), spoons and boxes of cast or repoussé copper alloy. A small pan scale allowed the balancing of weights on one side against gold dust on the other. These so called "gold weights" were in use into the 20th century.*

# PAMELA HOUK

I began collecting African art more than 30 years ago largely as a result of a close relationship with a former Director of The Dayton Art Institute, Tom Colt and his wife Priscilla, who were friends, neighbors and mentors. From the early 60s to the mid 80s, we spent many hours together talking about museum work and studying and discussing all kinds of art. Most particularly, the Colts taught me how to look at African art and to appreciate the many different cultures that had produced it. In fact, many of us in Dayton who have continued to collect this material, learned early on to sharpen our eyes and understanding from Tom and Priscilla's insightful influence. For example, while examining a particular piece of sculpture, we learned to look for certain kinds of patinas and patterns of wear. We spoke about the object's general use, even if its specific meaning and function remained a closely held secret among the society from which it came.

Dr. Roy Sieber was an important factor in my developing an interest in African textiles. Dr. Sieber, along with two of his graduate students generously provided guidance for an exhibition of art, artifacts and textiles of three different African peoples. Organized for the Living Arts Center Gallery in 1974, this project made me aware of the extraordinary quality and diversity of fiber arts that have flourished in many parts of Africa. It also involved working closely with colleagues from Ghana who introduced me to the remarkable kente cloths and other weaving traditions of the Asante and Ewe. I became aware of the two major types of looms used in West Africa—the women's relatively wide, upright heddle loom and the men's horizontal treadle loom used to sew woven narrow strips together to make whole cloths. The patterns made on the mens' looms could be quite complex, such as those in a kente weave. Because these elaborate kente cloths worn by men took a long time to make, they were highly valued and imparted a certain prestige to the wearer.

Subsequently, I discovered that African textiles served as inspiration for some European artists involved in the modern movement. For instance, both Paul Klee and Henri Matisse were drawn to the abstract appliqued motifs in women's wraps made by the Kuba people. The lively and dynamic shapes in these wraps, so full of symbolic meanings for the maker, can be seen in an entirely different context in Klee's paintings.

Not only are these traditional artifacts endlessly fascinating and a joy to live among, but as we have all seen, they have had a compelling impact on the art and crafts of the west.

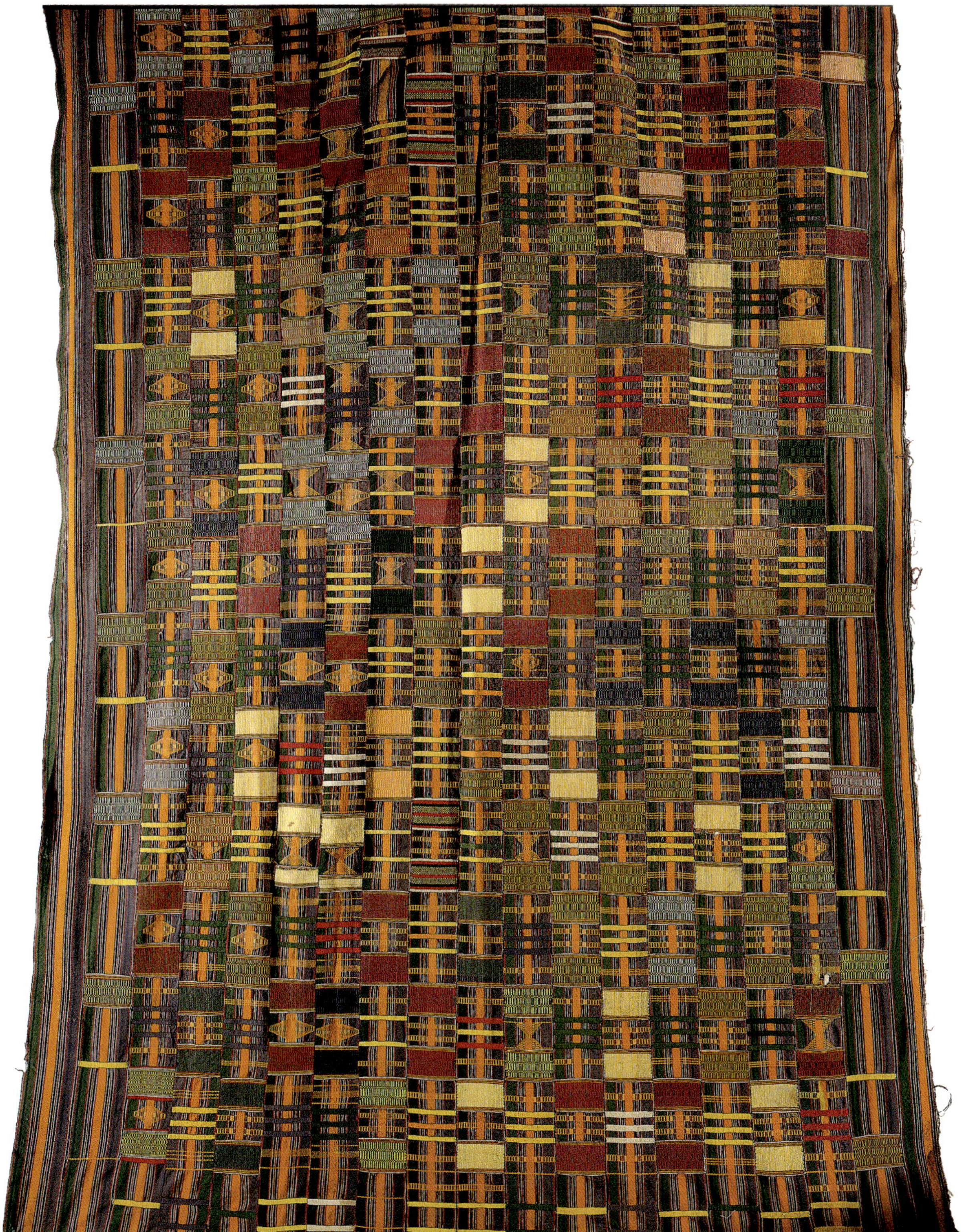

## Cloth (kente)

Ewe peoples, Togo, cotton, dye, w: 110 inches
Pamela P. Houk Collection

*Strip woven Ewe textiles for men are among the most complex and colorful in west Africa.*

# DIANNE KOMMINSK

I began collecting African art through my association with a friend who is also a collector. When I first met her, I was fascinated with these beautiful objects she wore around her neck. They turned out to be Pende ivories. The next time a dealer was in town, I came to "show and tell" at her home. At first, I could not afford to buy much, and I did not give a thought to building a collection.

There is a warmth about African art. Most of it is made of wood and I love living with wood, stone, marble, granite and other natural materials. When you look at my home, everything is natural. There is no Formica and little glass, except for the windows. These materials feel cold to me. African art was also the first art that I have been exposed to where the objects were a part of the original owner's daily or ritual life. I feel obligated to care for these objects because they were once important to someone else. Like a caretaker, I feel honored to keep these objects in my home. Because the pieces were used, there seems to be some heart and soul within them. This is a real draw for me.

There is a great deal of talent in the world. Yet, I am in awe of what African artists have been able to do with such minimal tools. I am also in awe of the universal aspects of African art. There are symbolic representations and imagery in many forms of tribal art that seem to appear and re-appear across cultures. The power in these forms is very attractive to me however, this power must be benign. I have purchased one or two pieces that appear to be a bit fierce. While I have grown to be less comfortable living with these pieces, I am still fond of them. I think perhaps they belong in a museum.

In choosing a piece, I have to love it first. I have to want it around me. Then, of course, the consideration is if I can afford it. If I think I can, I want to be sure I am not overpaying for the piece, or if I am, I want to know it in advance. I do not like to feel taken. If I choose to buy something I want so much that I choose to pay twice what it will be worth tomorrow simply because I feel I must have it, that is acceptable as long as I am aware of it in advance.

The world of African art dealers and collectors is a small and trusting one. Living in this cynical world, it is nice that so many of the people involved with buying and selling African art are willing to trust me enough to treat me as a friend would in similar circumstances. For example, many of the dealers have been wonderful about allowing me to live with a piece for a few days in order for me to be sure I want to purchase it. I have found this charming and reassuring and have enjoyed the sort of bond of trust that you simply do not find in many aspects of life. I have also found it fascinating that people from all walks of life have been receptive to my collection. It is truly enjoyable to share the artwork with anyone who is emotionally or intellectually taken with it.

When I began collecting, I was not intending to build a collection. Now, however, I have found that African art is quite accessible for me and that I enjoy the process of collecting. I have also found that I am truly a three-dimensional person. My main requirement is that I want a quality example of a form. It doesn't matter if it is little or inexpensive, I still want an excellent example.

I think it is important to see museum collections. I have many books, and this helps to develop my eye by seeing the variety of objects created. Nevertheless, I think that the more you see, the better your eye becomes. It seems that I buy a form with which I am taken, and if I haven't looked around or even gone through the books to see other examples, I find that I may have preferred to wait for a better example of that particular form. After collecting for 15 years, I can say there are objects that I would rather not possess unless I can have a truly good example of the form.

At this point, when I look around my collection, I am not interested in adding more to the collection, but rather, I am interested in trading off some of the things I have become less excited about. I don't have the space to adequately display more, and I don't want to put some in the basement and rotate pieces. I am not a museum, and I like the objects to surround me. My collection is a part of me.

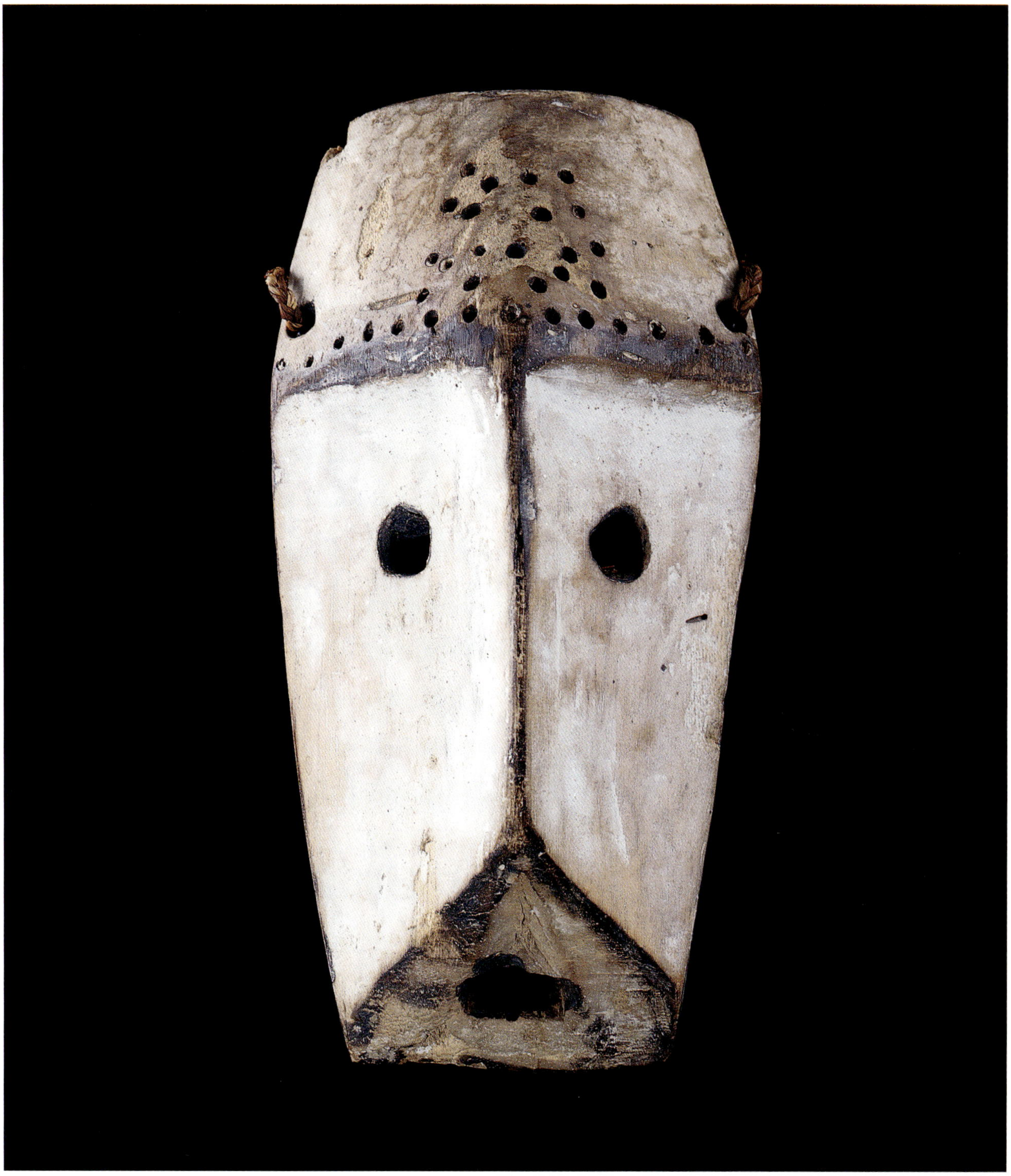

## Mask

Lega peoples, Democratic Republic of the Congo, wood, pigment, h: 8 inches
Dianne Komminsk Collection

*Every member of the highest grade of the Bwami men's religious and social association owns a small mask. Carved of wood, bone or ivory, it represents an ancestor and symbolizes the high moral code of the society.*

# WILLIAM ROGERS

I believe that I am the novice of this group of collectors, as I have only been collecting African art since early 1997. I try to keep very detailed records of my collection. All of my African objects have come from one dealer. Each item has been examined by Roy Sieber to assure, as best one can, that they are not fakes. I am not interested in what he says it is worth or if he thinks it is a good piece—I rely on my eye for that. Roy Sieber provides priceless knowledge through a lifetime of studying these objects, which enables him to say that a piece was made for tribal use rather than for export. Most collectors have made purchases they have later not been comfortable with. In African art, you cannot tell the age of a piece very easily. There are objects that have been falsified to look very used and old, and there are objects that have been in museum collections for 100 years that don't look old at all.

I began my African collection with a small ceramic piece and moved along to some masks and some iron works such as the Yoruba iron shrine piece. I scoured all of the dealer's books on African art and began reading some others to learn about the groups whose objects were of particular interest to me. I began my research with objects that were visually appealing to me, and then I set out to learn how the objects were originally used. This allowed me to narrow my choices further and I began to select from the items that my dealer was able to come by via runners—African traders who travel around with objects for sale—or from deaccessions from the collections of others.

Figures and masks are definitely preferred by most collectors and institutions that are interested in developing very good collections of African art. Most of the pieces I have collected are a bit different. They are ones that are not traditionally seen as the most popular pieces, yet they are authentic and considered to be good, representative examples of African art. I have a tremendous interest in the manner of fabrication of these pieces. For example, the Senufo mask that I have was carved from one piece of wood. If you went to a European artisan and asked him to carve something for you, routinely he would use multiple pieces of wood and piece them together. It is amazing how the Africans use such relatively crude implements to fashion such outstanding pieces.

African art is unique in many ways, but I have never been a focus collector. Most people find one area that they really love—Beanie Babies, coins or paintings—and they collect it. There is an advantage to this type of collecting because you become quite knowledgeable about one type of object throughout the time that you collect it. I, on the other hand, find many things interesting and am not only concerned with the objects themselves, but also how they relate to historical periods and themes. My collecting interests have moved through many different areas including African art.

My parents were quite eclectic in their tastes and I think that was an impetus for my interest in collecting today. I must make a distinction, though, in that most people who discuss collecting consider too many people to be collectors. To me, the majority of people we call "collectors" are really "acquirers." Imagine a scale. On this scale, I intentionally place the "acquirer" on the bottom because he sees an object and says, "Gosh, that looks nice and it would look good sitting in my living room. I think I will buy it." For most people, that is about all that they do. They do not do any research on the object; they do not understand how the object relates to history or what its intended use was.

The next level I will call the "collectors." A "collector" still acquires objects, but looks beyond the object itself to how it fits into historical periods, who the maker was and whatnot. Lastly, there is the pinnacle, which I will call the "connoisseur." Here the objects themselves become almost irrelevant. The ownership of the object becomes almost unnecessary for the connoisseur to be able to fully appreciate it. Achieving the level of connoisseur is predicated upon building one's knowledge and the sharing of that knowledge with others. The other things I collect—early firearms and early works on paper—are distinctly different from African art in content. Yet, the work I have done to develop my skills and move myself from a "collector" to a "connoisseur" has facilitated all of my collecting interests.

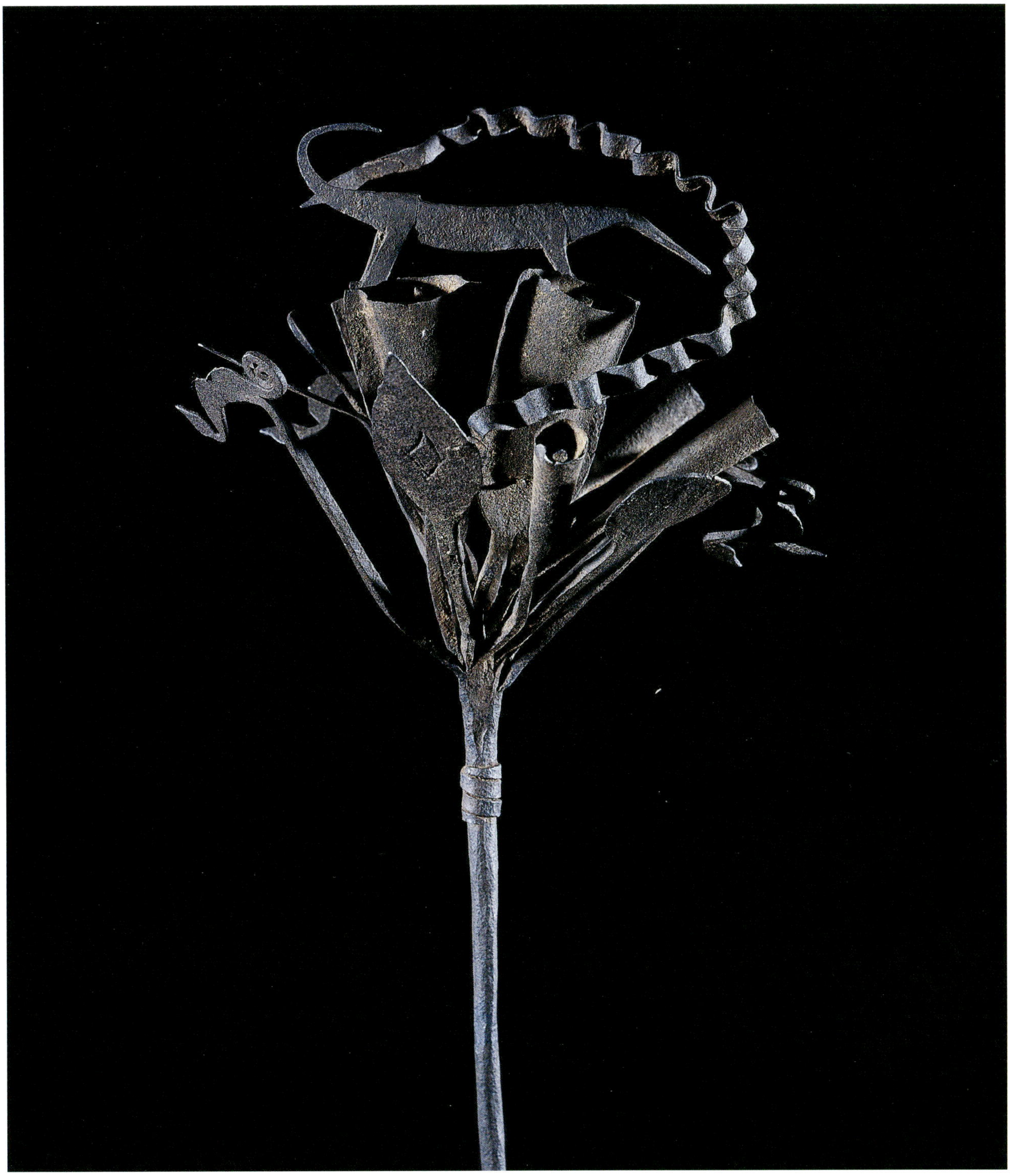

## Shrine staff
[Detail]

Yoruba peoples, Nigeria, iron, h: 71 inches
Dr. and Mrs. William E. Rogers Collection

*Among the Yoruba, iron staffs are dedicated to several deities (orishas). A priest or priestess may commission a staff that would function as the point of contact between the realm of the spirits and the world of the living. The specific meaning of this staff is unclear. The animal on top may be a chameleon or an anteater (a bird is more typical). Several gongs, usually found in shrines, and other forms are clustered at the top of the staff.*

# ARTHUR SHONE

The first thing that attracted me to African art was the form or abstraction and the energy that carvers put into pieces. The second was the materials...wood, stone, clay, metal. Then came an awareness that I was very lucky to own something that was important to someone else's culture more than 100 years ago, creating an amazing sense of custodianship.

I have found that research into the original intent or use of the object is extremely important, but I have never been able to do enough of that type of research. Hence, I do not necessarily have a scholarly understanding of the objects. I try to find out what it is, where it came from, its provenance, how old it is and then I stop. Before we [my ex-wife and I] could afford to buy any of the pieces—financially, intellectually or emotionally—we went to shows and bought books. Finally, we bought something."

When we bought our third object, I called my sister and announced that we now owned the largest collection of African art in Dayton because the museum only had two pieces at the time. So, there weren't many people to talk to. Everybody knows everybody in African art circles. It is a very small club. When we went to Europe, Roy Sieber gave us a couple of letters of introduction and suddenly there were people who would welcome us into their homes and their businesses.

One of the essential appeals of this material is that the objects were not made for me. I get a lot of pleasure from knowing they were made for other peoples' use in their daily life or for their rituals a long time ago in a place somewhat far away. When I find out that something has been made for me, or altered, it ruins my experience.

I am not a museum or a curator and therefore take a different approach to collecting. I do not look for the precedent or the antecedent of a piece in my collection. I understand the importance of seeing the differences between each of my pieces but my collecting is totally undirected.

I get an intense, immense, constant pleasure from living with African art. I like living in this space and sharing it with these objects. If you took all of the objects away from me, I would sell this house. For me, the pleasure one gets from going to New York, going to the auctions or having a dealer in my home is secondary to living with the objects...to having them here on my table.

I love going to other people's homes and seeing what they have, and I love to sit down and have a drink and talk about objects. So, I welcome people into my home in order to experience what I have here. I always wonder when someone comes into my home and does not ask me a question. I would never go into someone's home and not ask him or her questions about stuff as odd and as different as this. I would say, "Hey, what is this? How did you come to get this? And if you don't mind, how much did it cost?" I have kind of a perverse feeling when someone comes in here for three or four hours and then they go to leave and say, "Thank you very much. I really enjoyed the wine." I just think, "What are they thinking?"

I do not have a favorite piece in my collection...nor do I have a favorite child. Each one has a charm about it. I bought each one because I like it. I keep it around me because I like to live with it. I don't rate them. To me everything costs a dollar, is the same size and came from the same place.

In looking back over my experience, I would say if you are interested in starting to collect, I do not think you should wait until you can afford it. There are things available that do not cost a lot of money. Buy something good. Buy something real. Pick out an object or an area that appeals to you—that is all that really matters. If you only care about money, then you are only going to buy the *Mona Lisa*. But if you like objects, you have to pick an object and then there will be a range of quality. It varies from tribe to tribe and country to country. Value can be determined only with its immediate competition and should not simply be based on price.

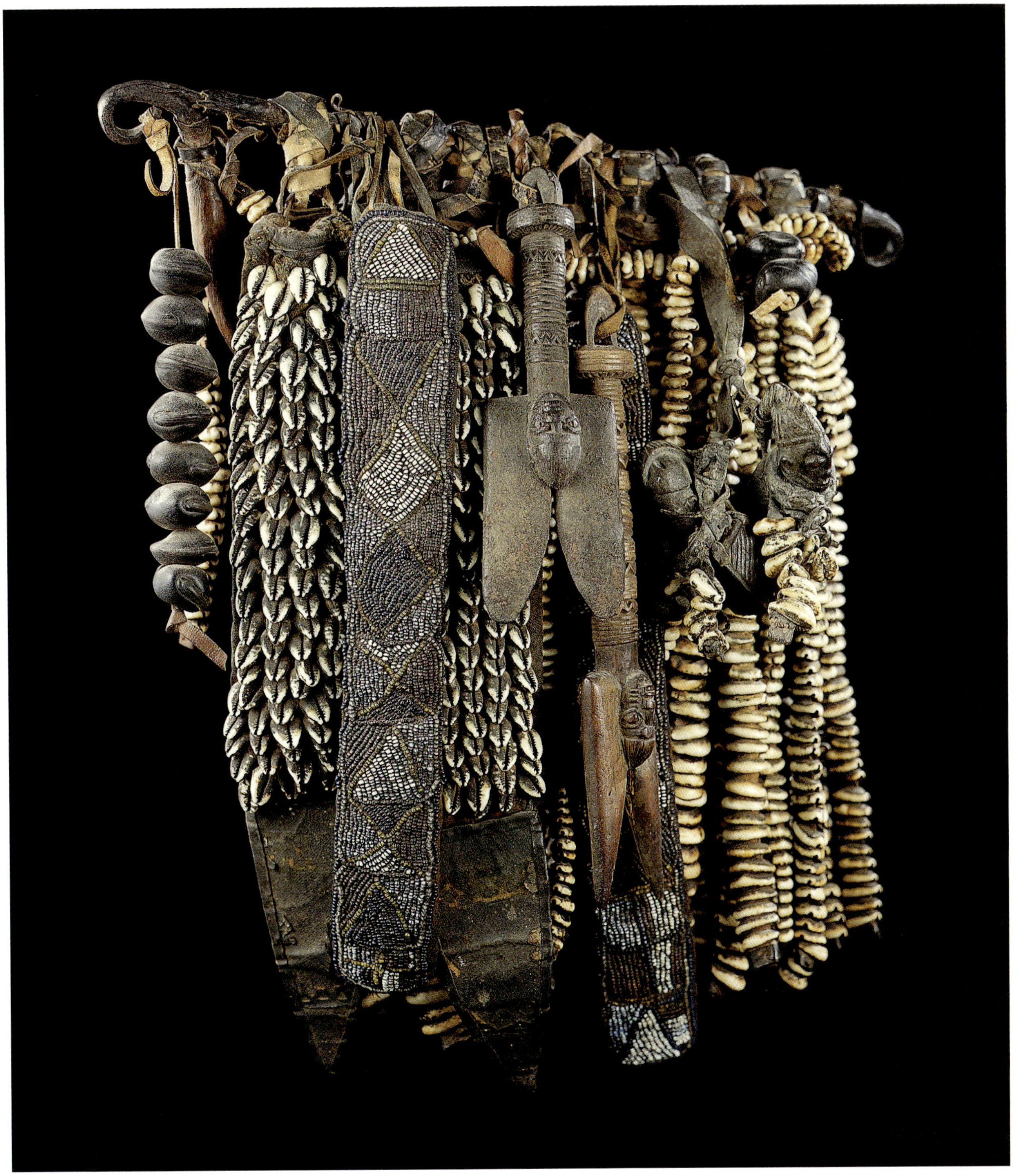

## Shrine object

Yoruba peoples, Nigeria, leather, cowrie shells, beads, metal, wood, h: 17 1/2 inches
Arthur Shone Collection

*This complex construction was hung on the wall of a shrine, possibly one dedicated to the deity Sango. Two staffs, carrying the double axe form of Sango, hang upside down. However, there are also cowrie shells and wooden emblems of Esu, the Yoruba messenger of the gods. Symbols of Esu and other deities (such as ibeji) are often found in Sango shrines.*

# LAVERNE SHONE

When we [my ex-husband and I] began collecting art, the first thing we collected was a painting. We had no furniture. We did not have the money to buy both. We discovered that our environment was changed or formed more by a painting than by a couch or chair. We hung it in the room, and we were perfectly comfortable with sitting on the floor and gazing at our painting.

Quickly, we found the need for sculpture. We wanted a mixture of materials and forms in our environment. Our love of African art was triggered by a number of things. We could not afford a David Smith or one of the other sculptors that we loved. We were attracted to the form and magic of African sculpture. The first thing that we brought home was a fake from a museum store. It was a Kurumba. It was not marked "in the style of a Bambara Kurumba." It said that it was Bambara. We thought, "Well, surely the museum wouldn't try to sell us a fake." But of course, a museum store only has fakes. Today, I would know what to expect.

Then our friends bought some fakes from a nearby dealer and the exciting question became "What is an authentic piece?" We told the people we were sent to see in New York that we wanted to see Asante dolls. They would bring out 30 and line them up. Well, I could say I knew which ones I liked but I did not know why. So I asked [the dealer], "Can you tell me what ones are the best?" This was all a part of cultivating my taste.

Our first Bambara piece sits on the coffee table in my living room. I remember carrying it home on the airplane from New York. I still sit and stare at the back of it. Now, I have seen better from the front, but the back is great. I would put the back of that piece up against any others. It has always held its strength for me. [After this piece], we were always hoping that we would not fall in love with something so that we could eat better. But every once in a while, we would just know we were in trouble.

When we first went to Brussels, we saw two little Luba ivories for sale. [The seller] let us take them without paying for them. We told him we were going to have them checked by someone and then decide if we were going to them. We called Roy Sieber when we got home and met him half-way between Dayton and Bloomington. We had spent two days in the British Museum's stacks studying Luba ivories and fakes. We thought our ivories were real, but were still unsure. I think we were in a Frisch's restaurant and Dr. Sieber looked at them and said, "Oh they're revolting—if you send them back—tell me where!" So we kept them.

In selecting a piece, it just has to speak to you. If it haunts you through the night, if you just cannot stop thinking about it, then you know you are hooked on it. I am very careful, though. I trust my eye only to a certain degree. Many people do not want to admit that they have made a mistake. If I purchased something because I loved it, and then was told that it was a "fake," I could try to convince myself that it was acceptable all day or night but I would grow to not like the piece.

For example, with an ivory, I have gotten to the point that I can shut my eyes and feel it. By doing this, I am trying to make sure that it was made for their [African] use. I don't want a piece that was "made for me." Even if I buy a wood tray or a wood bowl [to use] for salad or something, I want one that has been used. They smell different, they have a patina, they are worn and they have repairs that are great. To me, if they [the Africans] used it, and I can feel the use and the wear, this makes it more beautiful.

I do not plan my collection. I do not really consider myself a very big collector. I buy in spurts. I never know when I am going to be exposed to something that I am going to keep looking at and have a great desire to live with. It happens less and less now. The price of the quality pieces has changed to make many of them untouchable.

I love sharing my collection with people that love it, and I collect because it enriches my life—and it's exciting. Some people like gambling. Some people live on the fast-track. I love going through a Sotheby's catalogue before the auction, going there and seeing the things. It is exciting for me to go through the cases while [a dealer friend] is unpacking when he comes here for a visit. Collecting simply adds thrill and excitement to my life.

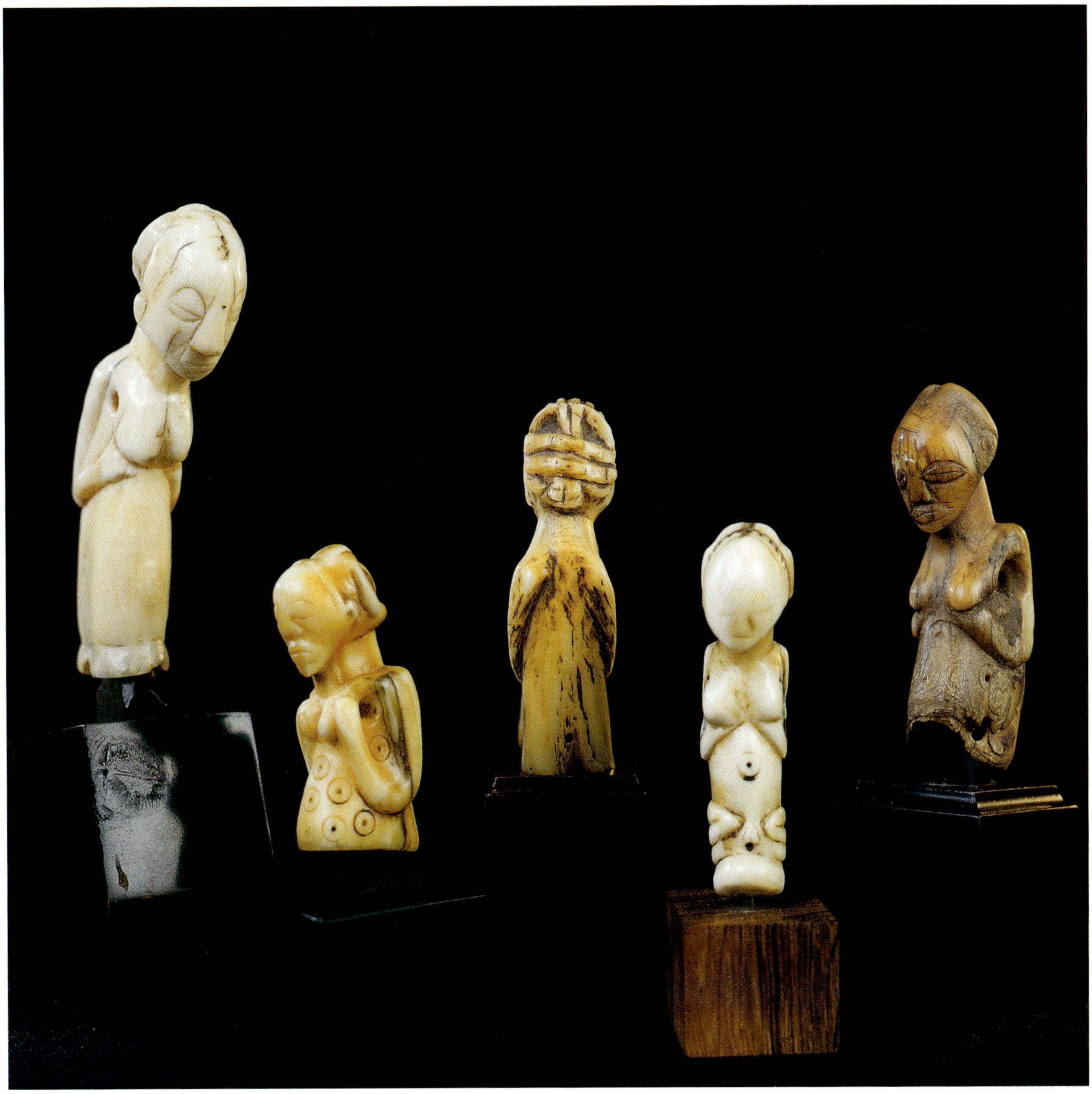

## Five figurative pendants (mikishi mihasi)

Luba peoples, Democratic Republic of the Congo, elephant and hippopotamus ivory, h: 4 1/4 inches
LaVerne Shone Collection

*Figurative amulets were long the most intimate and revered objects of the Luba, their soft forms, the results of long wear as pendants. Some, such as the one on the far right, date as early as the 18th century. The hands holding the breast symbolize an ancestor as the source of life and nourishment. For chiefs whose lineages mediate with the spirit world, these ivories established contact between the living and the beneficial spirits (mikishi mihasi).*

# CURATOR'S STATEMENT

When first conceived, this catalogue was to have had a more traditional format. There was to be an extended introduction followed by a listing of works arranged by collector. Fairly early, I suggested that statements by each of the lenders replace a long introduction, providing a fresh view of the objects as seen and admired through the eyes of the collectors. I would select the works of art for exhibition and the lender would choose a favorite work to accompany his or her statement. That plan would allow the objects to be arranged by type and meaning regardless of the collection they came from, although of course the lender of each work would be acknowledged.

Thus, the lenders' statements establish one "window" on African arts and the objects another. The result is a somewhat unusual, possibly unique, presentation of African art: through the tastes of the collectors and the lens of art history.

Now, it is my turn to offer a few thoughts on the history of attitudes toward African art and its collecting.

It is currently something of a cliché that collectors are modern-day hunters and gatherers. The challenge and delight in acquiring works of art has replaced the urgent need to search for food, clothing and shelter. Yet, there is a great variety of goals among collectors, including those devoted to African art. Some "need" to have one work from each major art-producing group south of the Sahara. Some limit their search exclusively to one form: figures, masks, jewelry or textiles, for example; others are dedicated to the arts of a particular region, country or ethnic group. Some choose only objects that reach out to them, regardless of type, origin or meaning. Yet there is a common thread and that is the Western focus upon the aesthetic of the object: the work of art. (I avoid the word beauty because it has far too much associative baggage as conventionally pretty, pleasing or attractive.)

In contrast to an intensive focus on the aesthetic, there has emerged a concern for a fuller understanding of the works of art that can only result from the knowledge of their origin and meaning. Thus an increased emphasis on the cultural context of the art works has developed during the past half-century.

A brief look at the history of these differing yet parallel views must begin with the often repeated tale of the discovery of African art by Picasso, Braque, Derain, Matisse and others in the first decade of the 20th century. Less well-known, however, is that their interest was nearly exclusively with the formal aspects of the objects. During World War I, the *Dada* movement in Zurich, Switzerland and its *Surrealist* successor perceived romanticized magical aspects in the arts of Africa. Concern with precise origins and meanings only came a generation later and the concept of the importance of the work in its parent culture nearly two generations later. Thus, African sculpture first became a justification for the avant garde artists' break with the classical and naturalistic norms of European art and later with European religion and mythology. Both of these perceptions were totally ethnocentric: in truth, Africa had no history of classical or naturalistic forms to break with, nor did they have a basis in European religion or mythology. Both attitudes neglected the real origins of African art in African history and culture.

However, the artists who recognized African art *as art* deserve many thanks for alerting the West to the excellence of those art forms. Earlier, African material culture, including what we now consider art, had been the province of anthropologists. Some, including the German adventurer, explorer and ethnographer, Leo Frobenius, observed, reported and collected African artifacts, mostly for museums of natural history. French, Belgian and American expeditions also collected works usually for national museums. But the goal of such collections was to survey material culture with little or no attention to aesthetics. This attitude prevailed well into the 20th century.

Two major events in the mid-1930s effectively cracked that mold. In 1935, the Museum of Modern Art in New York held the first major exhibition of African art in an art museum. It paved the way for other art museums in the

United States to offer exhibitions and build collections. Further, it encouraged private collectors to consider African arts worthy of their attention. This exhibition is the logical result of the expanding interest among private collectors and public institutions.

At the same time as the Museum of Modern Art exhibition, Carl Kjersmeier began publishing a four-volume study on the centers of African styles. It was the first systematic presentation that defined what were called tribal styles. "Tribe" and "tribal" have since been rejected by Africans and Western scholars as too judgmental as well as inaccurate. Yet the stylistic designations assigned still apply, although "tribes" are now termed ethnic groups or peoples.

I am old enough to recall a surprisingly large number of theories in art history and in anthropology that paralleled the growth of interest and collecting of African arts. Members of each generation of scholars feel it incumbent on them to reject the views of their fathers. Rather than building on their legacy—standing on their mentor's shoulders—they prefer to reject, modify or warp it, delivering a quick swift kick to their predecessors.

This attitude is neither new nor even recent. I admit that a half-century ago I delighted in excoriating the pet ideas and enthusiasms of my elders. These included art history studies based solely on style and on objects in museums (why go to Africa if everything worthy is already in the West); others equated "primitive" art with that of children and the insane, and never equal to the "high" arts of literate cultures. Many, theories I admit, I have forgotten, usually without regret. One still lives with me: relativism, not in the native form where a scholar was encouraged to become a blank slate (*tabula rasa*) when viewing another culture and to bring none of his prejudices or beliefs with him. In contrast, I live with the constant reminder that like all inhabitants of this time and place, I have deeply rooted prejudices, but I do attempt to bring them to bear knowingly as little as possible! To attempt, in short, to impose neither taste nor theory on the African or his art, is a difficult perhaps never fully realized goal.

Obviously one can never set aside, much less lose all one's prejudices nor one's aesthetic judgment. Despite the temptation to believe otherwise, taste is learned, not intuitive; but it can be so imbedded, so deencephalized as to seem intuitive. Not only is there individual taste but there is the taste of one's time that identifies what is "best" in the arts. Yet all such judgments are bound by time and place.

All who deal with African art—collectors, historians, anthropologists—live in the present and carry with them all the baggage of modern life. Our taste is deeply rooted in our own time, modified to the degree that we understand the meanings of the arts in Africa. But that is as it always has been, each historical moment has had its own take on the arts of other times or places. The Romans made their judgment of the Greeks (positive) and of the barbarians (negative); art beginning in the 12th century has been called Gothic, a term that meant at first crude or barbaric. Similarly many of the now fully accepted terms for early modern movements were originally pejorative, such as Impressionism and Pointillism, or insulting to the artists, for example calling them Fauves (wild beasts).

In much the same fashion, the arts of Africa or Oceania were termed primitive. The word means primary, indigenous or aboriginal and by inference crude, rude and unsophisticated. In both meanings, it is inaccurate. None of the arts of Africa are or were original (primary): thousands of years separated the appearance of the arts and what the West has experienced from the 15th century to the present. Nor were they crude: great technical and aesthetic sophistication exists. It is true that there are—both in our eyes and those of the Africans—works of lesser or greater skill. Not every adze cut is the stroke of genius, any more then every work of Western art is equally fine.

Unfamiliarity breeds contempt; familiarity breeds comfort. Indeed, one's eye will sharpen with a growing concern for African art, a constant search for examples (in private and public collections and with dealers) and much reading and looking at photographs. One's aesthetic judgment will become more critical and, inevitably, admiration will grow. But that takes time, energy, focus and commitment. However, the rewards are great as one moves from unfamiliarity and confusion to knowledge and clarity.

Roy Sieber
GUEST CURATOR

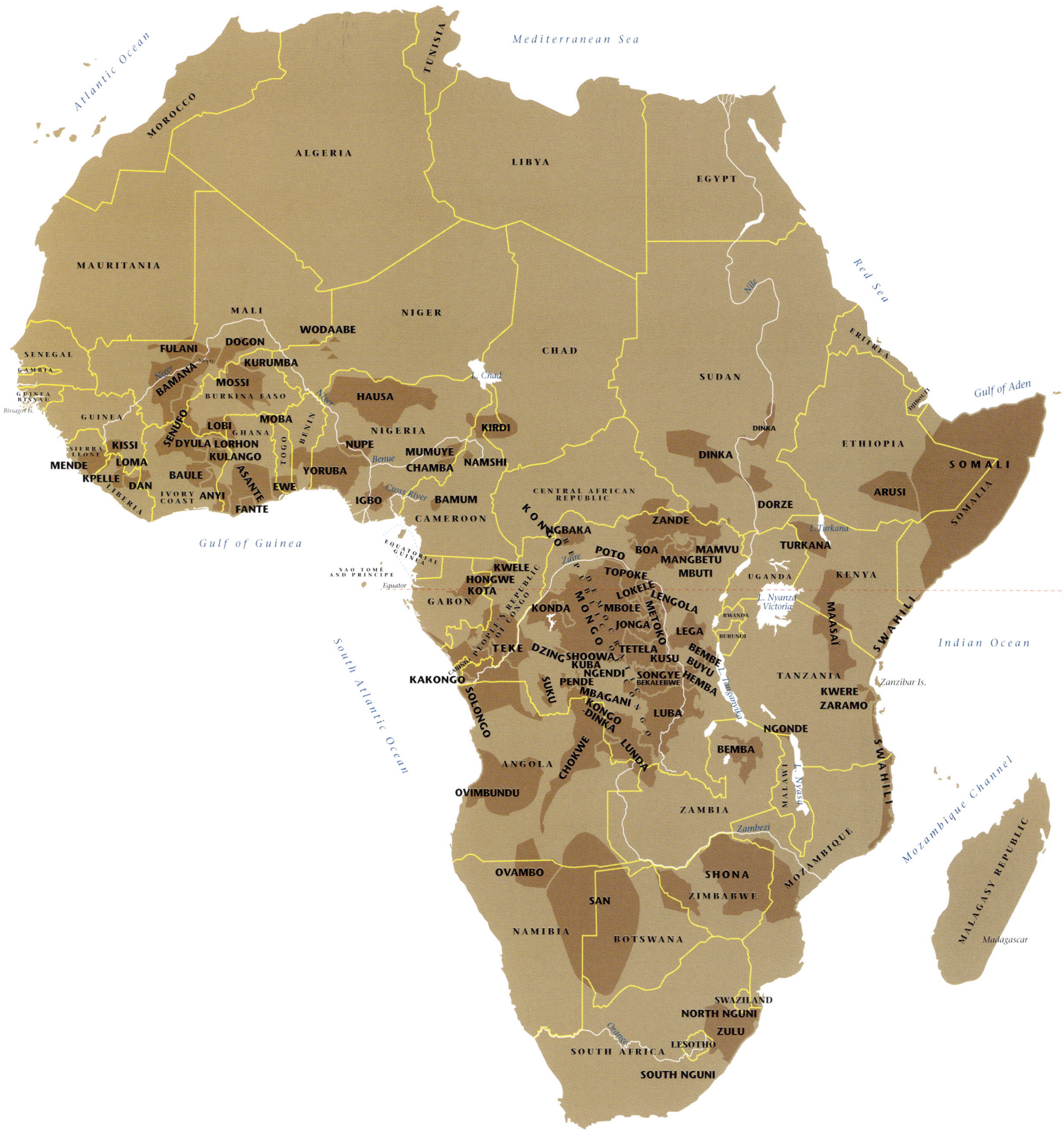
Mediterranean Sea
Atlantic Ocean
MOROCCO
ALGERIA
TUNISIA
LIBYA
EGYPT
Red Sea
Nile
MAURITANIA
MALI
NIGER
CHAD
SUDAN
ERITREA
Gulf of Aden
DJIBOUTI
SENEGAL
GAMBIA
GUINEA BISSAU
Bissagos Is.
GUINEA
SIERRA LEONE
LIBERIA
IVORY COAST
BURKINA FASO
GHANA
TOGO
BENIN
NIGERIA
Niger
Mopti
L. Chad
Benue
Cross River
CAMEROON
CENTRAL AFRICAN REPUBLIC
ETHIOPIA
SOMALIA
KENYA
UGANDA
RWANDA
BURUNDI
TANZANIA
Zanzibar Is.
Indian Ocean
Gulf of Guinea
EQUATORIAL GUINEA
SAO TOMÉ AND PRINCIPE
Equator
GABON
PEOPLE'S REPUBLIC OF CONGO
DEMOCRATIC REPUBLIC OF CONGO
Zaire
Cabinda
South Atlantic Ocean
ANGOLA
ZAMBIA
MALAWI
L. Nyasa
L. Tanganyika
L. Nyanza Victoria
L. Turkana
MOZAMBIQUE
Mozambique Channel
MALAGASY REPUBLIC
Madagascar
Zambezi
ZIMBABWE
NAMIBIA
BOTSWANA
SWAZILAND
LESOTHO
SOUTH AFRICA
Orange
FULANI
DOGON
WODAABE
KURUMBA
BAMANA
MOSSI
SENUFO
LOBI
MOBA
DYULA
LORHON
KULANGO
KISSI
LOMA
MENDE
KPELLE
DAN
BAULE
ASANTE
ANYI
FANTE
EWE
YORUBA
HAUSA
NUPE
MUMUYE
CHAMBA
NAMSHI
KIRDI
IGBO
BAMUM
KONGO
NGBAKA
ZANDE
BOA
POTO
MAMVU
MANGBETU
MBUTI
TOPOKE
LOKELE
LENGOLA
MONGO
KWELE
HONGWE
KOTA
KONDA
MBOLE
JONGA
METOKO
LEGA
TEKE
DZING
SHOOWA
KUBA
TETELA
KUSU
BEMBE
BUYU
HEMBA
NGENDI
SONGYE
BEKALEBWE
PENDE
SUKU
MBAGANI
KONGO-DINKA
LUBA
KAKONGO
SOLONGO
CHOKWE
LUNDA
BEMBA
OVIMBUNDU
OVAMBO
SAN
SHONA
DINKA
TURKANA
DORZE
ARUSI
SOMALI
MAASAI
SWAHILI
KWERE
ZARAMO
NGONDE
NORTH NGUNI
ZULU
SOUTH NGUNI

# EXHIBITION OBJECTS

The peoples of Africa have long been aware of the importance of maintaining a balance between the sacred and secular worlds. Community leaders, diviners, priests and healers execute complex rituals to secure the aid of ancestral and nature spirits to ensure a more secure world.

Sacred works of art, such as masks, figure sculptures, shrine pieces and some objects of personal adornment are imbued with supernatural power and were used to appeal to the ancestors and spirit forces.

Secular works of art, including textiles, dress, musical instruments and furniture reflect the human desire for prestige, comfort and entertainment.

# MASKS

Masks hide the identity of the wearer who assumes the persona of the spirit embodied in the sculpture. Masqueraders appear in many contexts: to dispel evil forces that bring disease and infertility; to ensure the success of the harvests and hunting; to validate coming of age ceremonies; and to supervise the installation of priests and leaders. Masks are made from a wide variety of materials, including wood, fiber, basketry and metal. They are only complete when the performer is in costume and dances accompanied by music in front of an audience.

1

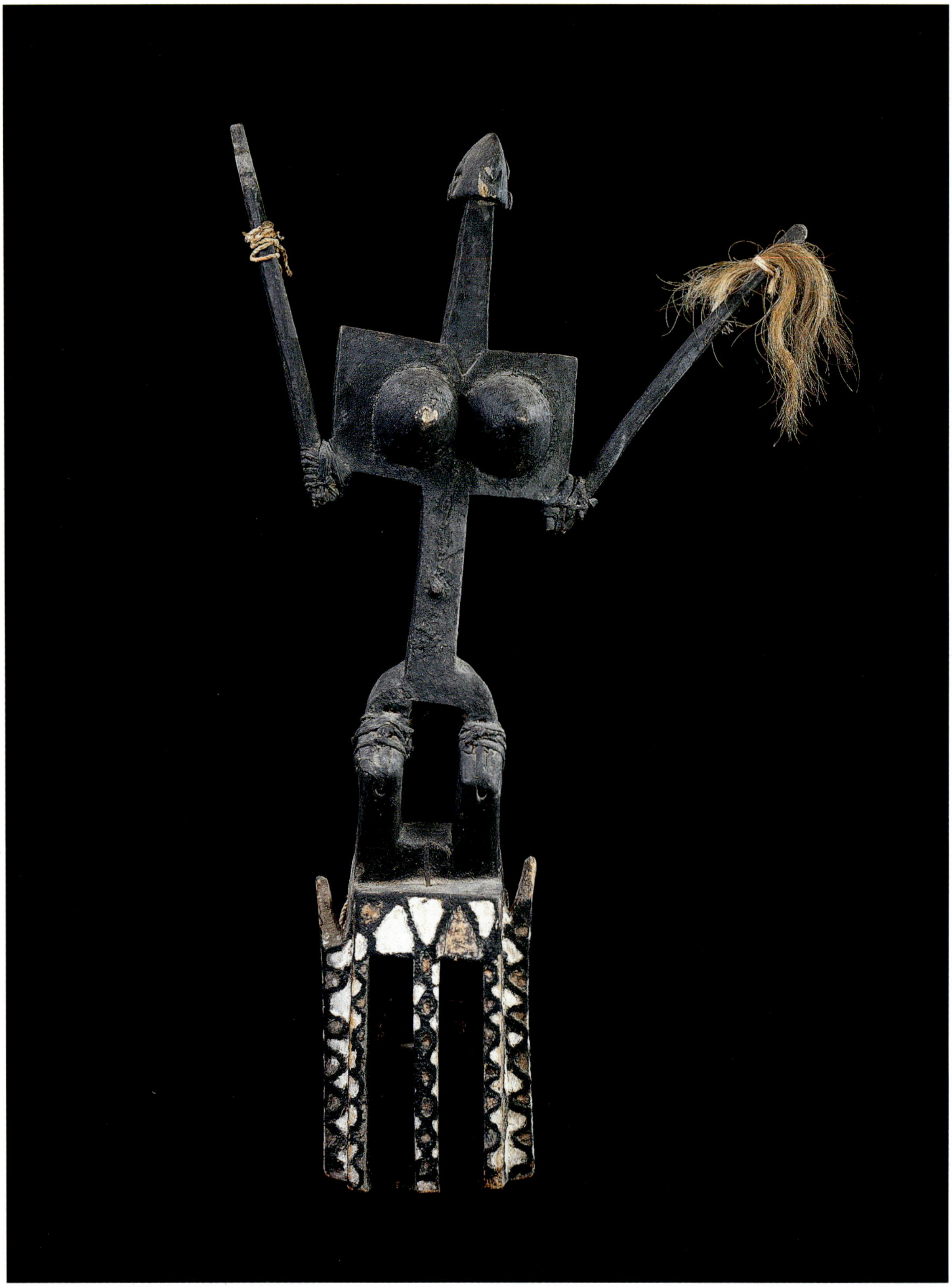

1

## Mask (satimbe)

Dogon peoples, Mali, wood, pigment, raffia, h: 40 inches
Vincent and Elana Bolling Collection

*A great number of Dogon masks appear at the Dama ceremony that honors recently deceased members of the Awa men's society. Satimbe is the only Dogon wood sculpture that combines a mask and the figurative image of a woman. It celebrates the only female member of the Awa society and is called the elder sister of masks. Like nearly all masks in Africa, it was carved by a male sculptor and danced by a man.*

2

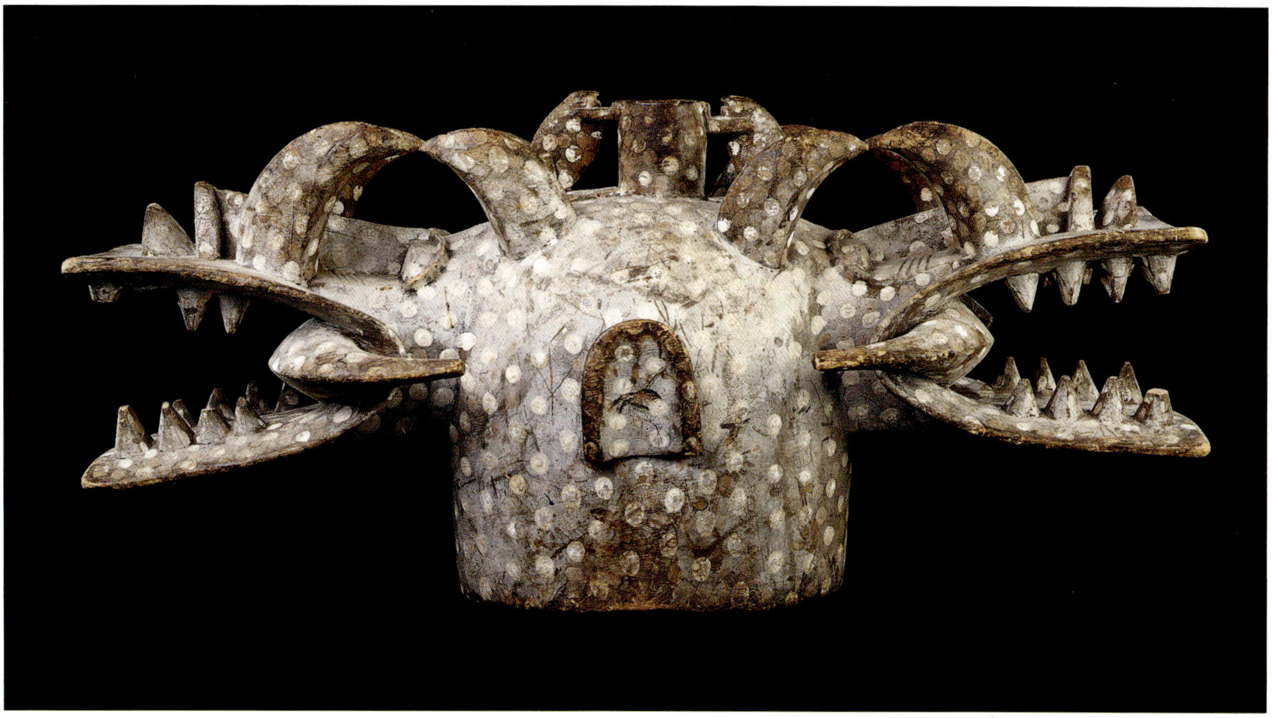

2

## Horizontal helmet mask

Senufo peoples, Côte d'Ivoire
wood, pigment, l: 32 1/2 inches
Willis Bing and Audrey Davis Collection

*There are both animal and human aspects to this Poro men's society mask. The zoomorphic elements include crocodile, bush cow and antelope. Each depicts a powerful bush spirit.*

3

## Kono mask

Bamana peoples, Mali
wood, sacrificial patina, h: 26 inches
Dianne Komminsk Collection

*The Kono association is an organization of male elders that focuses on civic morality and family relationships. This elongated abstract animal form is typical of the Kono aesthetic.*

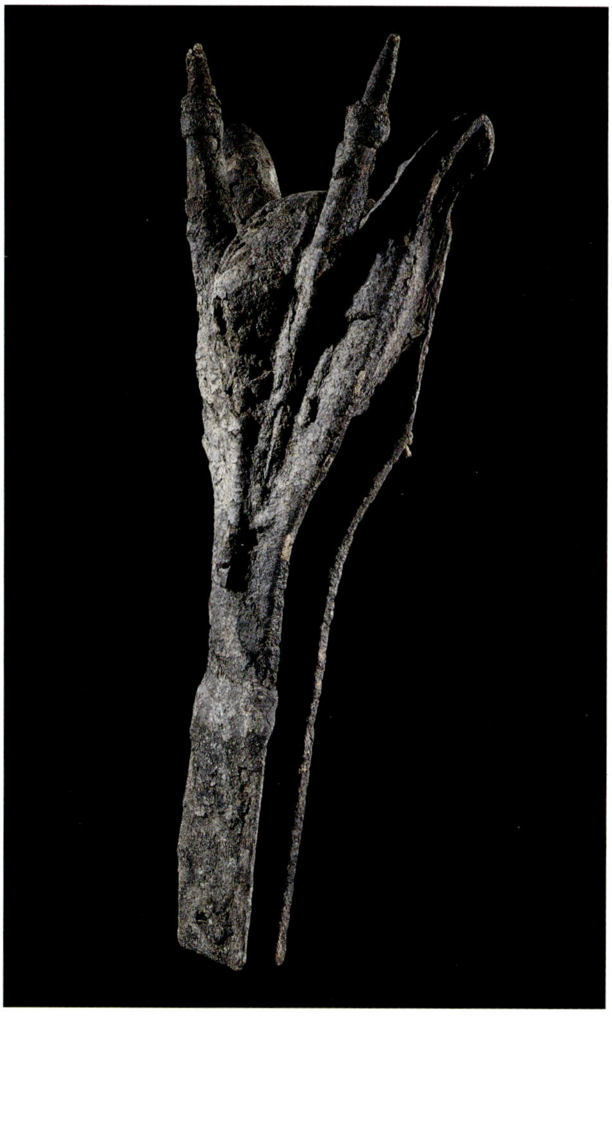

3

4

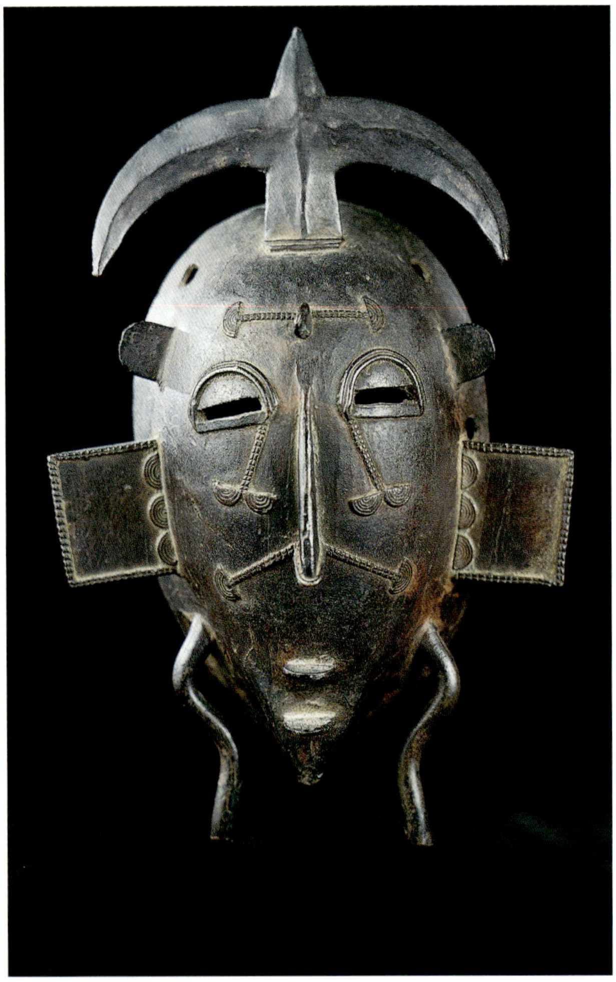

4

## Face mask (kpelie)

Senufo peoples, Côte d'Ivoire
metal, h: 11 inches
Arthur Shone Collection

*Unlike the aggressive and massive forms of the Senufo horizontal helmet masks, kpelie masks of the Poro society have small features depicting composure and dignity. Only rarely were they made of metal rather than wood.*

5

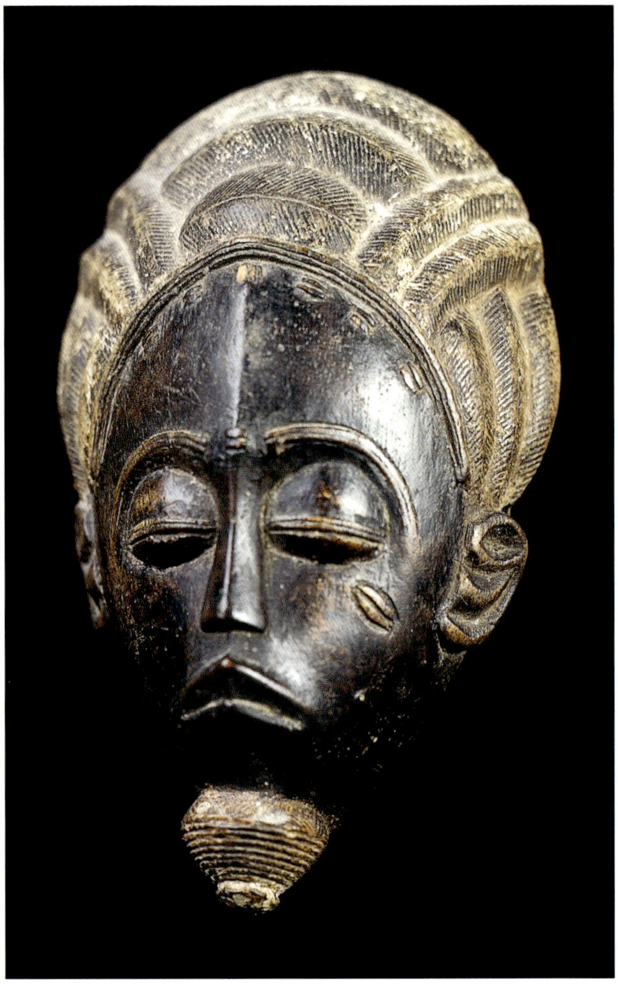

5

## Mask (mblo)

Baule peoples, Côte d'Ivoire
wood, h: 5 1/2 inches
LaVerne Shone Collection

*Mblo masks are used for entertainment purposes. The delicate features and downcast eyes depict a pensive expression often found in masks such as this unusually small example.*

6

## Mask

Dan peoples, Côte d'Ivoire or Liberia
wood, h: 9 inches
Arthur Shone Collection

*Among the Dan peoples, masks associated with the men's society are owned and controlled by families or individual lineage members. Therefore, the function and importance of a mask may change as the status of the owner changes.*

7

## Passport masks (ma go)

Dan peoples, Côte d'Ivoire or Liberia
wood, h: 5 inches
Vincent and Elana Bolling Collection

*Small masks, which embody protective spirits, are miniature versions of larger Dan masks. They are sometimes used as sacred objects for oath-taking and offering sacrifices or to identify the owner as a member of the Poro men's society; hence they are called passport masks.*

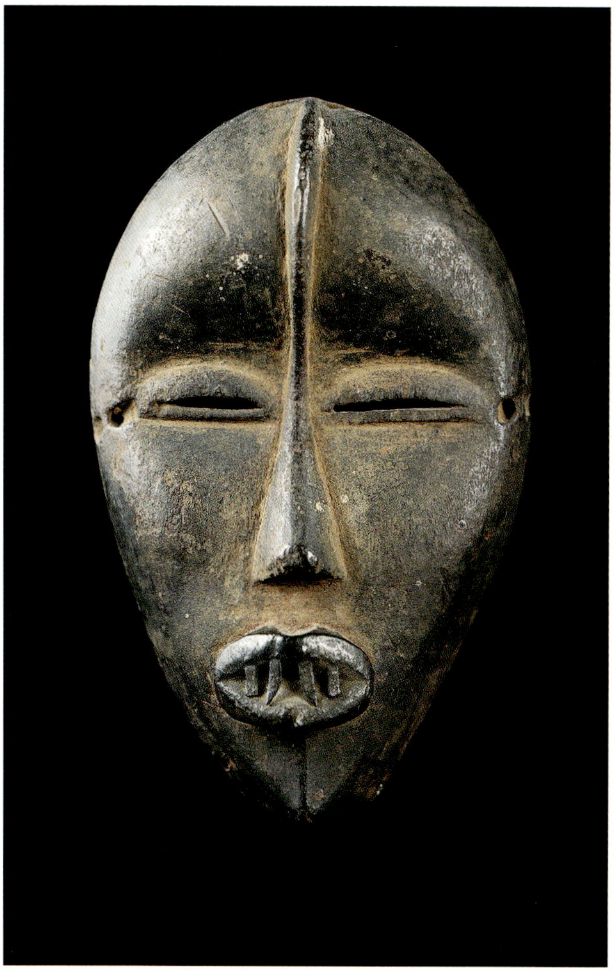

6

7

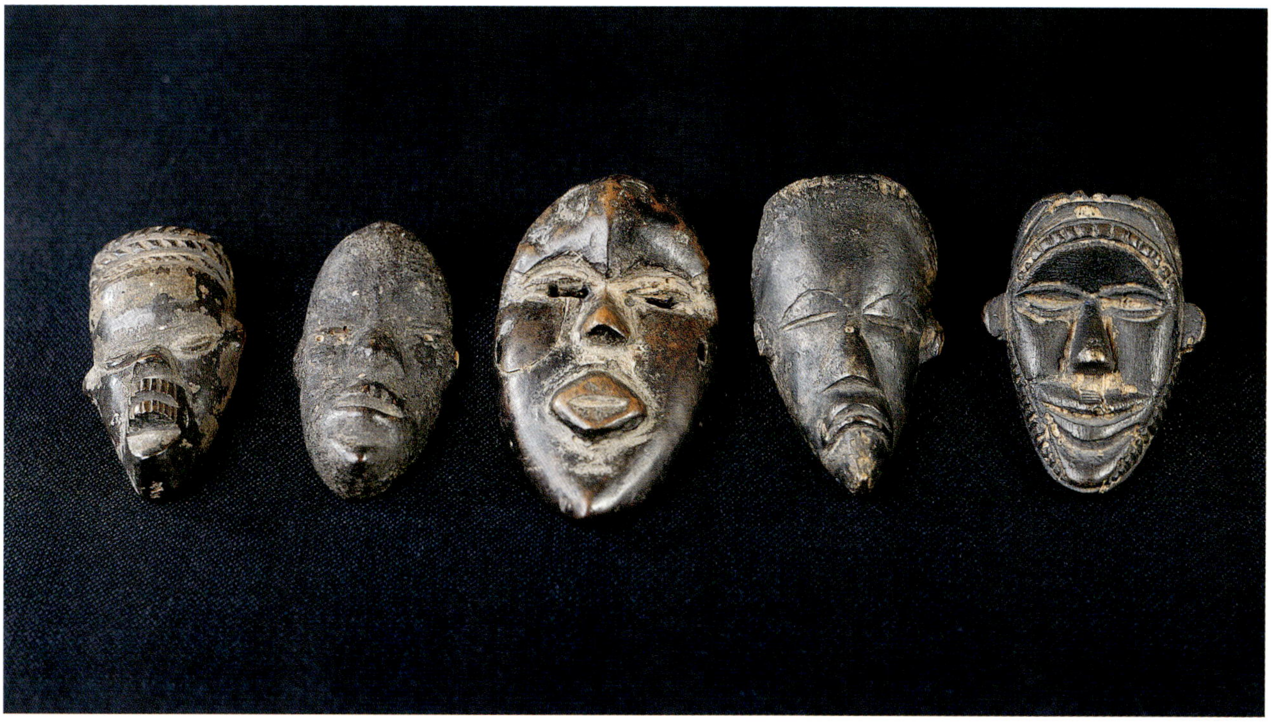

8

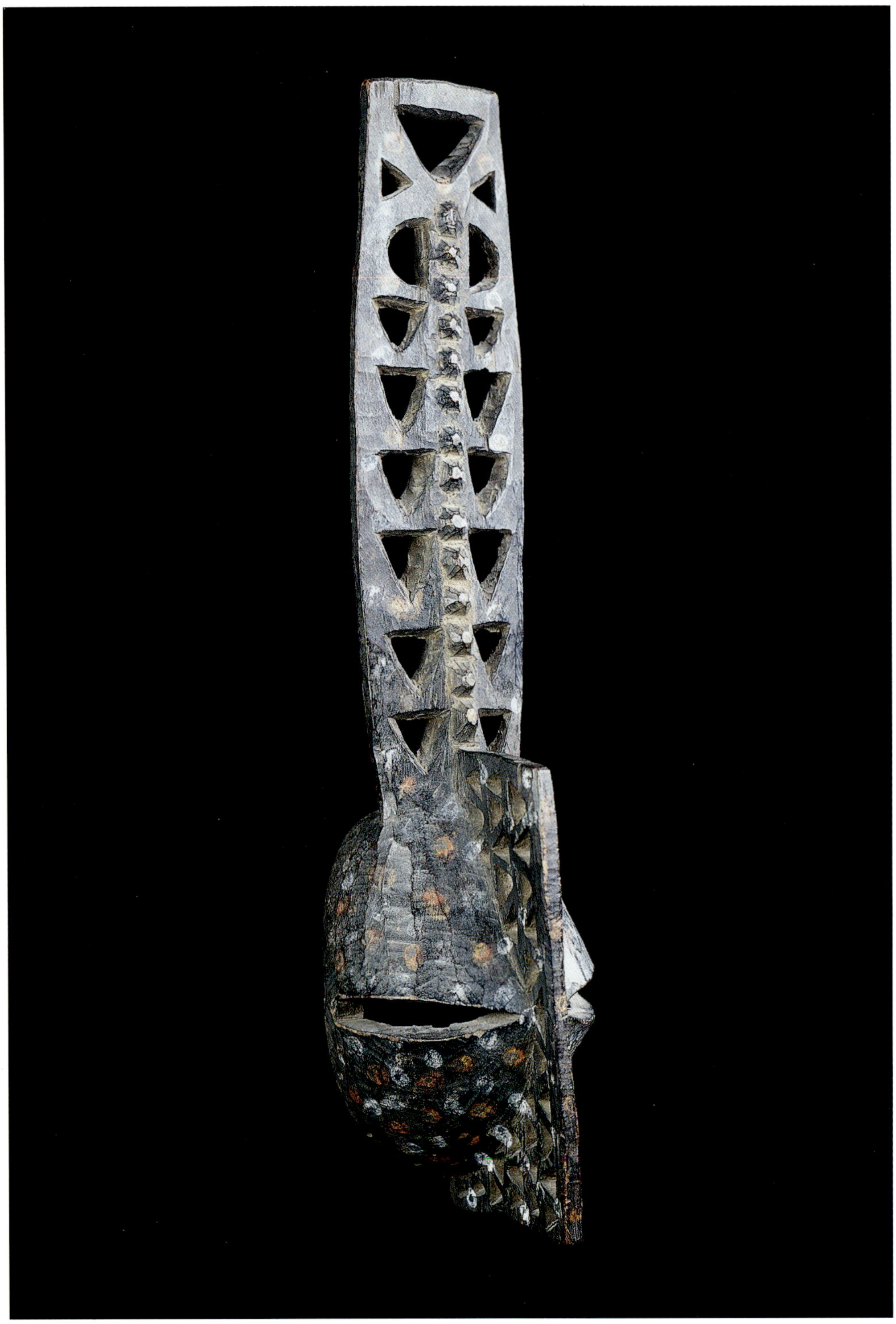

8

## Mask

Igbo peoples, Nigeria, wood, pigment, h: 25 1/2 inches
Dianne Komminsk Collection

*The Igbo are the largest ethnic group in southeastern Nigeria and demonstrate a tremendous variation in regional masking traditions. Patrons often seek out and reward carvers who produce new and unusual mask forms.*

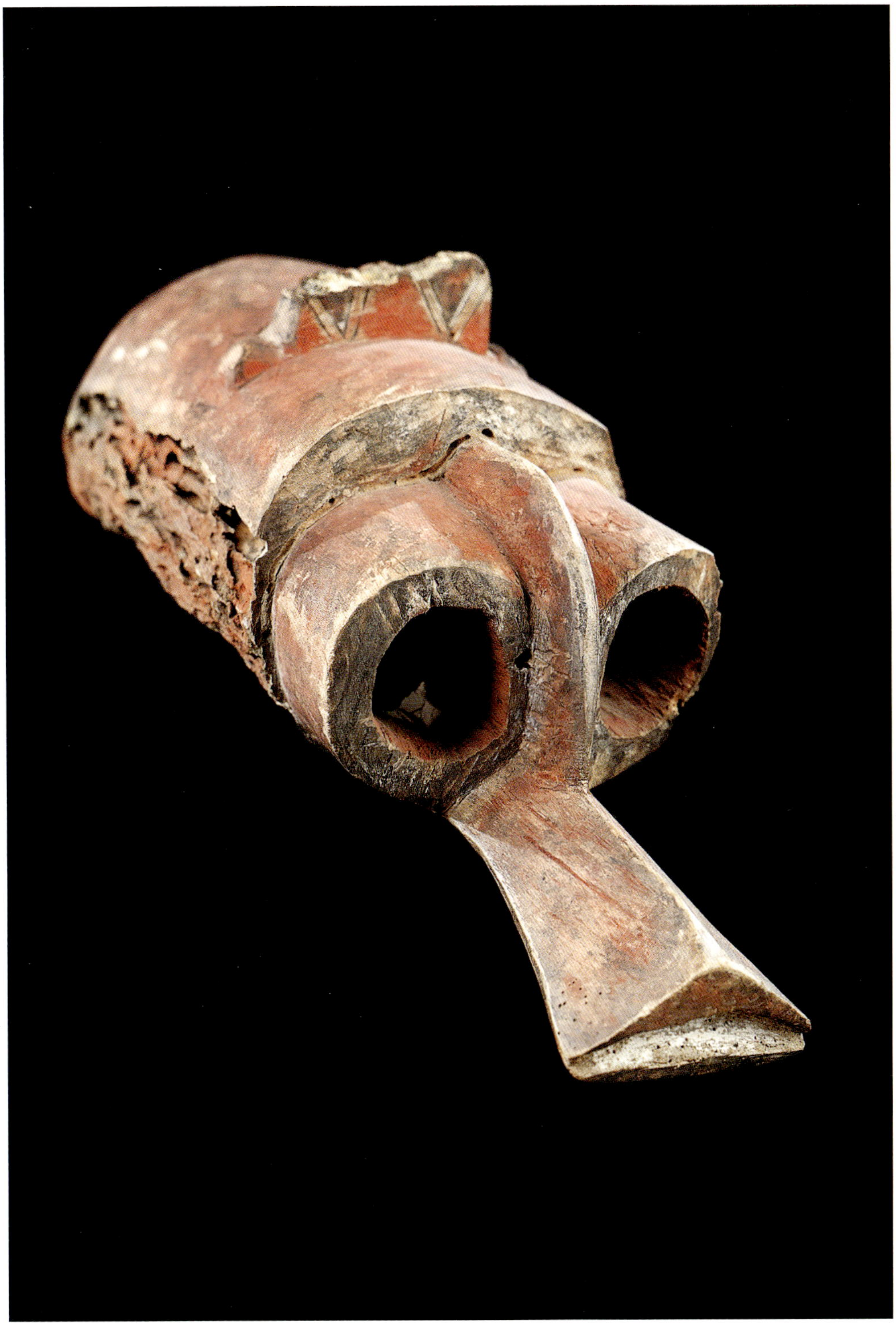

9

## Mask

Mumuye peoples, Nigeria, wood, pigment, l: 16 inches
Vincent and Elana Bolling Collection

*This female mask appears at Vabo men's society initiations. During public performances, a male mask accompanies it. Although the pair depict highly stylized animals, they refer to gender relationships in Mumuye society.*

10

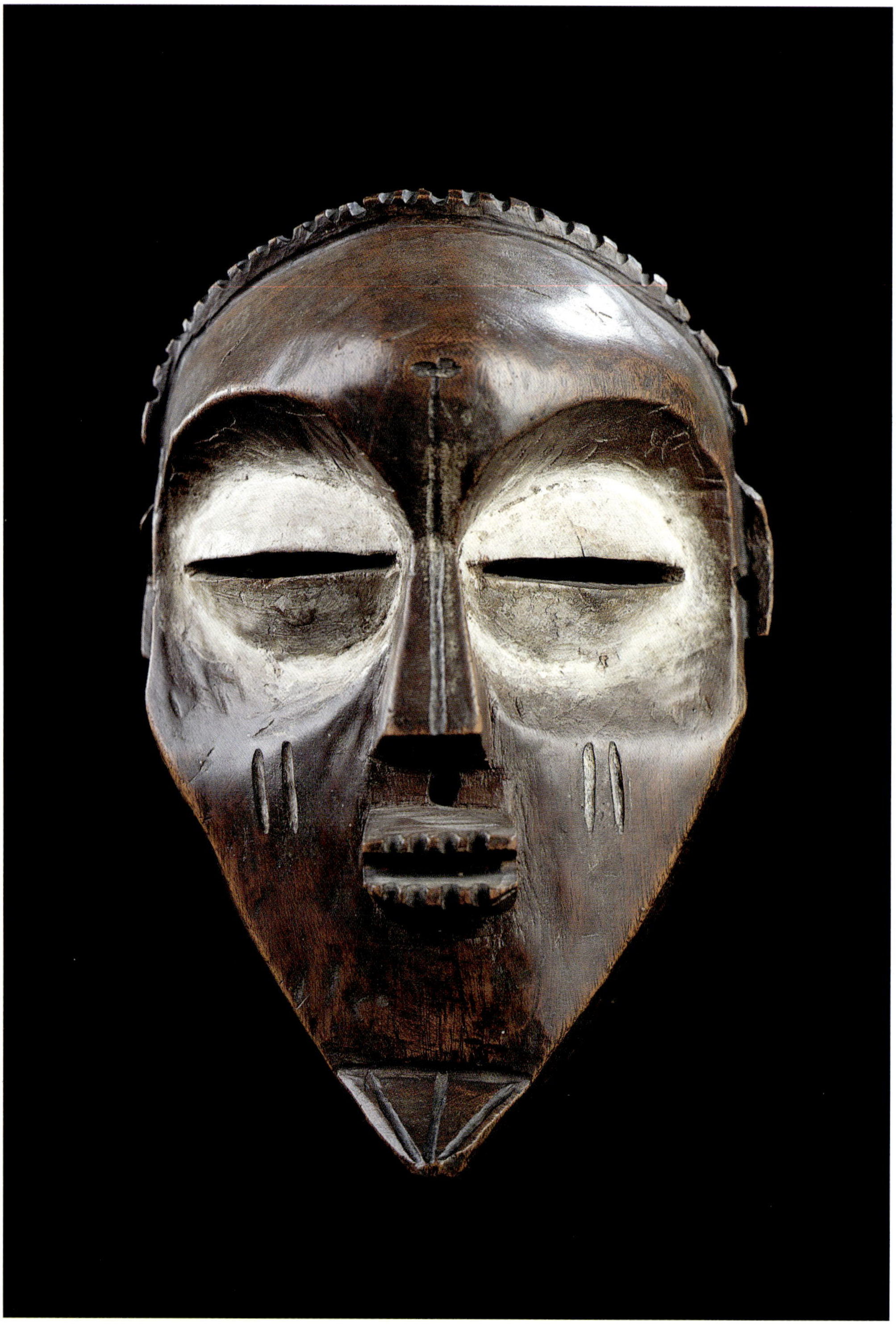

10

## Face mask (gashiga)

Mbagani peoples, Democratic Republic of the Congo, wood, pigment, h: 11 inches
Vincent and Elana Bolling Collection

*Probably danced at the end of a boy's initiation rites and normally hidden, these masks would appear in public to ensure successful hunting or to combat female sterility. The opposition of red (evil) and white (beneficial ancestor spirits) symbolizes the struggle of life and death.*

11

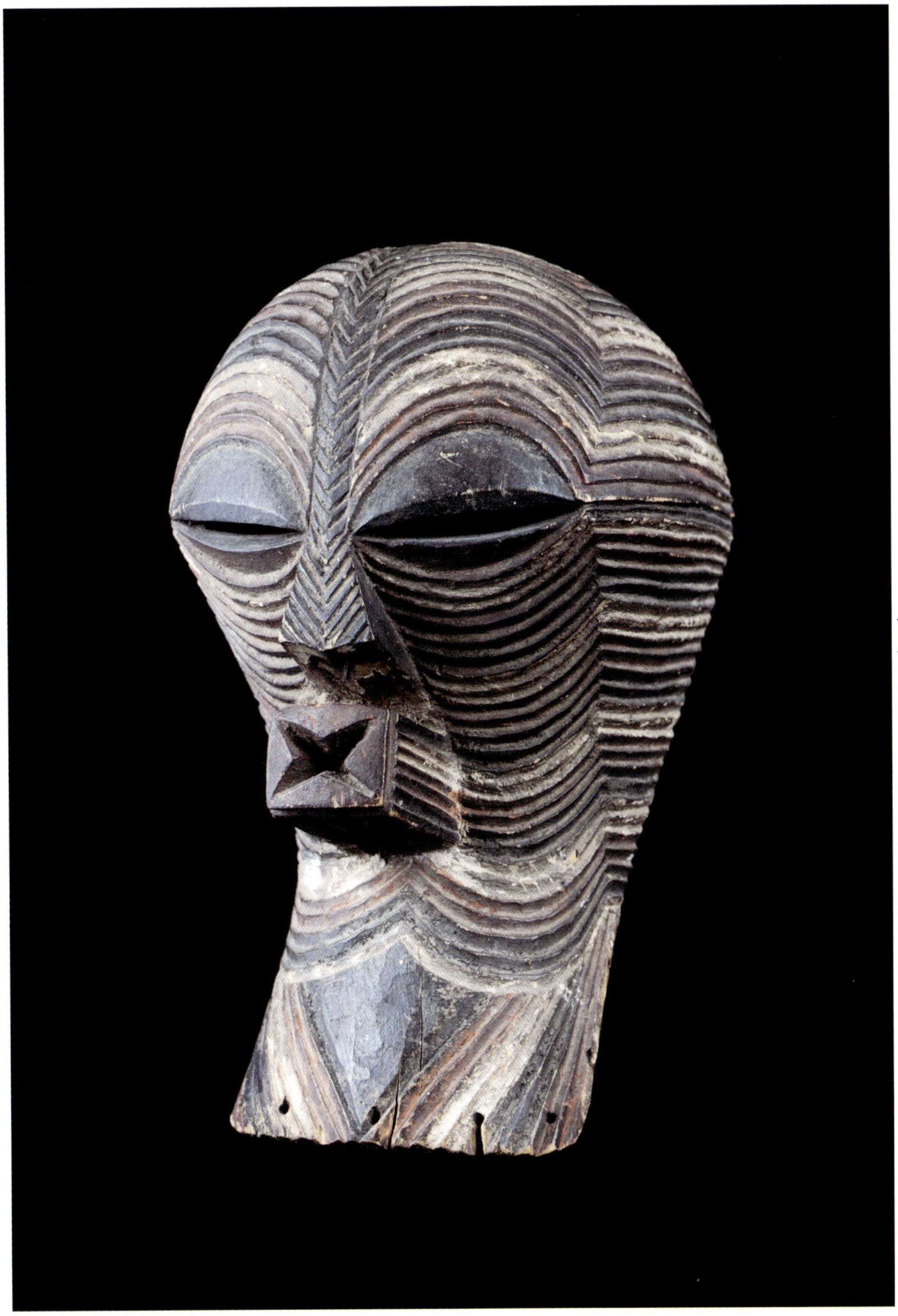

11

## Female mask (kifwebe)

Songye peoples, Democratic Republic of the Congo, wood, pigment, h: 14 inches
Dianne Komminsk Collection

*The mask is part of a pair of male and female masks used by members of the men's Bwadi Bwa kifwebe association in charge of social control. This mask is recognizable as a female by its flat sagittal crest and elegance of form. Female kifwebe masks are the seat of beneficial powers and perform less aggressively than their male counterparts.*

12

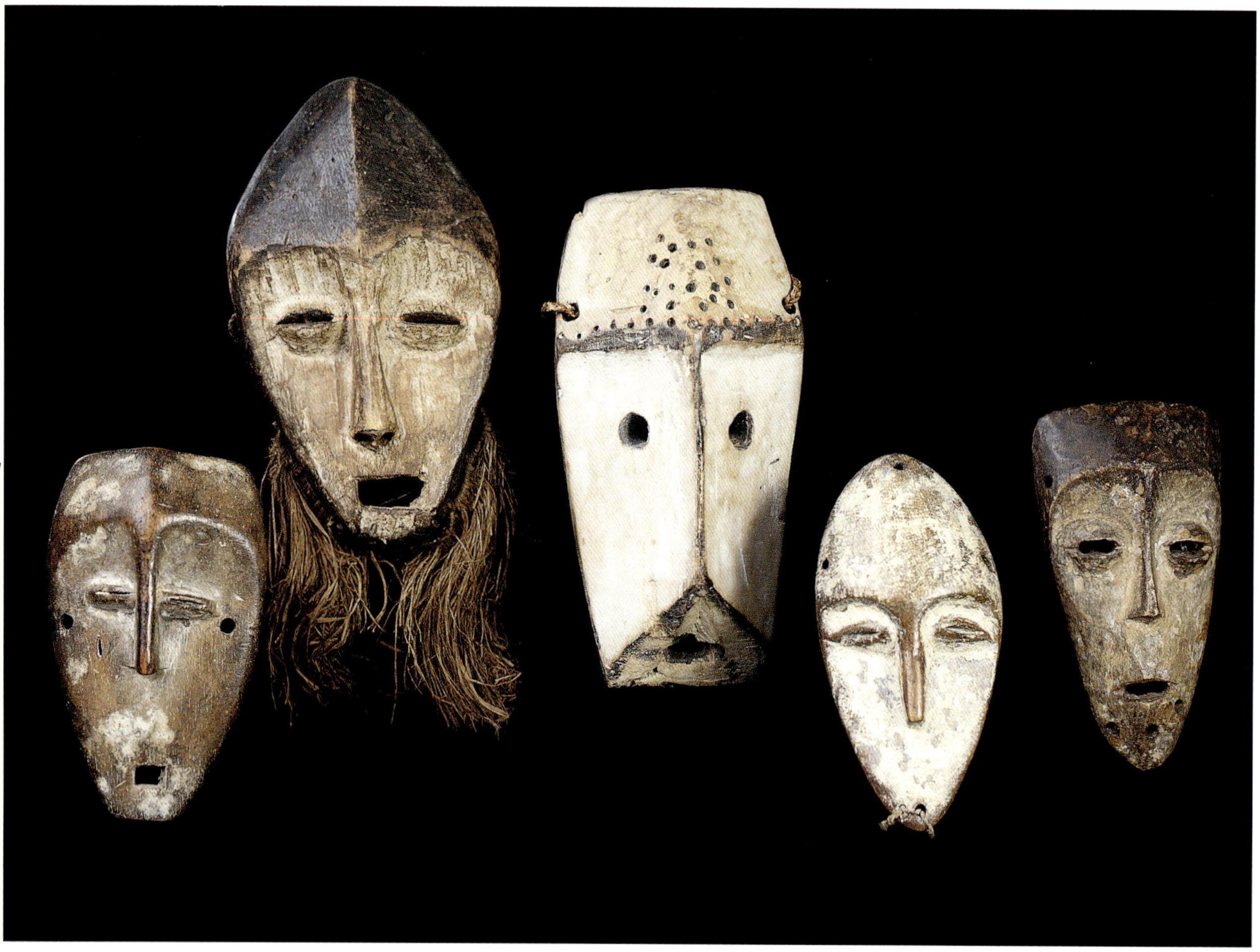

12

## Five masks

Lega peoples, Democratic Republic of the Congo, wood, pigment, raffia, h: 11 inches
Dianne Komminsk Collection

*Small masks were used as status emblems by young initiates within the Bwami men's association. During ceremonies, they were fastened to the cheeks, arms, knees or belt; hung on a lattice; or laid on the ground.*

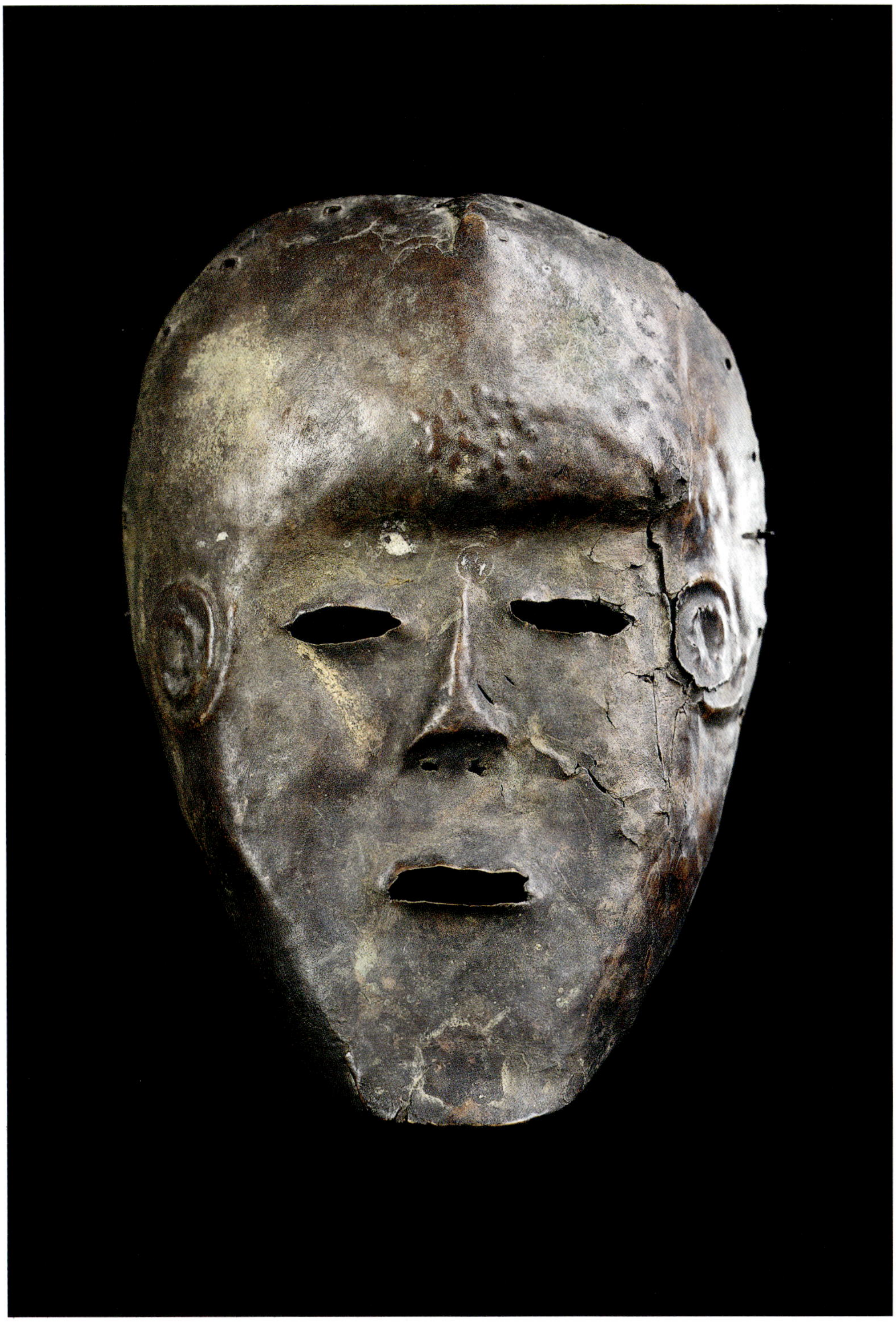

13

13

## Mask

Kongo-Dinga peoples, Democratic Republic of the Congo or Angola, copper, h: 11 inches
Dianne Komminsk Collection

*The Kongo-Dinga are unusual in their use of repoussé copper masks used to maintain order and enforce social control. During funerary rites, they are laid next to the corpses of the members of the ngongo secret society as a sign of respect for the deceased.*

14

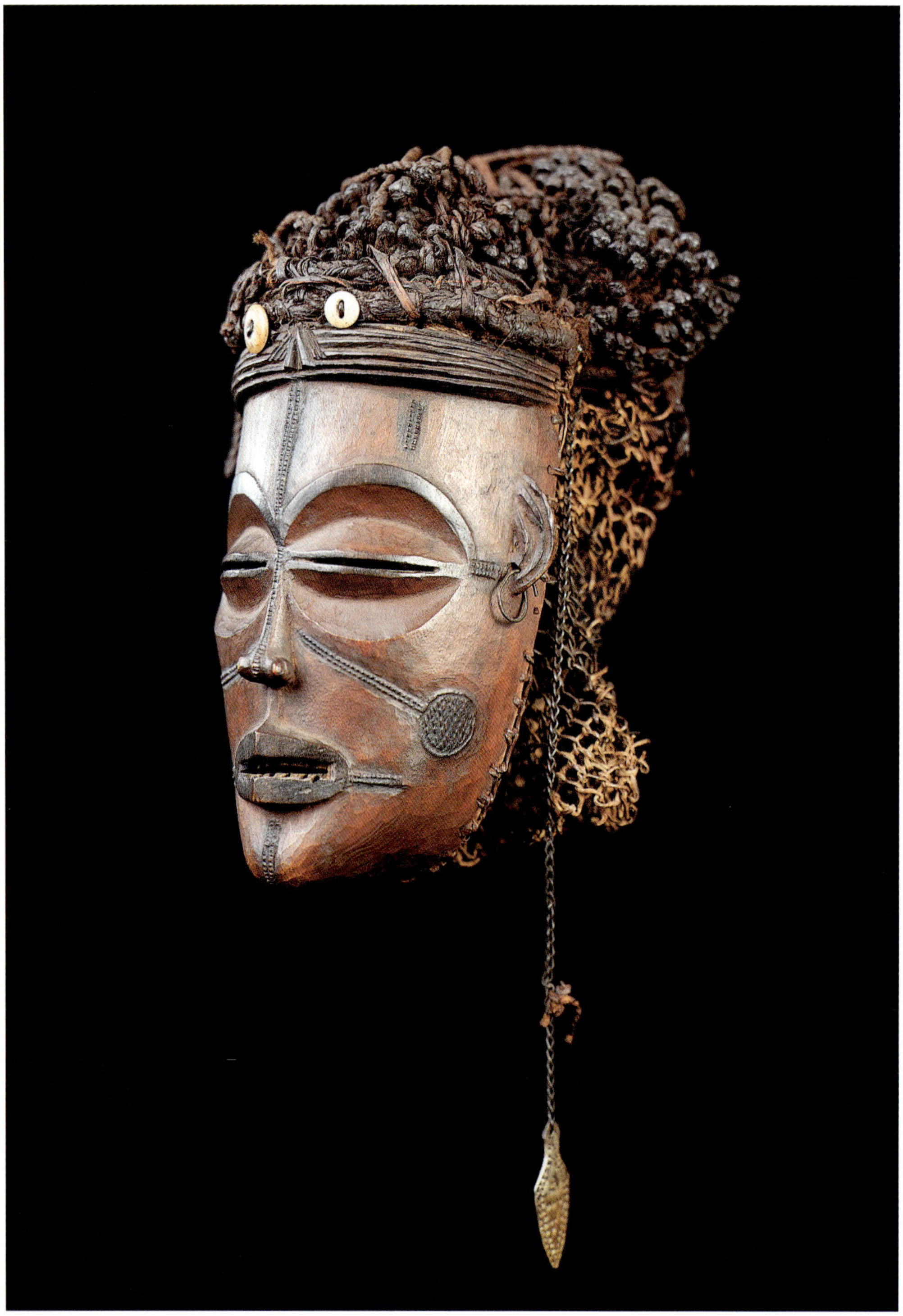

14

## Female mask (pwo)

Chokwe peoples, Democratic Republic of the Congo, wood, metal, buttons, fiber, pigment, h: 16 1/2 inches
Dianne Komminsk Collection

*The refined beauty of this mask expresses the Chokwe vision of the ideal woman: the ancestor mother, the female chieftain, the lovely girl or the fertile woman; provider of nourishment. The pwo mask embodies all the female virtues, exalted in songs and dances particularly during the ceremonies of initiation of young men.*

# INITIATION

Initiation rites are designed to teach young men and women ideal adult behavior. The rites that reinforce this ideal employ a variety of objects in addition to masks. Generally, initiation masks are owned and controlled by men, but there are rare exceptions such as the Sande women's society of Sierra Leone and Liberia.

15

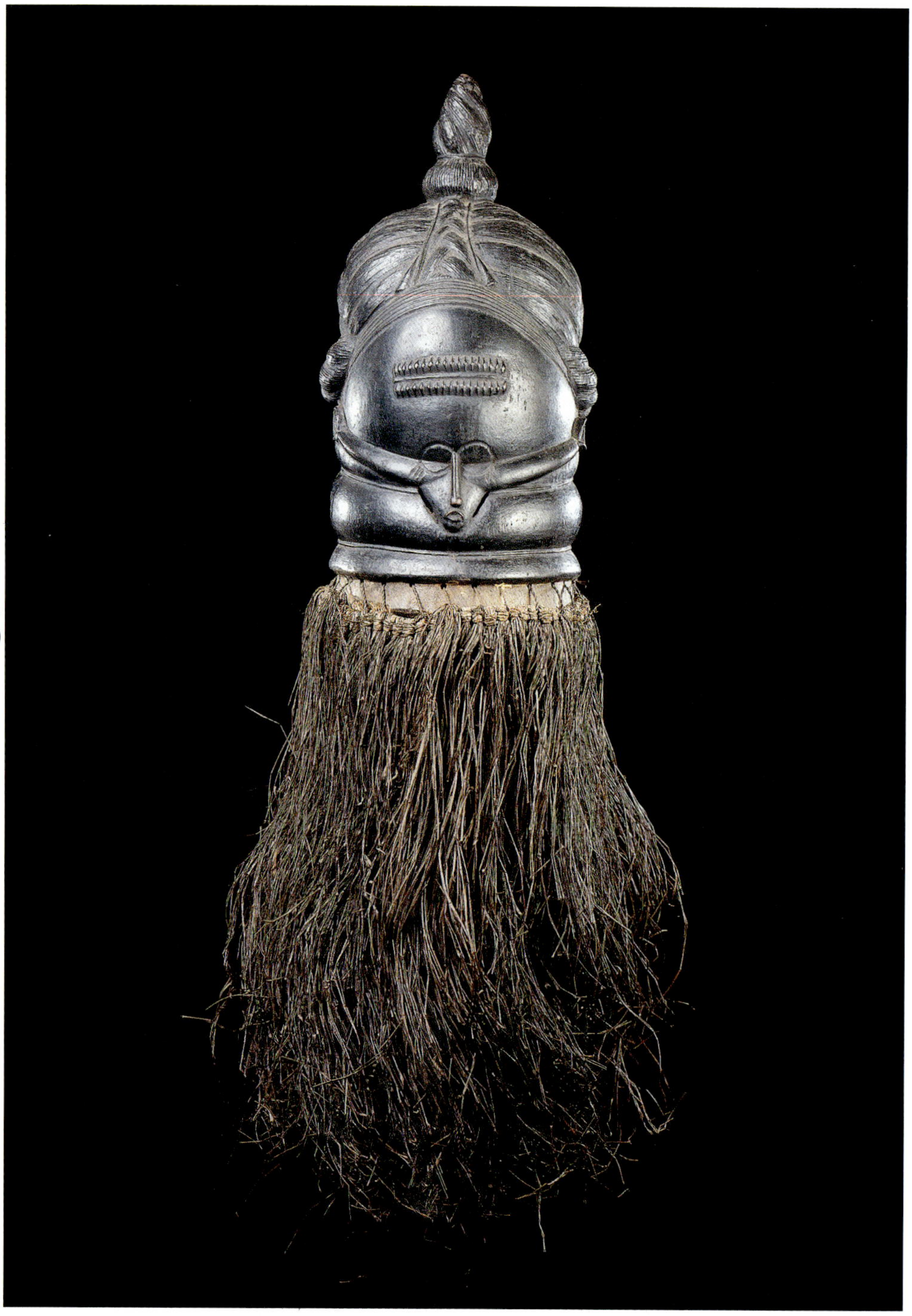

15

## Sowei mask

Mende peoples, Sierra Leone, wood, raffia, h: 36 inches
Dayton Society of Natural History/Boonshoft Museum of Discovery Collection
Gift of Mr. and Mrs. Irvin G. Bieser, Jr.

*Sculptors are almost without exception male, as was the creator of this mask. However, this example was commissioned, directed and danced by the women of the Sande association. The association oversees the initiation rituals and education of young Mende women.* *(see p. 12)*

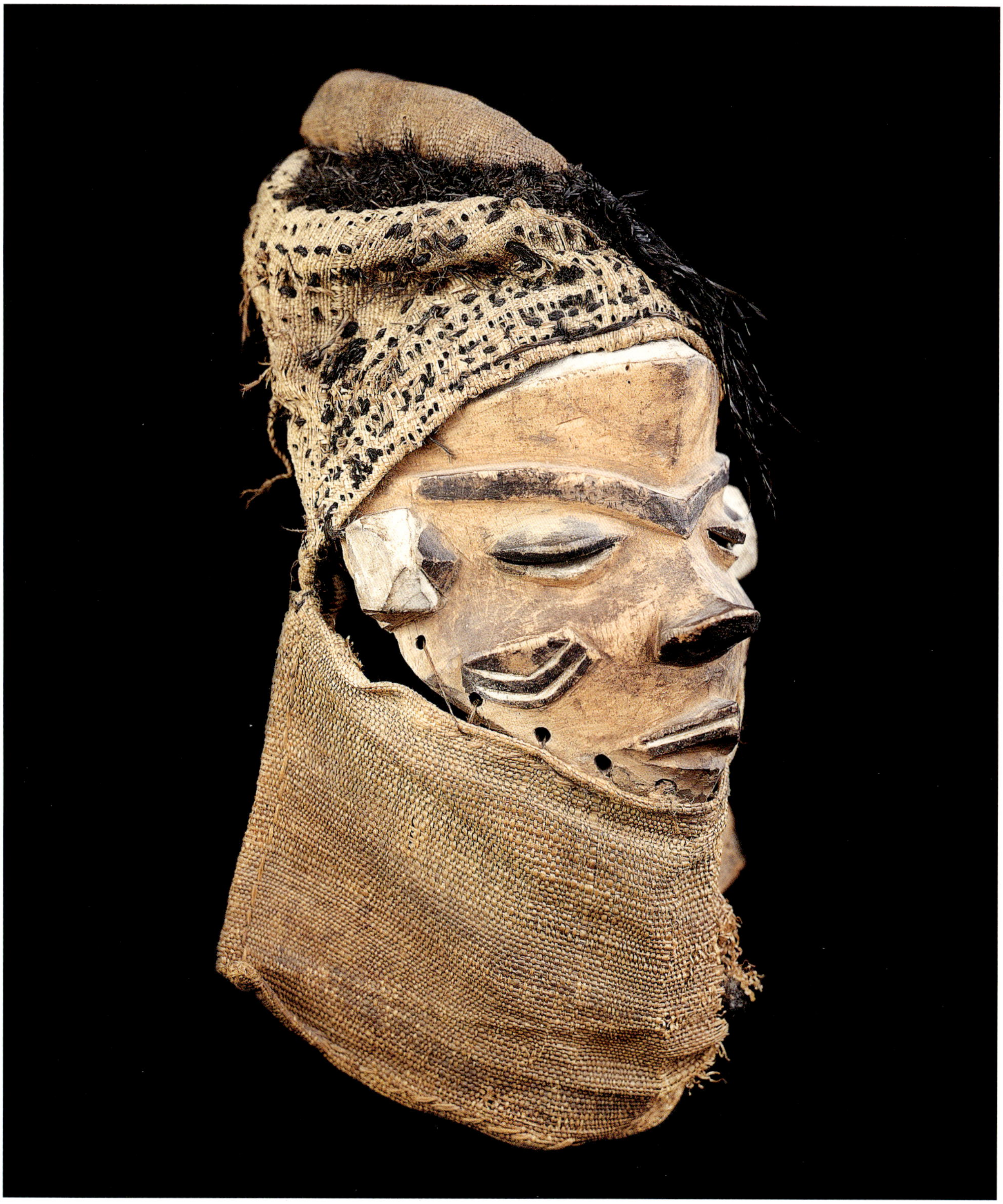

16

16

## Face mask (mbuya)

Pende peoples, Democratic Republic of the Congo, wood, pigment, raffia, h: 16 inches
Dianne Komminsk Collection

*Various characters, displayed in a humorous, satirical manner, appeared during the celebration of the passage of young men into adulthood.*

17

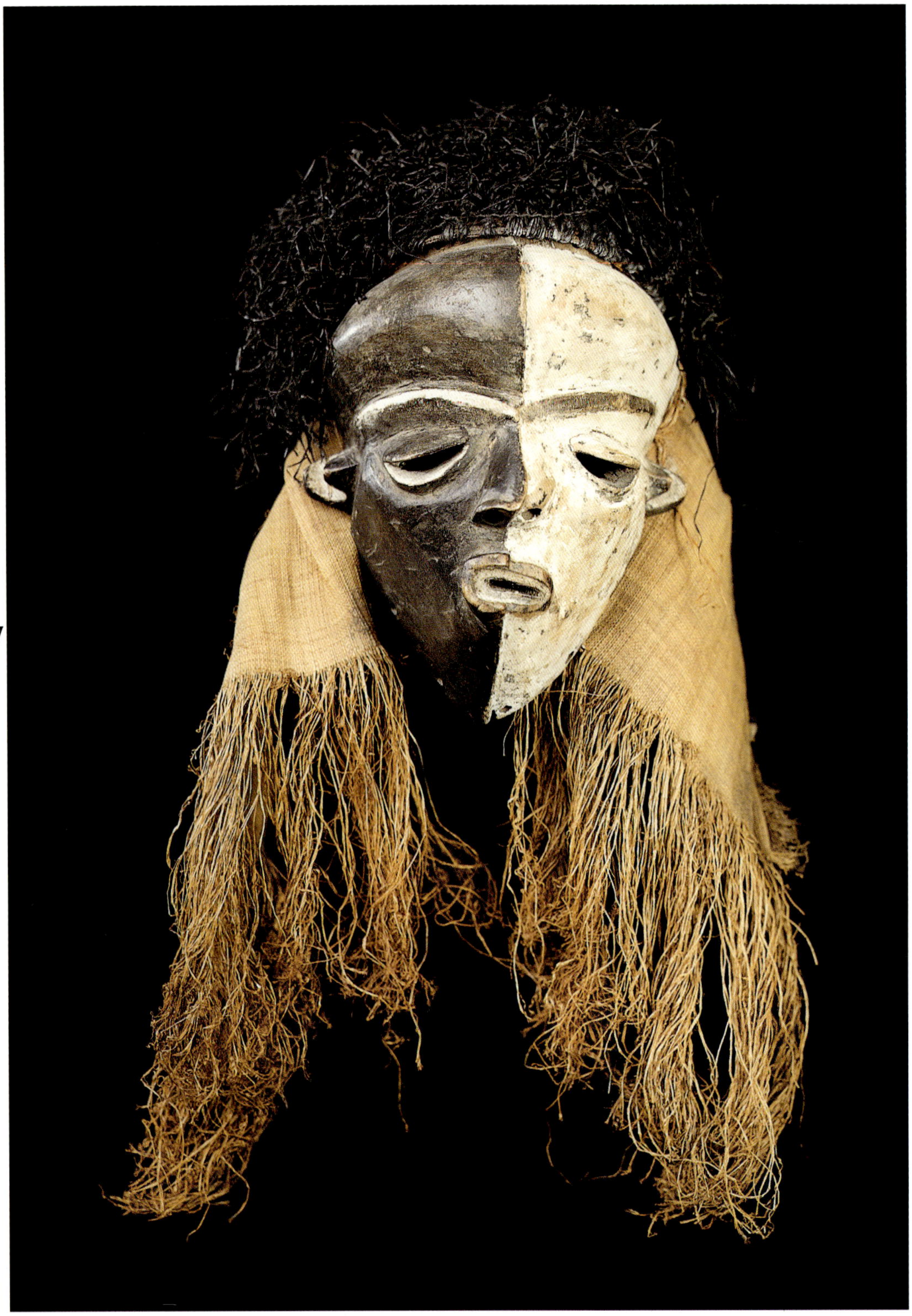

17

## Face mask (mbuya-mbangu)

Pende peoples, Democratic Republic of Congo, wood, pigment, raffia, h: 21 inches
Dianne Komminsk Collection

*Through deformity, the mbangu masked character expressed the evil caused by sorcery. Half of the face is depicted as having been burnt and crippled by fire. For the Pende and other central African people, the opposition between black and white symbolizes the struggle between death and life, suffering and well-being, despair and hope.*

# DOLLS

Dolls are found throughout Africa and are created from a wide variety of materials. They encourage girls' desire for children and help shape maternal skills. Motherhood is the normal, indeed required, role for women in Africa. Some dolls are commissioned by Asante and Fante women after conception to ensure a healthy and beautiful child. Others may be carried to ensure or restore fertility.

18

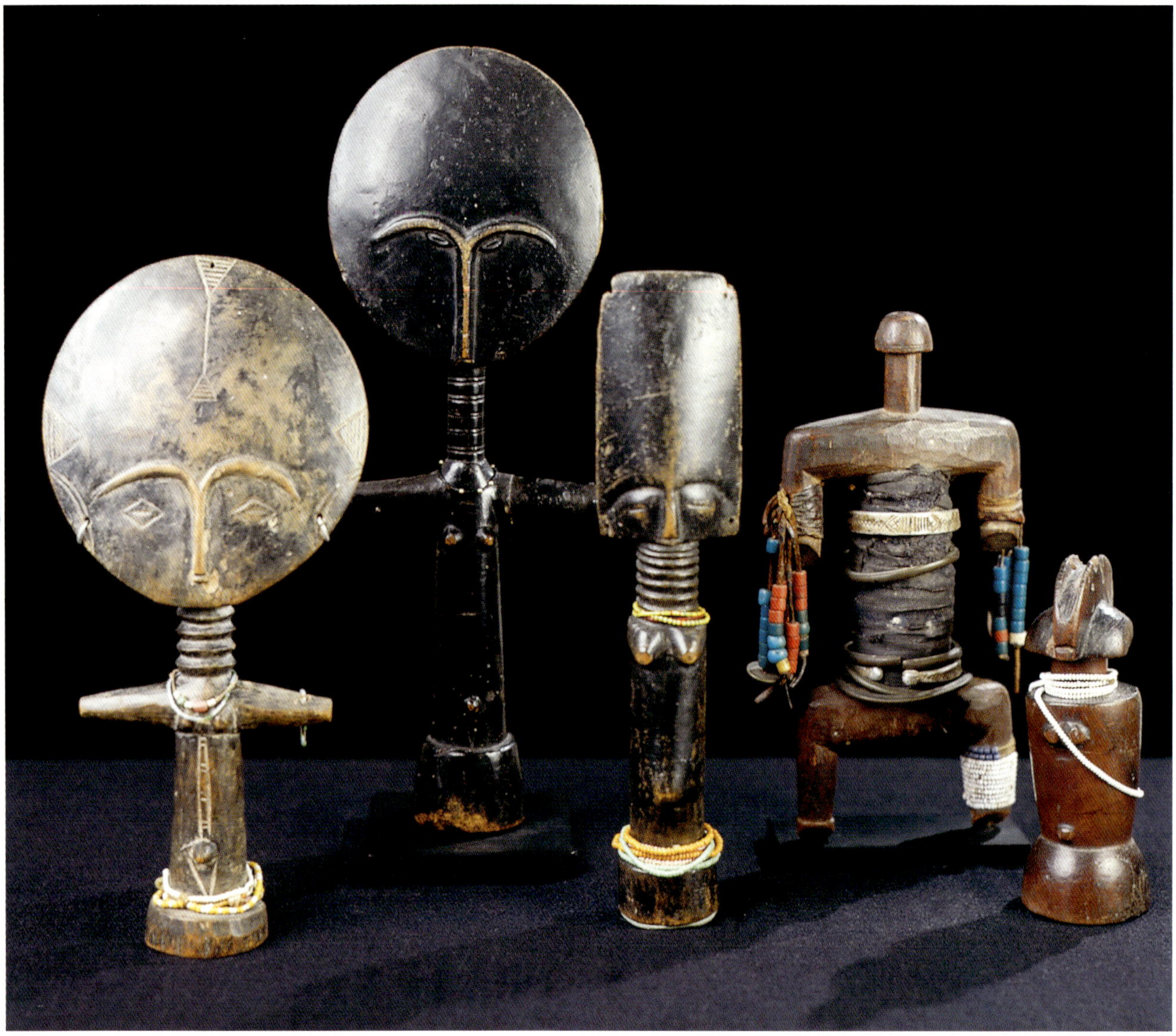

18

## Doll (akua'ba)
Asante peoples, Ghana, wood, beads, pigment
LaVerne Shone Collection

## Doll (akua'ba)
Asante peoples, Ghana, wood, h: 14 inches
Arthur Shone Collection

## Doll (akua'ba)
Fante peoples, Ghana, wood, beads
LaVerne Shone Collection

## Doll
Namshi peoples, Cameroon, wood, beads, metal, fiber
Arthur Shone Collection

## Doll (mwana hiti)
Zaramo or Kwere peoples, Tanzania, wood, beads
LaVerne Shone Collection

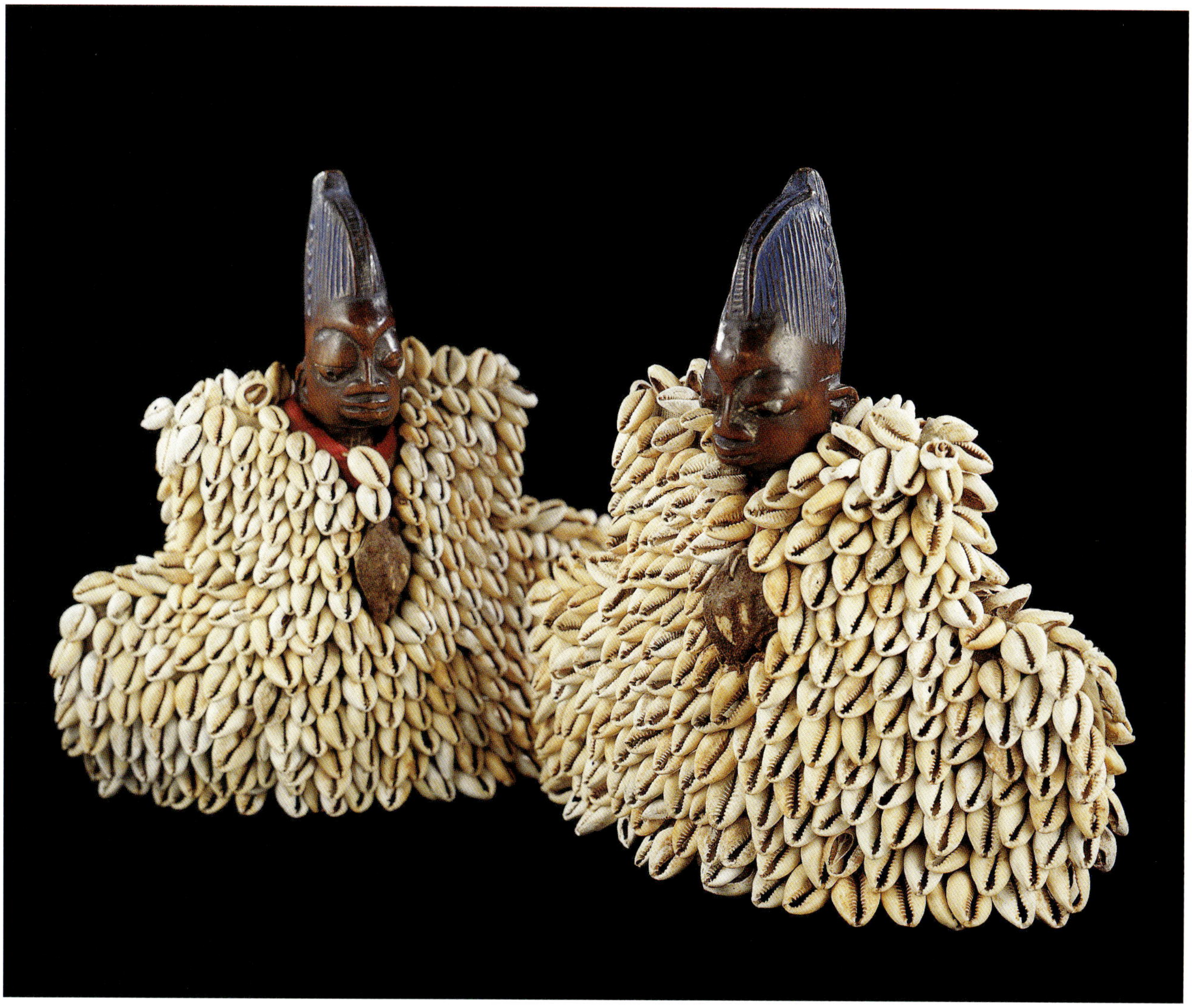

19

19

## Twin figures (ibeji)

Yoruba peoples, Nigeria, wood, cowrie shells, fiber, symbolic substances, pigment, h: 11 inches
Arthur Shone Collection

*Ibeji, unlike other dolls, represent deceased twins. The sculptures are washed, dressed and fed like a living child. Twins are highly desired by the Yoruba who have a higher rate of twinning than any other peoples.*

# FIGURES

Many groups in Africa use figure sculptures. Ranging in size from a few inches to larger-than-life size, they can be enhanced visually and spiritually with cloth, shells, metal, beads and sacrificial offerings. Their functions vary: they may depict ancestors, be found on shrines, appear at funerals or be used in divination and healing ceremonies. They serve as the contact points between the human and spirit realms to receive human requests and prayers and to transmit them to the world of the spirits whose aid and support ensure a secure world.

20

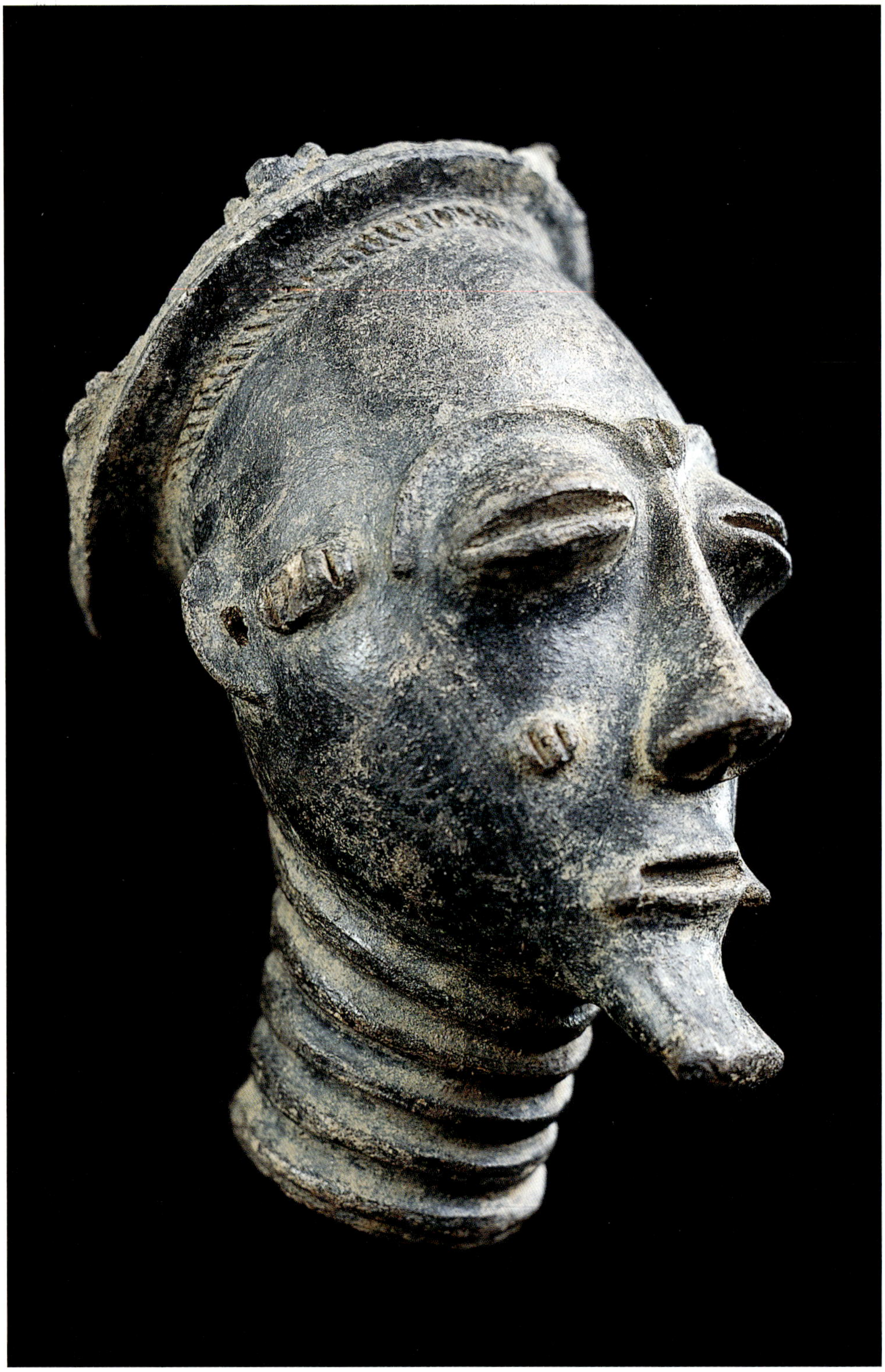

20

## Funerary figure

Anyi peoples, Côte d'Ivoire, terra cotta, h: 8 1/2 inches
Dianne Komminsk Collection

*Fired clay images in Ghana and Côte d'Ivoire commemorate deceased men and women. The figure appears at the formal funeral of the deceased as a means of honoring the dead and may provide a resting place for the spirit.*

21

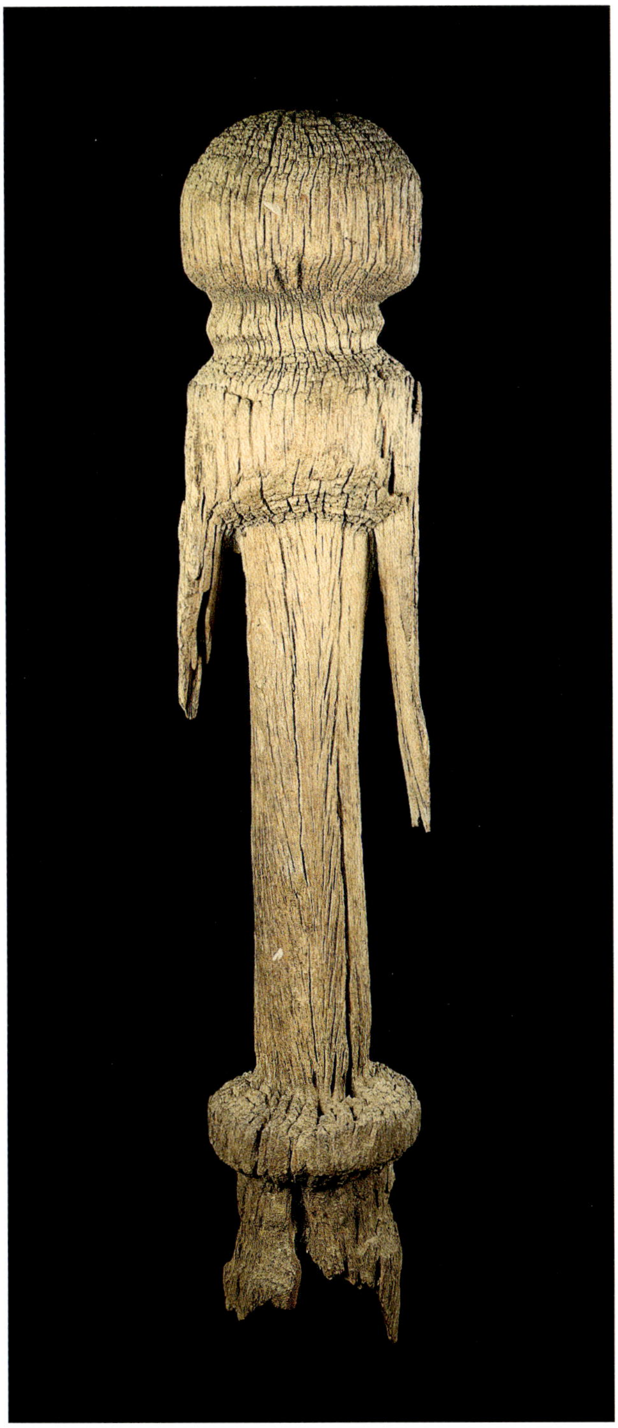

22

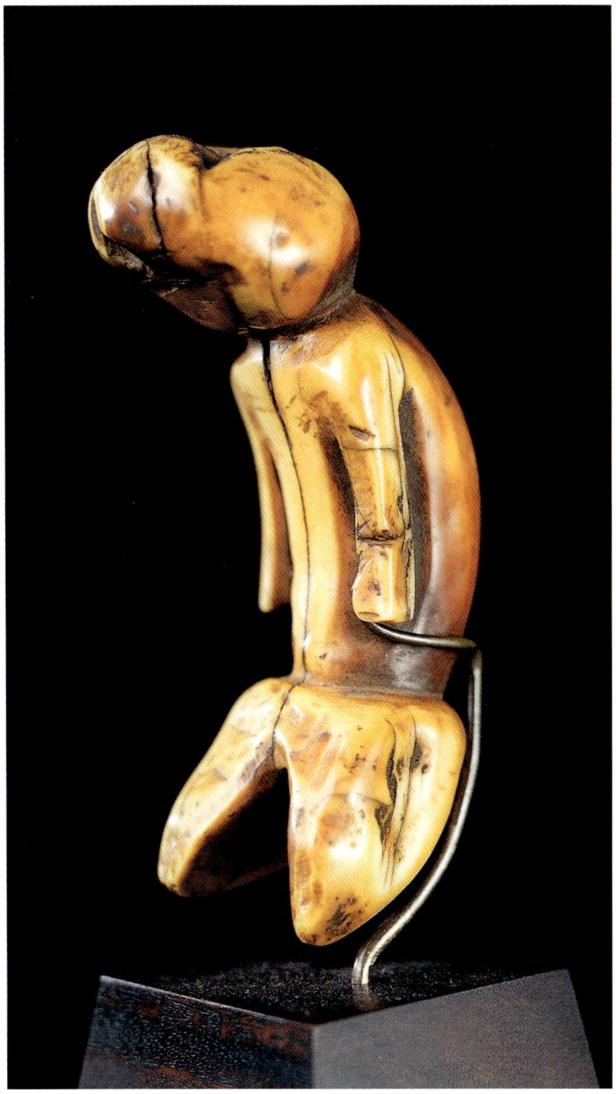

22

## Figure

Moba peoples, Togo
ivory, h: 4 inches
Arthur Shone Collection

*This figure conforms to abstract conventions common in Moba sculpture. It is unusual because it is carved of ivory rather than wood and is in the form of an armlet.*

21

## Figure

Moba peoples, Togo
wood, h: 38 inches
Dianne Komminsk Collection

*This figure represents the founding ancestor of a clan and serves to protect the living. Diviners are consulted to determine if they are to be made for use on personal, household or village shrines.*

23

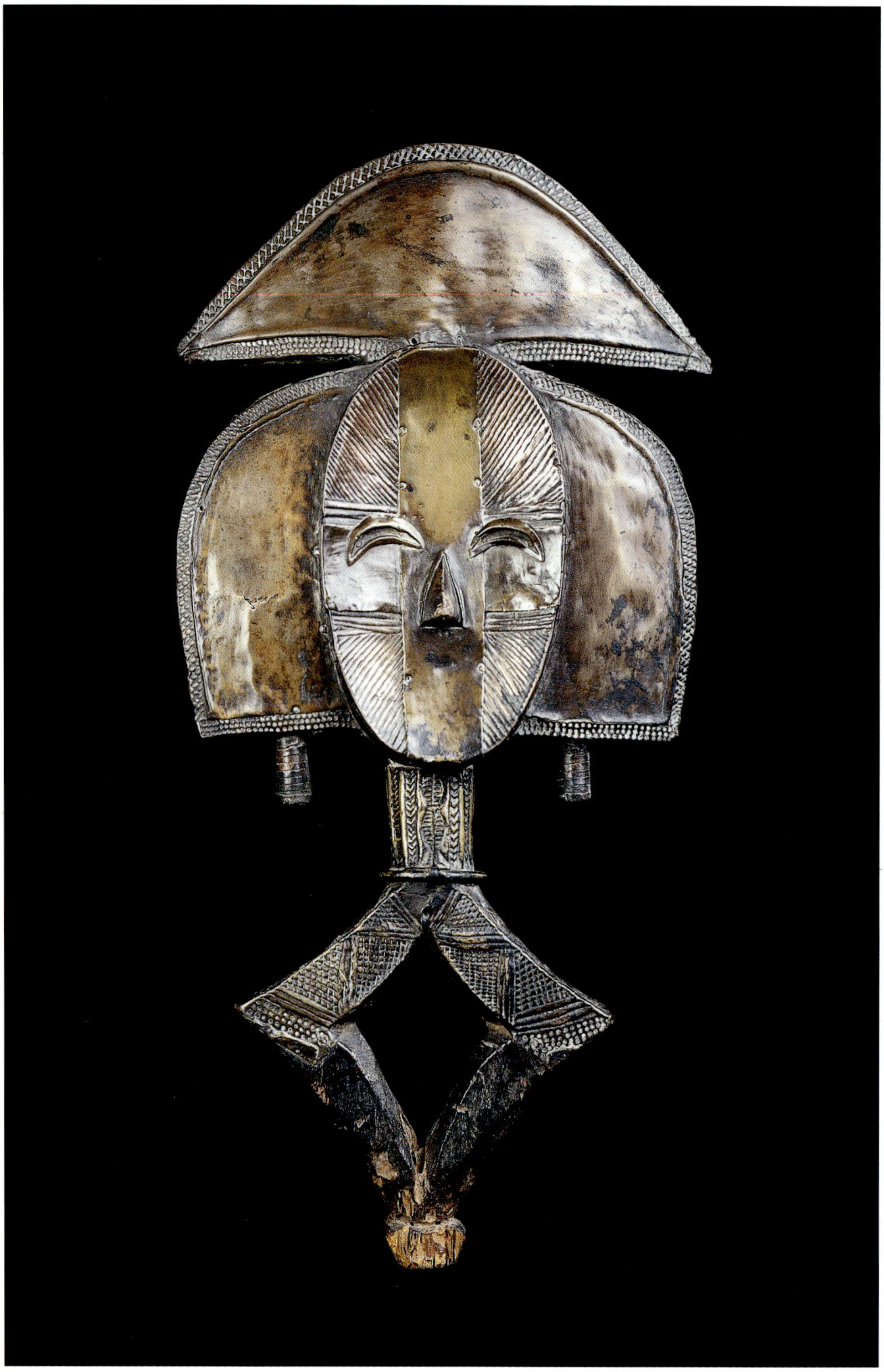

23

## Reliquary figure (mbulu)

Kota peoples, Gabon, wood, metal, h: 21 inches
Dianne Komminsk Collection

*This highly stylized sculpture is made of wood covered by hammered brass and copper. The metal may have derived from large basins imported by European traders. The figure served to protect the relics of ancestors.*

24

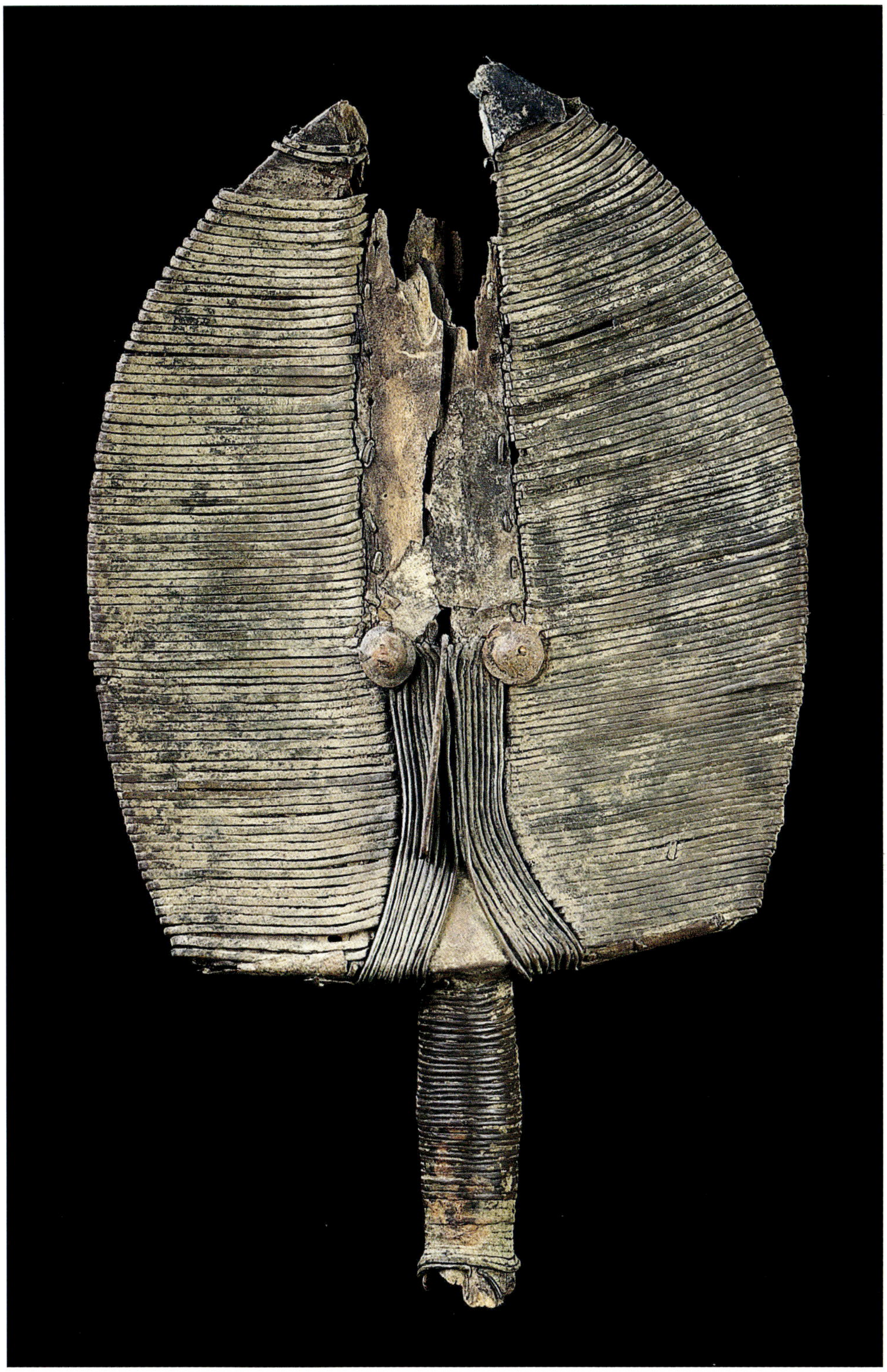

24

## Reliquary figure (bwiti)

Hongwe peoples, Gabon, wood, metal, h: 14 1/2 inches
LaVerne Shone Collection

*Bones of ancestors, preserved in bark boxes, baskets or cloth bags, are protected by bwiti figures. The bwiti may be a highly abstract 'portrait' of the deceased or a device to ward off evil forces.*

25

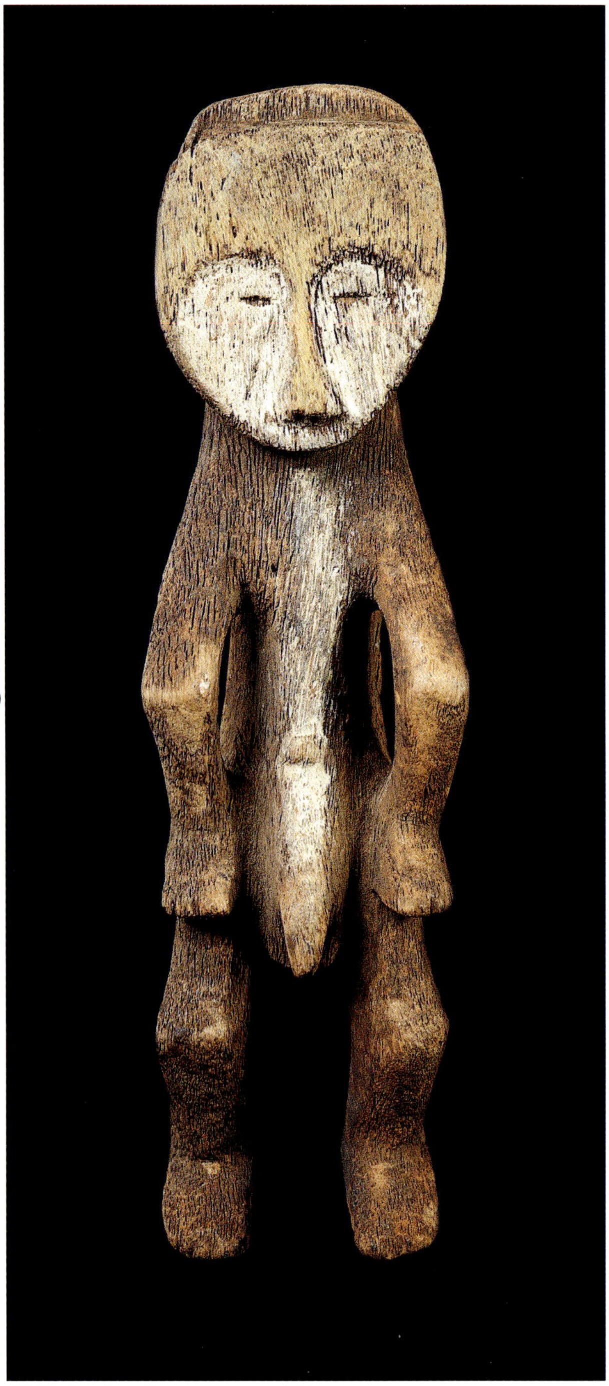

26

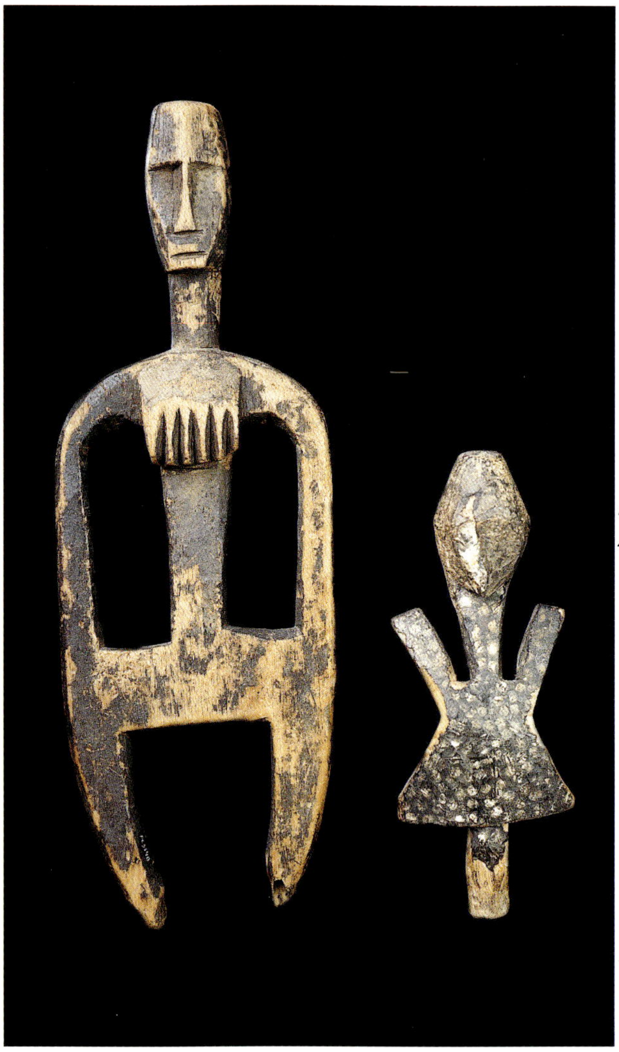

26

## Female figure

Lengola peoples, Democratic Republic of the Congo
wood, pigment, h: 16 inches
LaVerne Shone Collection

*One of the rare sculptures of the Lengola peoples, it is characteristic of figures used by forest dwelling people. Although its use is unknown, it may represent a female spiritual entity (with its six breasts) probably used in a fecundity cult.*

25

## Figure (ofika)

Mbole peoples, Democratic Republic of the Congo
wood, pigment, h: 15 inches
Dianne Komminsk Collection

*Such stylized figures exert an enormous influence on the members of the Lilwa male secret association. They represent an executed criminal or a man sacrificed by hanging when a dignitary is elevated to the rank of high priest, (isoko). As a result, they are both cautionary and instructive.*

## Post

Lengola or Metoko peoples, Democratic Republic of the Congo
wood, pigment, h: 9 inches
Dianne Komminsk Collection

*Used in the initiation/circumcision rites of the Bukota men's secret association, the initiator-priest and the chief would carry such posts as scepters and emblems of their functions. The white dots on the sculpture are characteristic of the neighboring Lengola and Metoko peoples and might refer to the leopard, an emblem of chieftainship.*

27

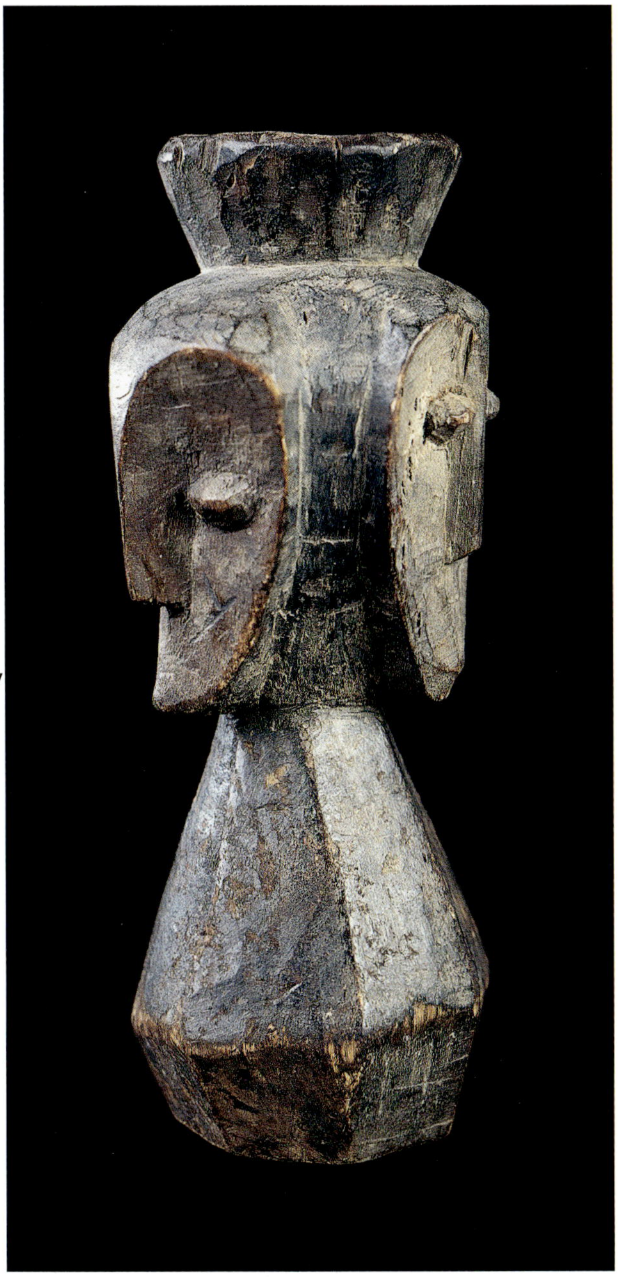

28

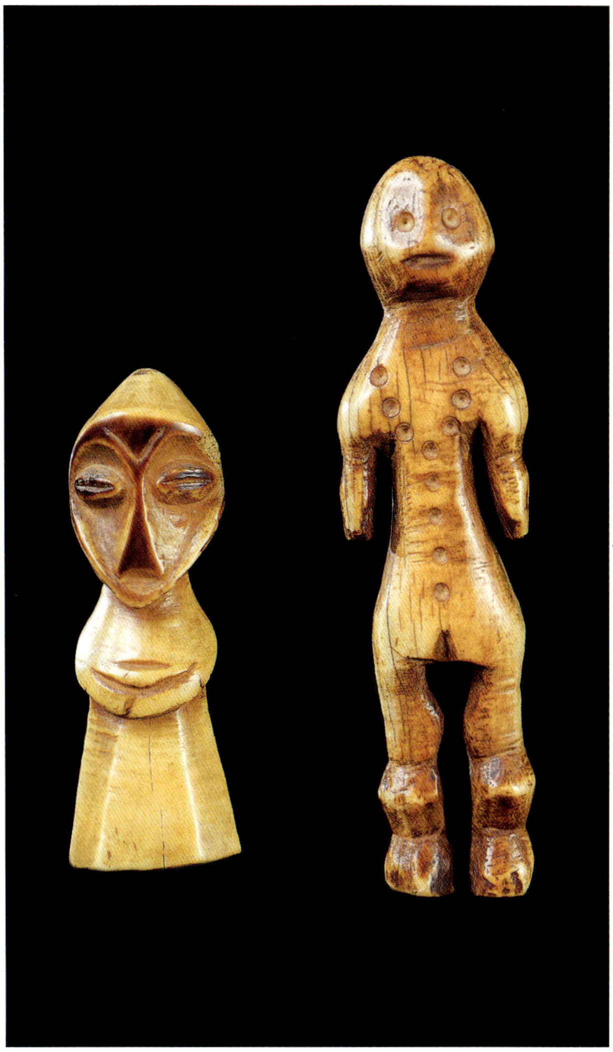

28

## Two figures

Lega peoples, Democratic Republic of the Congo
ivory , h: 7 inches
Arthur Shone Collection

*Small ivory figurines are owned by members of the highest rank of the Bwami society. Each had a meaning often expressed in a title or parable associated with the Lega philosophy of wisdom and moral excellence. The precise meaning of a figure could have been learned only from its original owner.*

27

## Three faced wooden figure (sabitwe-bitwe)

Lega peoples, Democratic Republic of the Congo
wood, h: 11 inches
Bonnie H. Bozorgi Collection

*This figure was used by the highest grade (kindi) of the Bwami society. The society transmitted social virtues through the generations. The several heads could refer to the power of clairvoyance that the members acquire by the end of their initiation. Alternatively, one face may be male, another female and the third, without facial features, could symbolize the primal ancestors.*

29

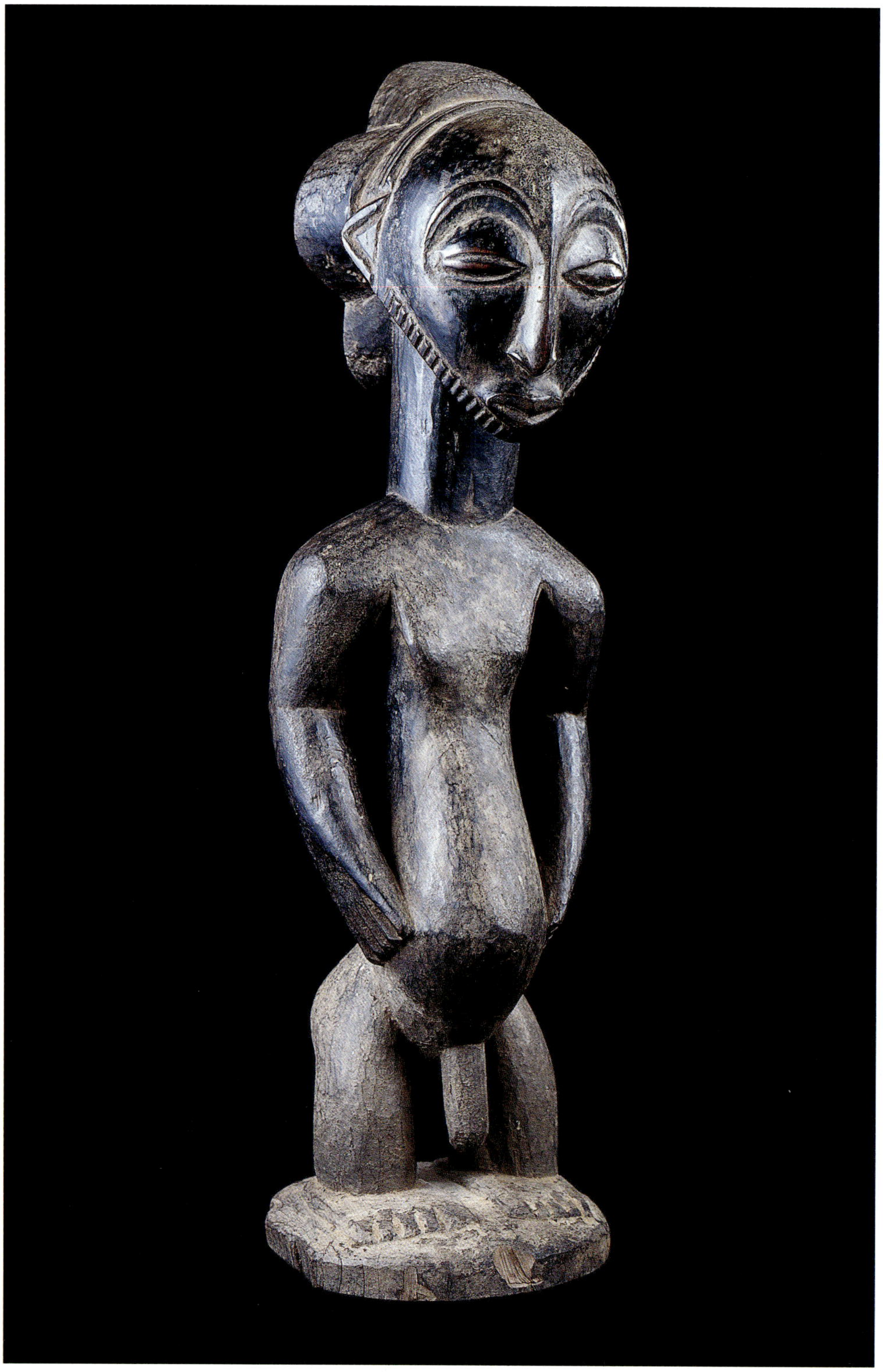

29

## Male figure (singiti)

Hemba peoples, Democratic Republic of the Congo, wood, h: 23 inches
Dianne Komminsk Collection

*This figure in Niembo style represents a clan ancestor. Clan members rely on the religious power of the ancestors. Clan chiefs keep ancestor figures, possibly idealized portraits, in memory of deceased chiefs whose names they may inherit.*

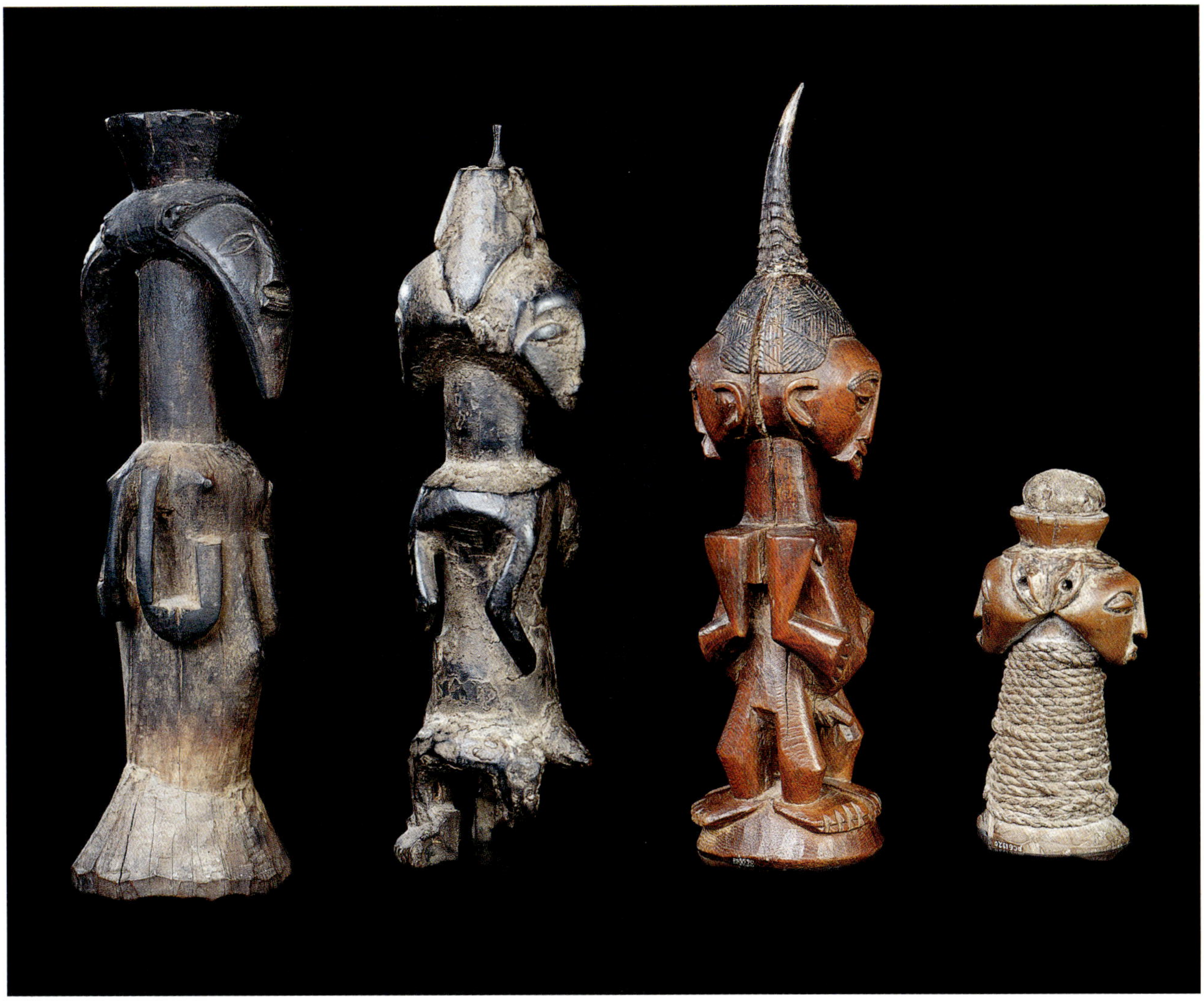

30

30

## Janus figure
Kasongo peoples, Democratic Republic of the Congo,
wood, h: 14 inches
LaVerne Shone Collection

## Janus head figure (kabeja)
Hemba peoples, Democratic Republic of the Congo,
wood, metal, traces of red and white pigment
Dianne Komminsk Collection

## Janus power figure
Songye peoples, Democratic Republic of the Congo,
wood, antelope horn, metal
Dianne Komminsk Collection

## Janus figure (kakudji)
Luba peoples, Democratic Republic of the Congo, wood, fiber
Dianne Komminsk Collection

*Janus figures depicting males and females back to back often represent the mythical primordial couple, founders of the group. Ancestral spirits are believed to insure health, well-being, human and animal fertility. Although some symbolize antagonistic or opposing spiritual forces, the primary meaning of these figures as used by the healers and diviners was to insure a more secure world.*

31

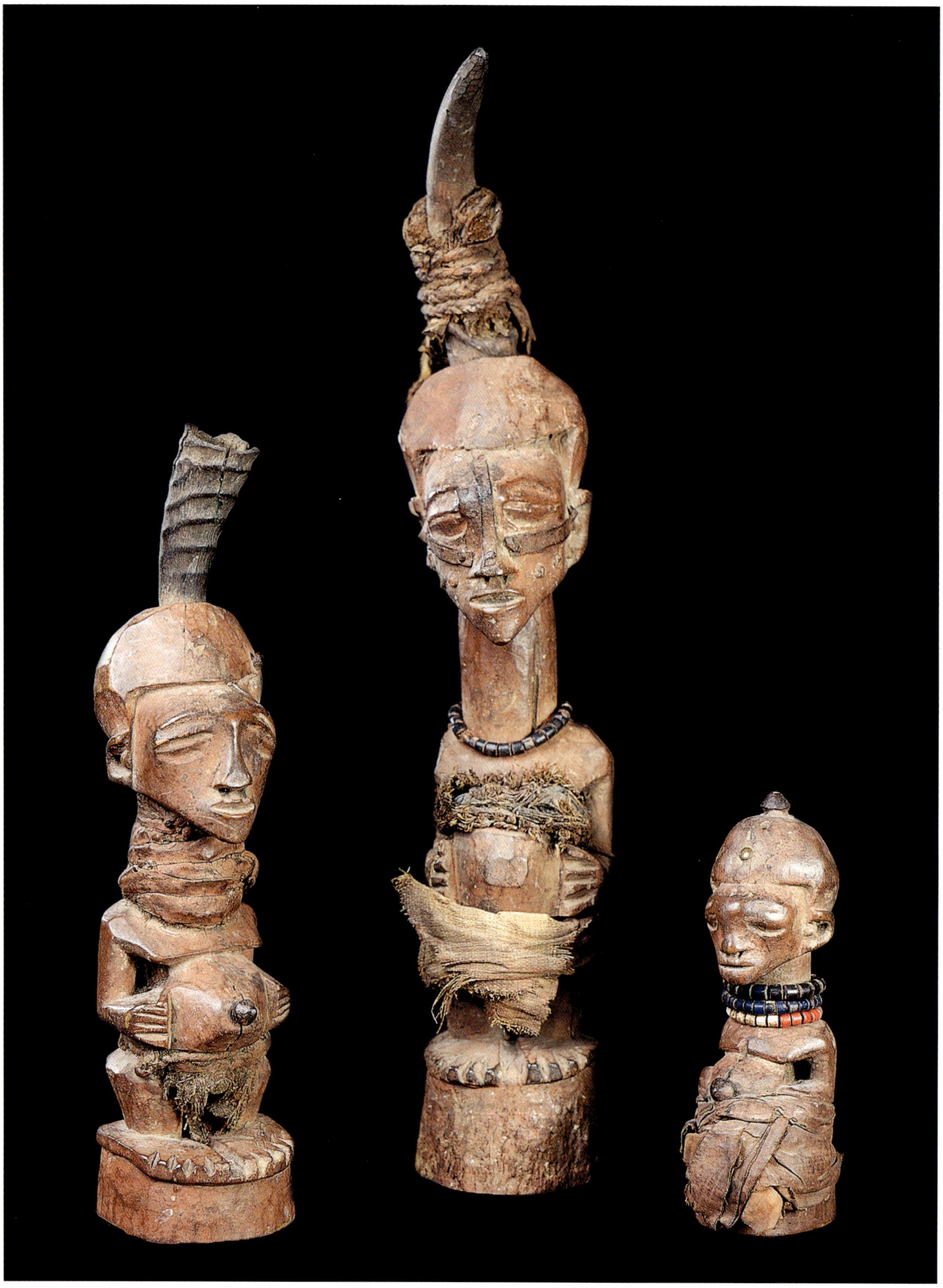

31

## Three power figures (mankishi, singular nkishi)

Songye peoples, Democratic Republic of the Congo, wood, fiber, beads, horn, pigment, h: 21 inches
Dianne Komminsk Collection

*The style of these three northern Songye figures indicates that they were made by the same artist. They are personal power figures vested with spiritual forces. They would have been in a family or lineage sanctuary in a basket together with symbolic substances for protection against illness, bad luck, death and infertility. They thereby ensured health, success and fertility.*

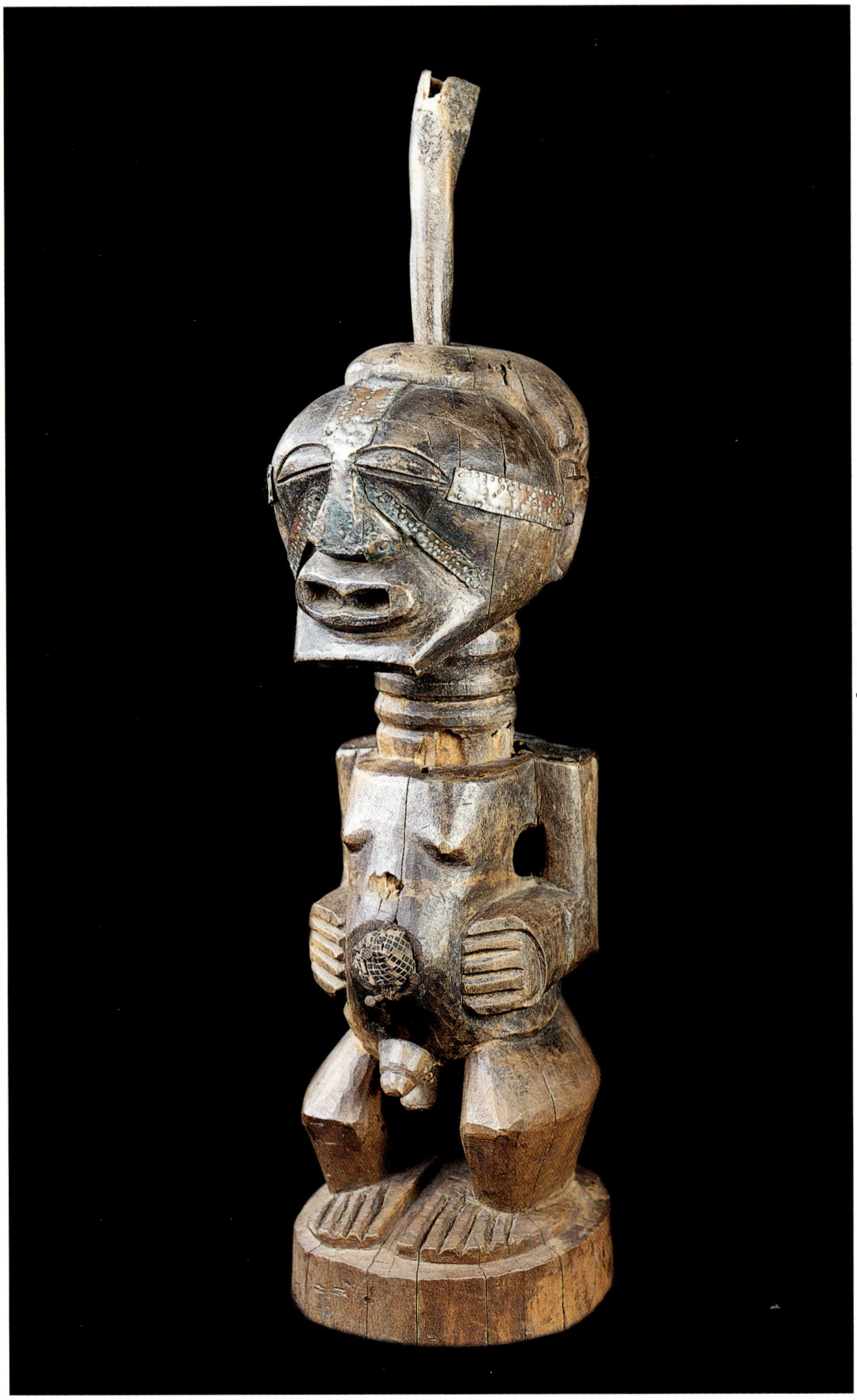

32

32

## Male figure (nkishi)

Songye peoples, Democratic Republic of the Congo
wood, horn, copper, iron, cloth, h: 26 inches
Dianne Komminsk Collection

*The horns planted in the head of this and other Songye figures serve as depositories of magic or religious elements called bishimba. The figures thus acquire the status of a spiritual entity, (nkishi). It protects the community against negative forces, including sorcerers and ensures fecundity, health and success in hunting and agriculture.*

33

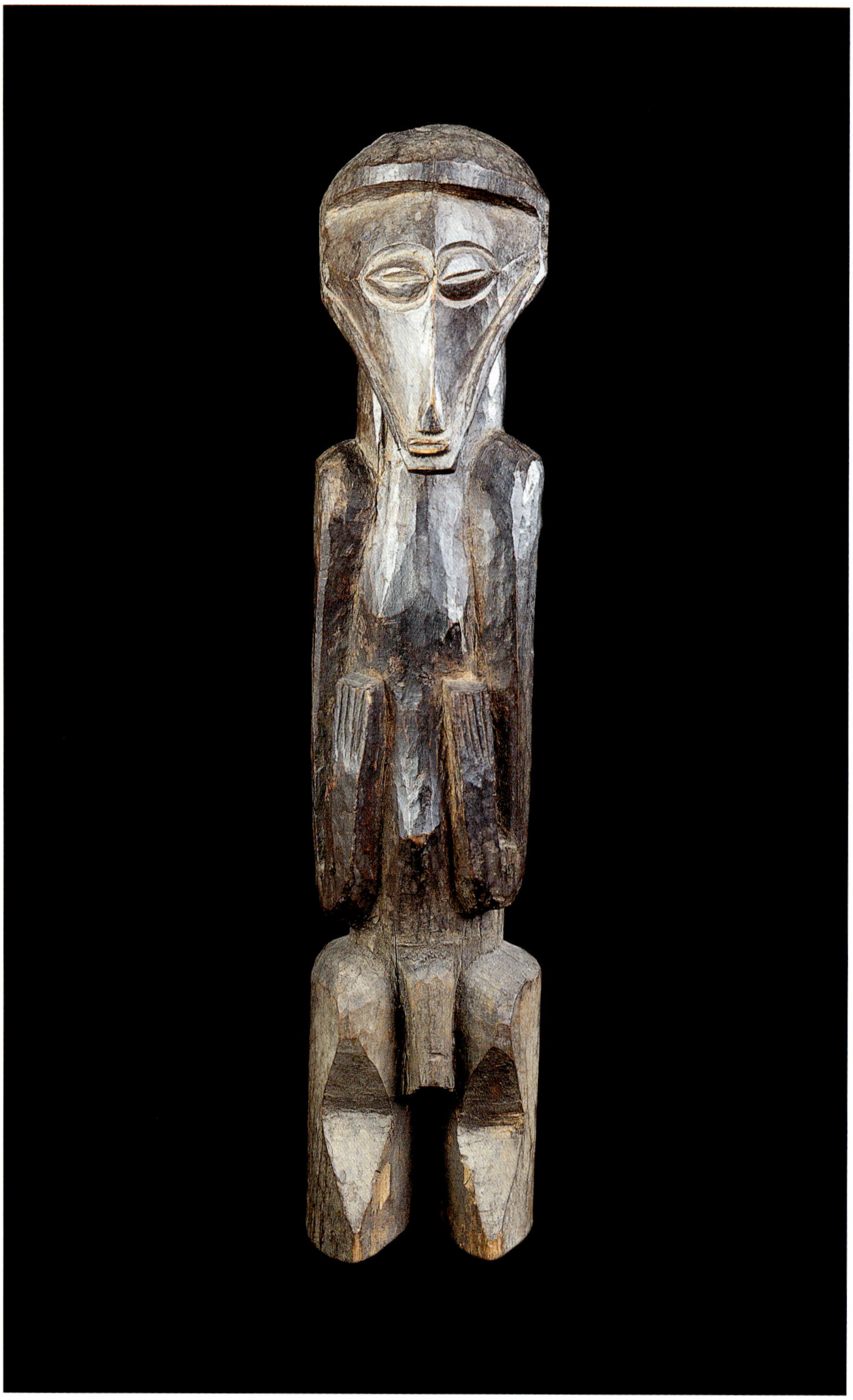

33

## Male figure

Buyu peoples, Democratic Republic of the Congo, wood, h: 24 inches
Dianne Komminsk Collection

*An imposing, hieratic ancestor figure of simplified, geometric style, this example was kept in a special house together with other ancestor figures of both genders.*

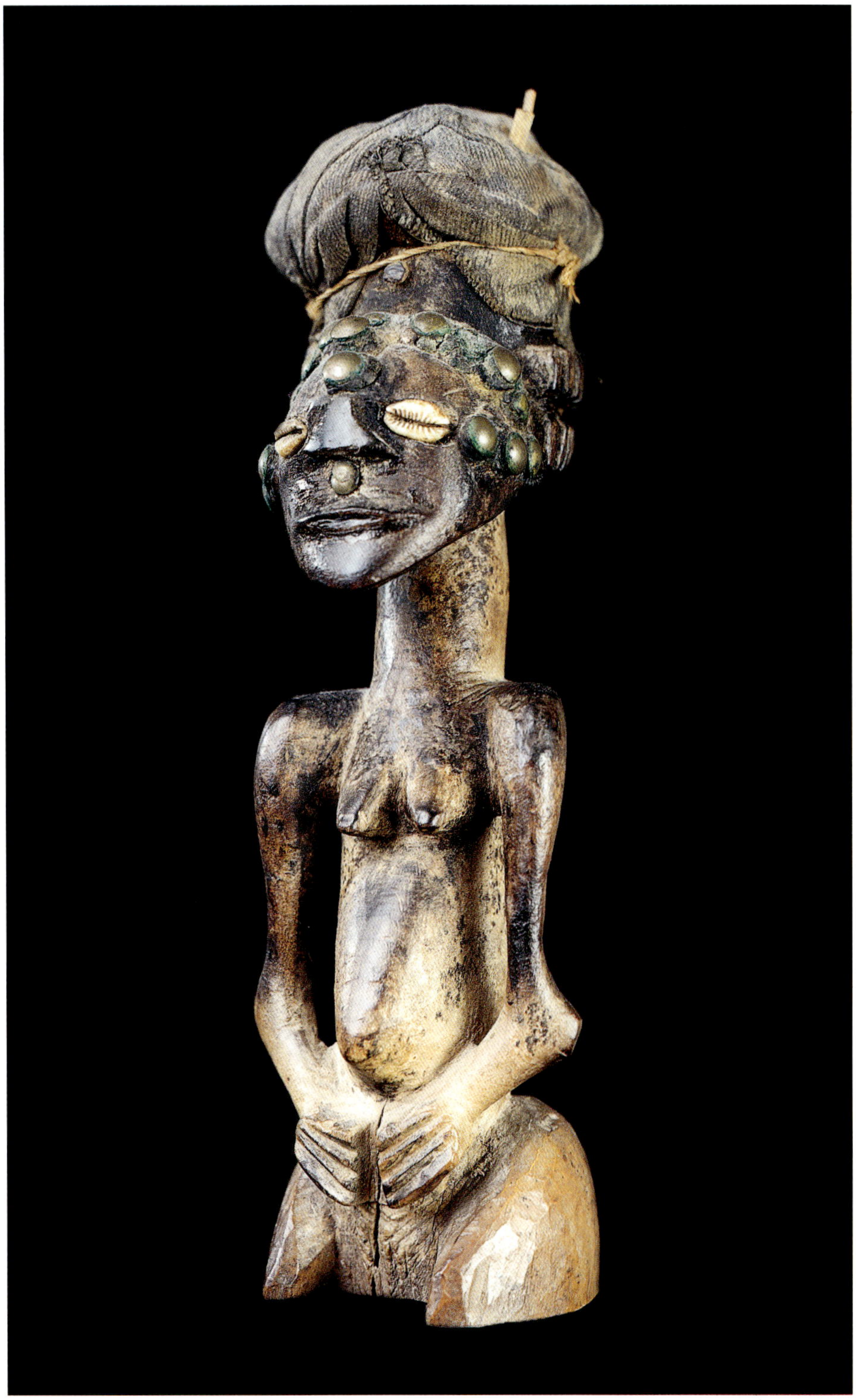

34

34

## Power figure

Kusu peoples, Democratic Republic of the Congo
wood, cowrie shells, brass tacks, cloth, pigment, h: 12 inches
LaVerne Shone Collection

*For the Kusu, these figures embody the spirits of nature manipulated by the cult specialist for many social ends. The head is surmounted by a bundle of magical substances, the face is decorated with brass tacks and the eyes are encrusted with cowries. Each of these attributes endows the figures with magical powers.*

35

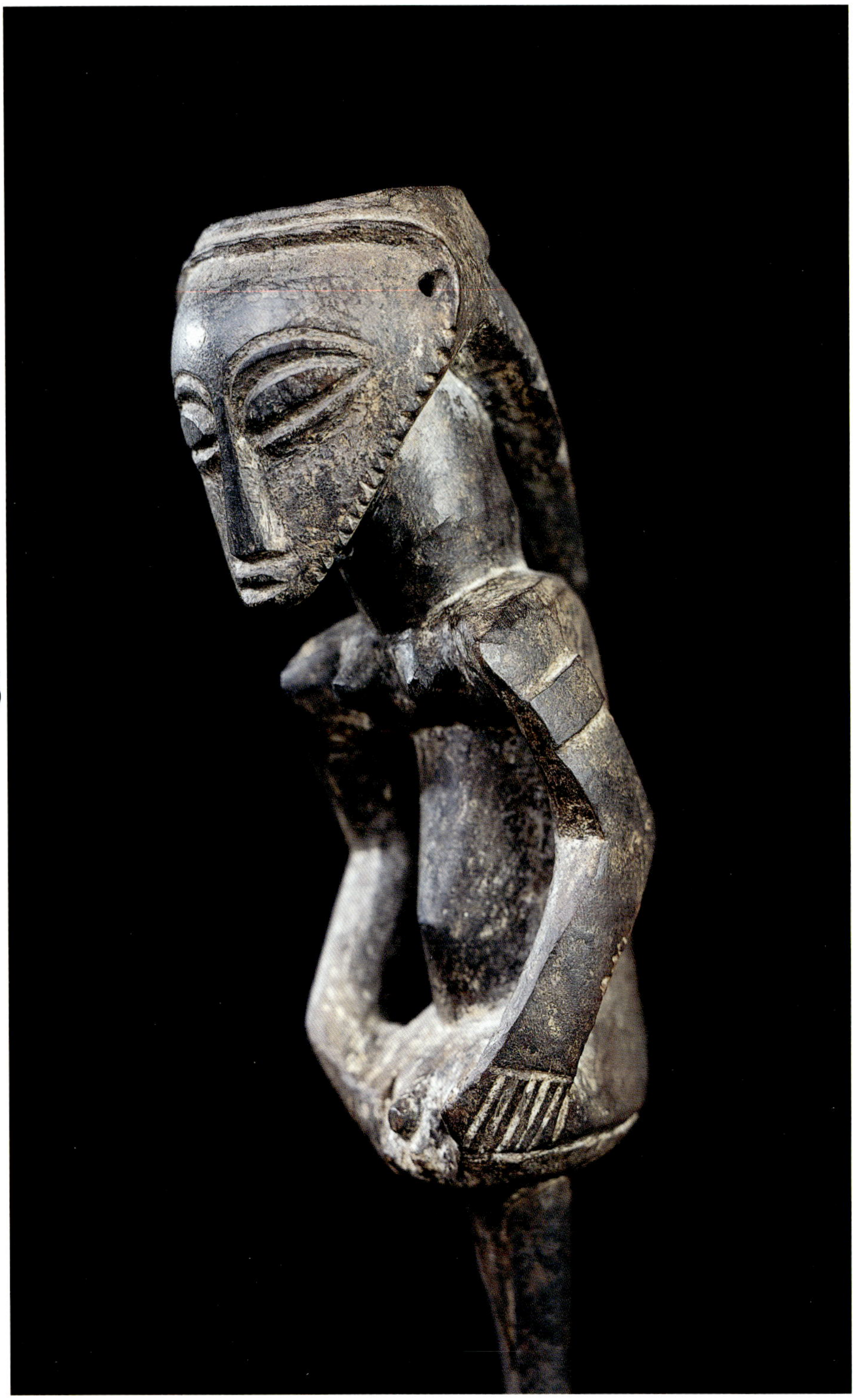

35

# Figure

[Detail]

Bembe people, Democratic Republic of the Congo, wood, iron, h: 18 inches
LaVerne Shone Collection

*This male half-figure ending in a spike is at the same time a scepter and a post, an emblem of power and a royal ancestor figure. The shape of the head, the coiffure and the beard evoke ancestor figures from other nearby peoples.*

# SHRINES

There are hierarchies of deities and spirits throughout Africa. The creator god is remote and rarely appears in the visual and performing arts. Other deities and spirits are the conduits by which humans make contact with the spirit world. Shrines and altars are dedicated to them to solicit their intervention for community and personal well-being.

36

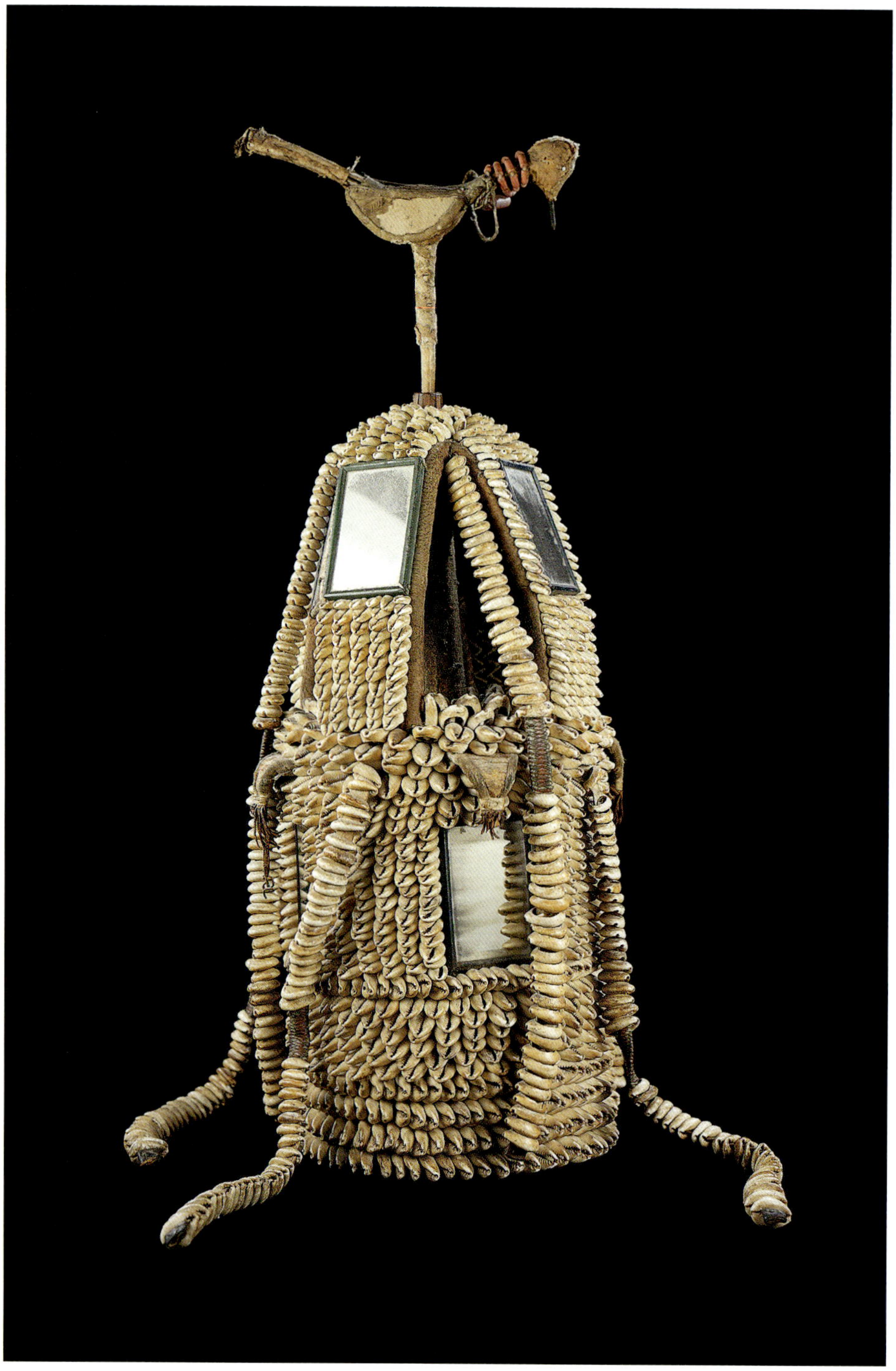

36

## Sango crown

Yoruba peoples, Nigeria, leather, fiber, cowrie shells, beads, mirror, wood, h: 33 inches
Arthur Shone Collection

*Many personal and community shrines are dedicated to Sango, a powerful Yoruba orisha (deity). Devotees who oversee his most important shrines commission cowrie-studded crowns to honor this deity of thunder, lightning and human fertility.*

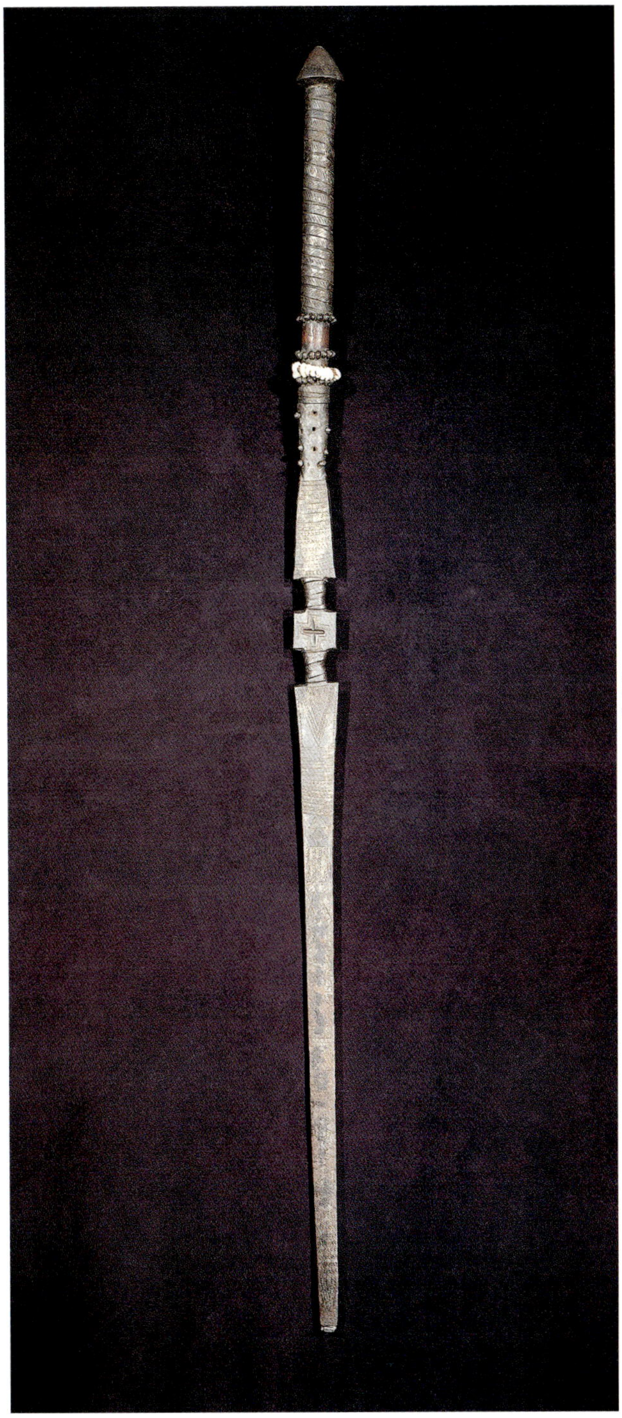

37

37

## Shrine sword (opa orisha oko)

Yoruba peoples, Nigeria, iron, leather, cowrie shells, h: 59 inches
Dr. and Mrs. William E. Rogers Collection

*Dedicated to Oko, the orisha of agriculture, this symbolic sword is made from worn-out hoe blades. It protects farm crops from damage and thieves, and helps to ensure a good harvest.*

38

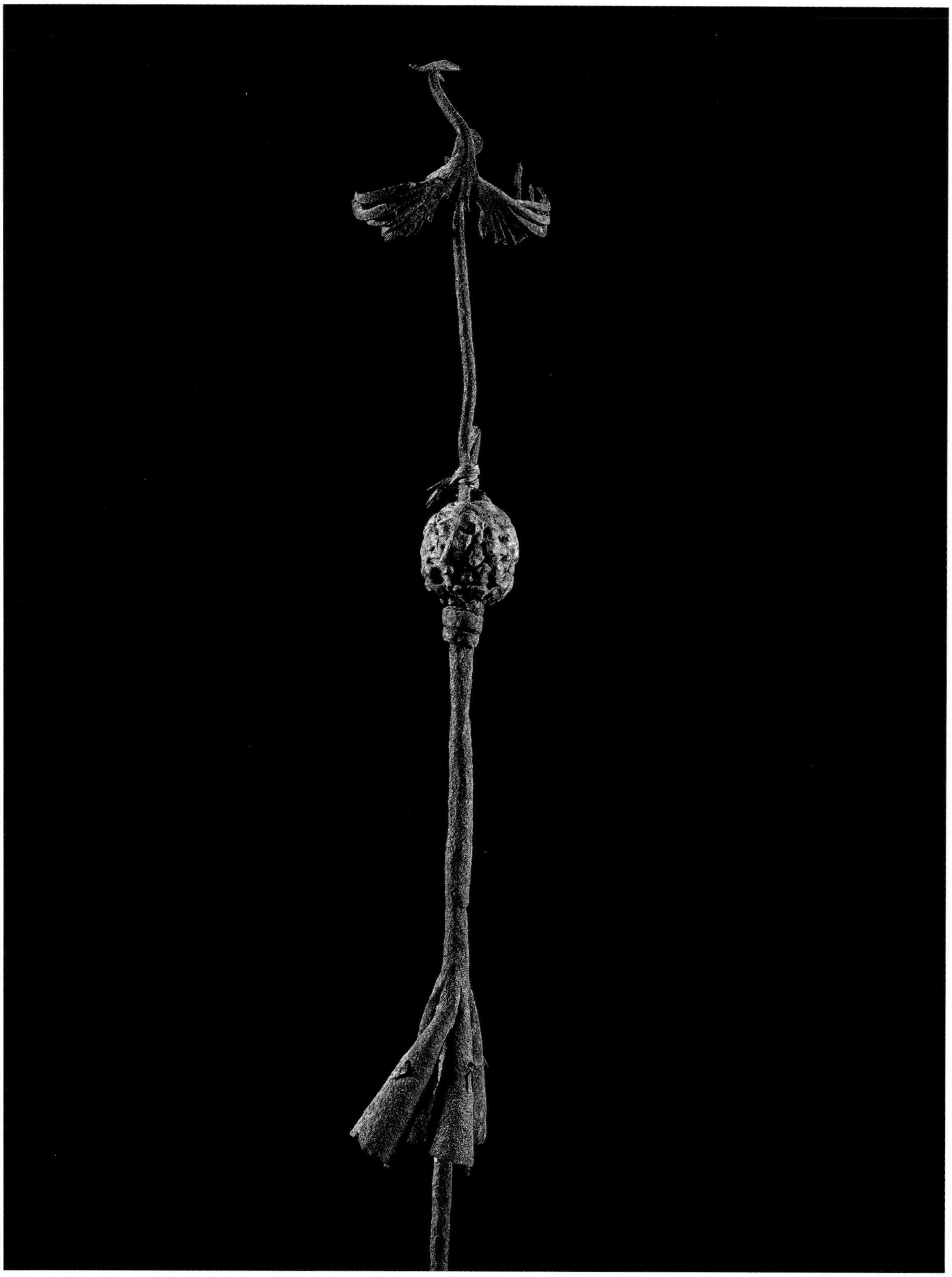

38

## Shrine staff (opa Osanyin)

[Detail]

Yoruba peoples, Nigeria, iron, h: 49 inches

Arthur Shone Collection

*The bird on this staff is associated with herbalists and diviners who are followers of the cult of the orisha Osanyin. These professionals seek out and combat witches who are the source of human disease, infertility and misfortune.*

# DIVINATION

Divination is an ancient art practiced throughout Africa. A variety of systems have been designed to tap into the spirit world to assist the living in determining the cause of illness, infertility, crop failures or other personal and community problems. Diviners are religious and spiritual specialists who use a wide variety of paraphernalia.

39

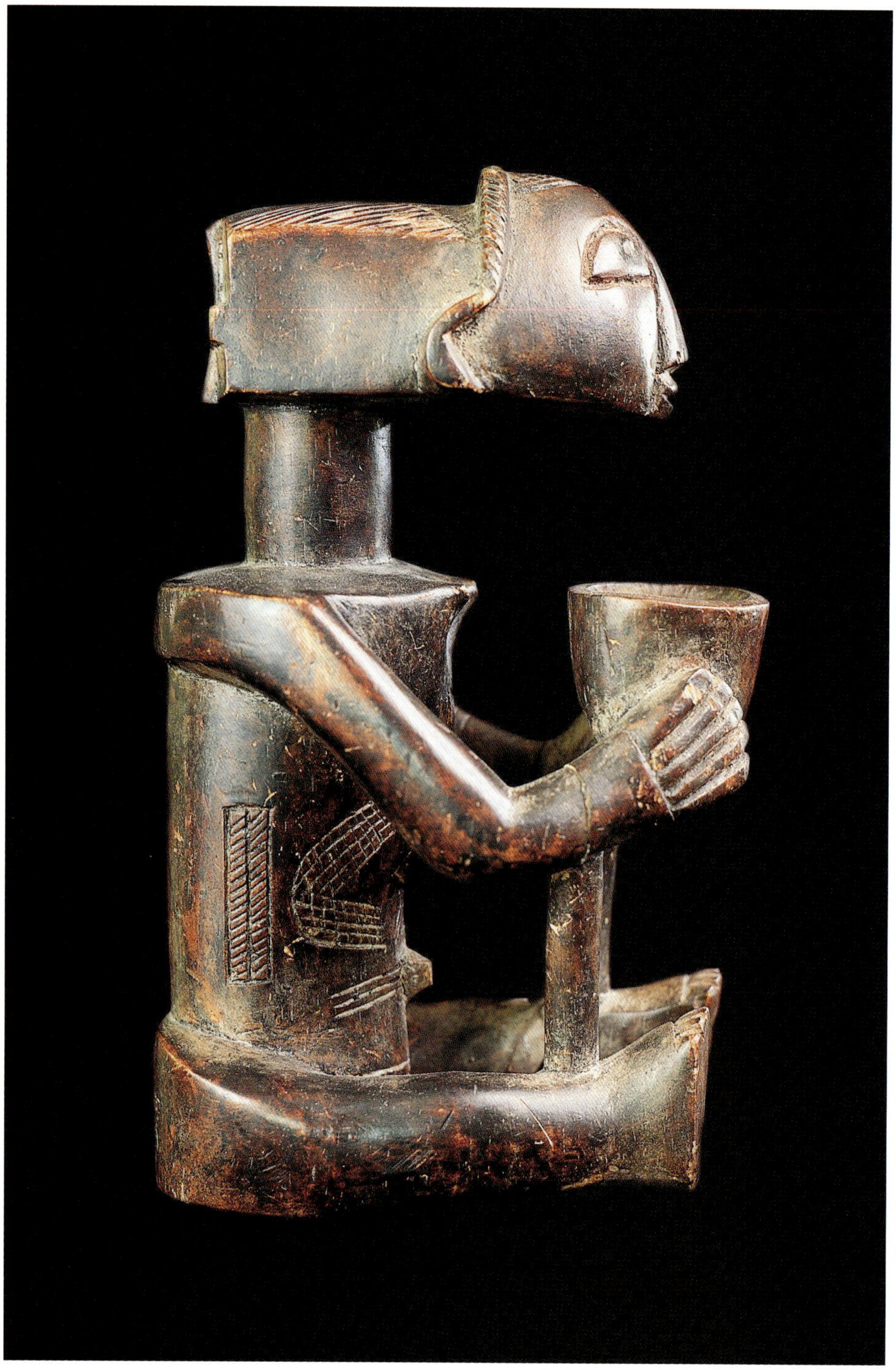

39

## Bowl (mboko or kabila)

Luba peoples, Democratic Republic of the Congo, wood, h: 10 inches
Dianne Komminsk Collection

*This bowl bearer with a headdress reminiscent of the Hemba style is an essential divination tool. The territorial chief and the medium-diviner use it as a container for the sacred kaolin (white clay) powder called pembe. Because the figure has clairvoyance and protective powers, it functions as a dispenser of positive procreation forces.*

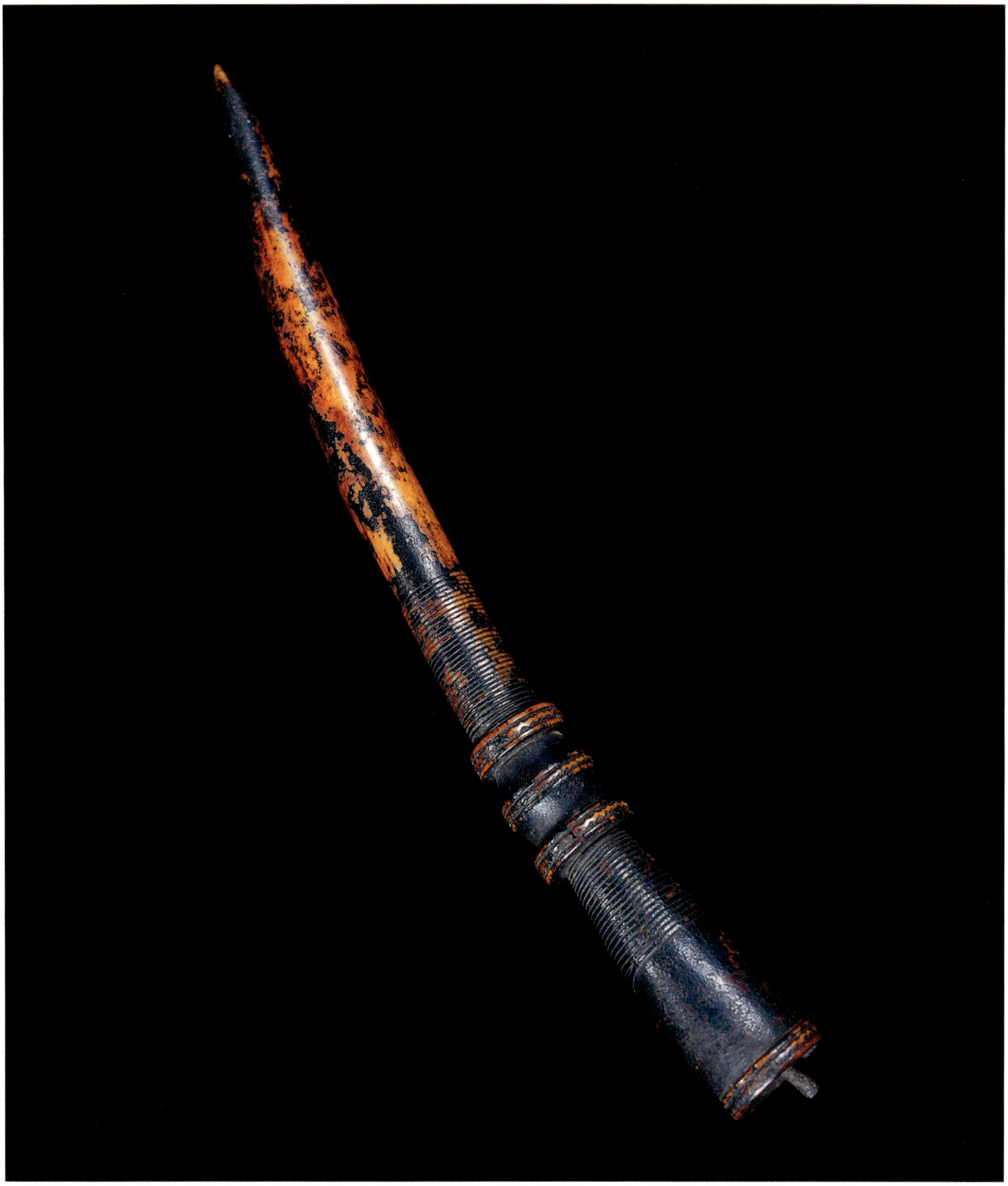

40

40

## Divination tapper (iroke ifa)

Yoruba peoples, Nigeria, ivory, h: 14 inches
Arthur Shone Collection

*A babalawo (diviner-priest) uses a tapper in conjunction with a divination tray and 16 palm nuts to appeal to Ifa, the Yoruba god of divination. The tapper is rapped on the tray to attract Ifa's attention before the divination process begins.*

41

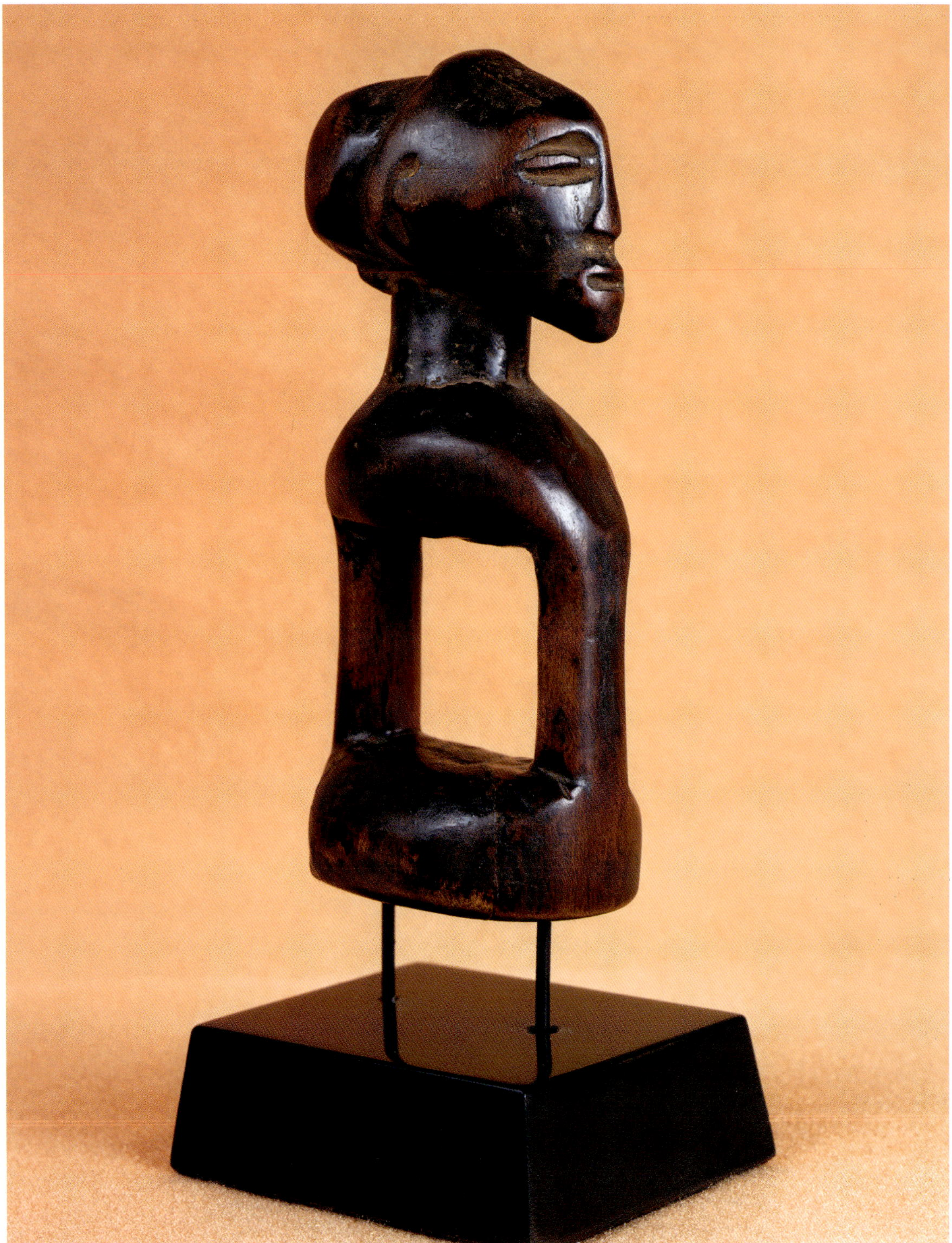

41

## Divination device (kashekesheke)

Luba peoples, Democratic Republic of the Congo, wood, h: 5 inches
Dianne Komminsk Collection

*These small sculptures are considered female and are used to consult the ancestors. The diviner and his or her client take hold of the device with two fingers and thumb of their right hands. The Divination device will move to respond yes or no to questions concerning, for instance, the cause of misfortune.*

# PERSONAL OBJECTS

Jewelry, clothing and other personal objects enhance the appearance of the wearer and signify his or her gender, age, marital status and ethnicity. The materials and designs of the objects declare wealth and status in the community. Many of these artworks are prized possessions that are cared for and used throughout an individual's life and, at times, are buried with the owner.

42

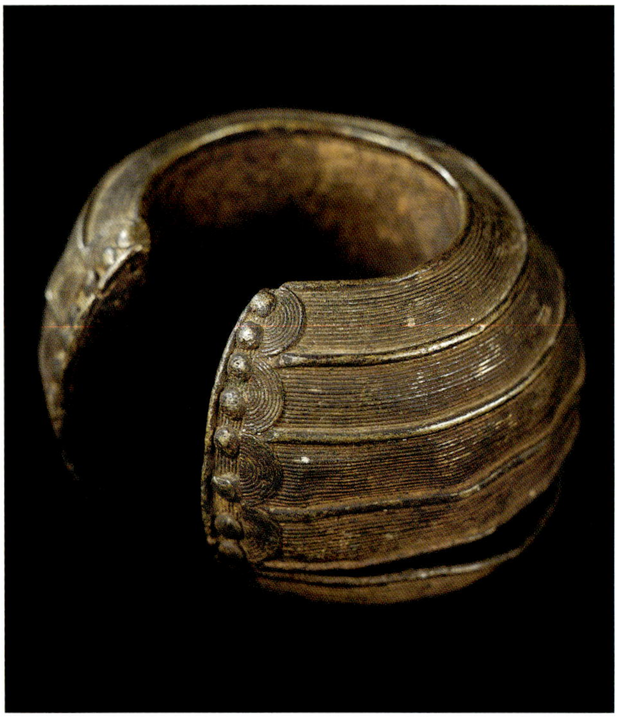

43

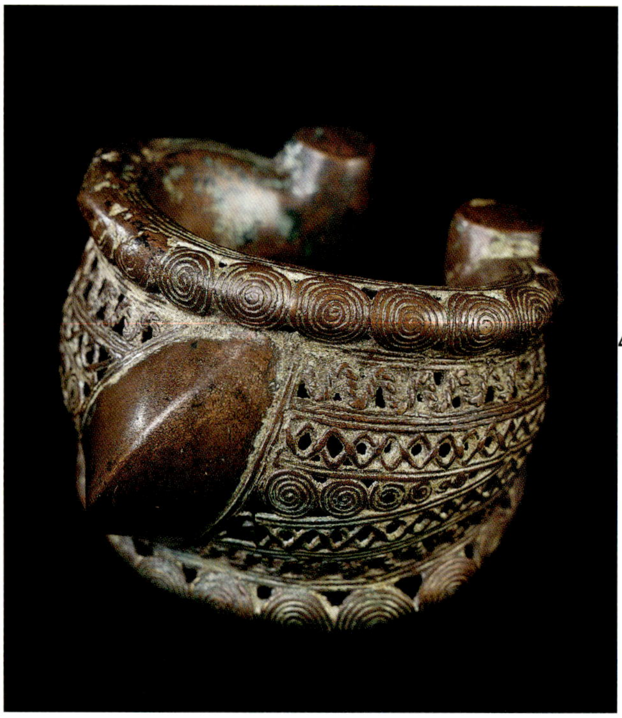

44

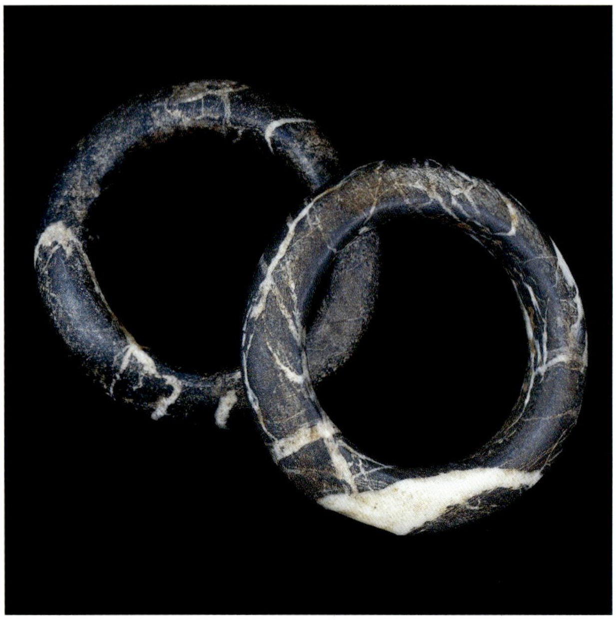

42

## Anklet

Baule peoples, Côte d'Ivoire
copper alloy, h: 6 inches
Arthur Shone Collection

*There is a long tradition among the Baule of wearing metal ornaments, such as brass and gold on the ankles, wrists, neck and in the hair. The Akan peoples in nearby Ghana introduced many of the metalsmithing techniques used by Baule artists.*

43

## Bracelet

uncertain origin, copper alloy, w: 4 1/2 inches
Willis Bing and Audrey Davis Collection

*This handsome bracelet was collected in Senegal, said to be from Guinea, and resembles lost-wax casting from as far away as the Cameroon Grassfields.*

44

## Bracelets

Northern Ghana or Southern Burkina Faso
stone, w: 4 1/2 inches
Arthur Shone Collection

*The natural marbling of the stone in these examples adds an elegant design element.*

45 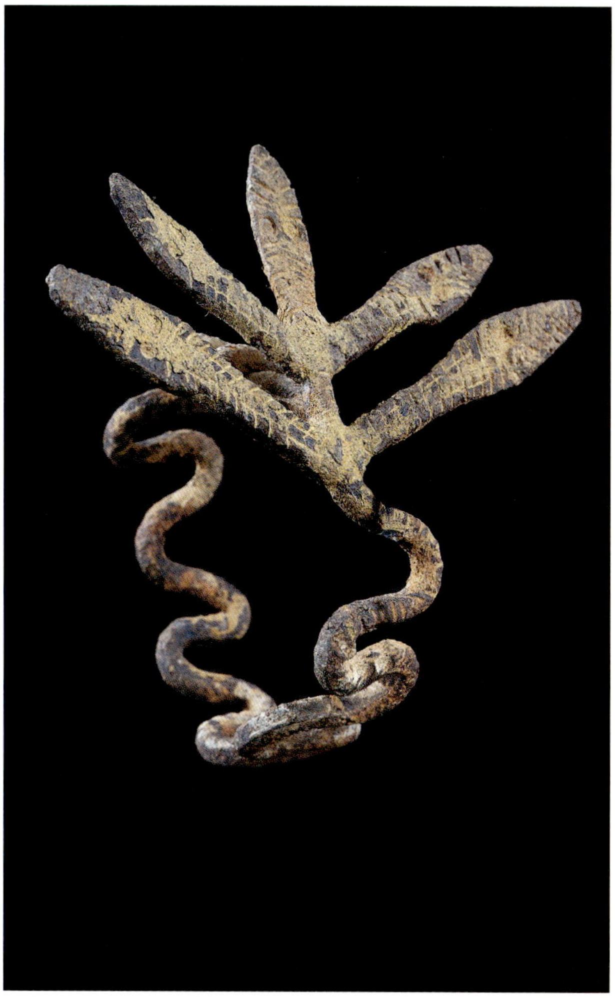

45

## Bracelet

Lorhon peoples, 18th century, Burkina Faso or Côte d'Ivoire
copper alloy, h: 5 1/2 inches
Dianne Komminsk Collection

*The Lorhon peoples have long been known for the fine prestige castings they created for the Lobi and Kulango peoples.*

46

## Bracelet

Yoruba peoples, Nigeria
copper alloy, w: 6 inches
Arthur Shone Collection

*This bracelet is probably an emblem of office associated with Ijebu chieftaincy or the society of elders called Osugbo.*

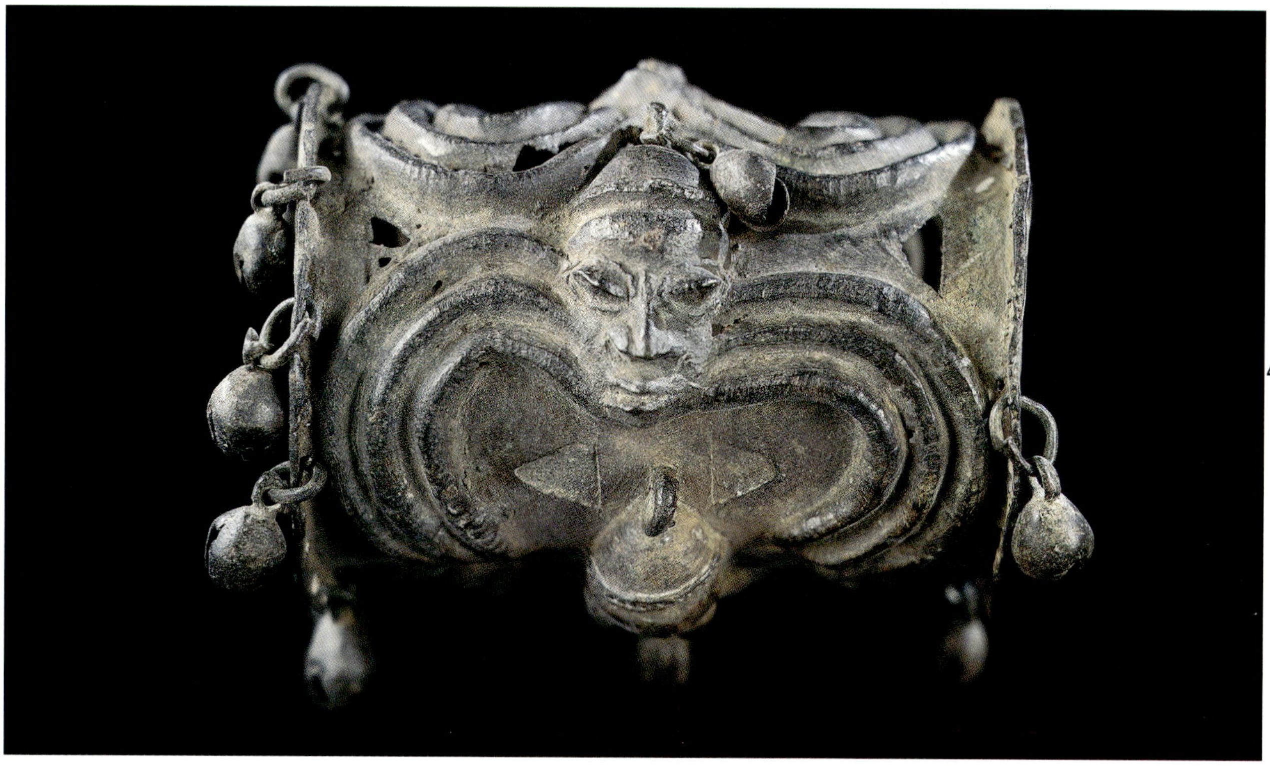 46

47

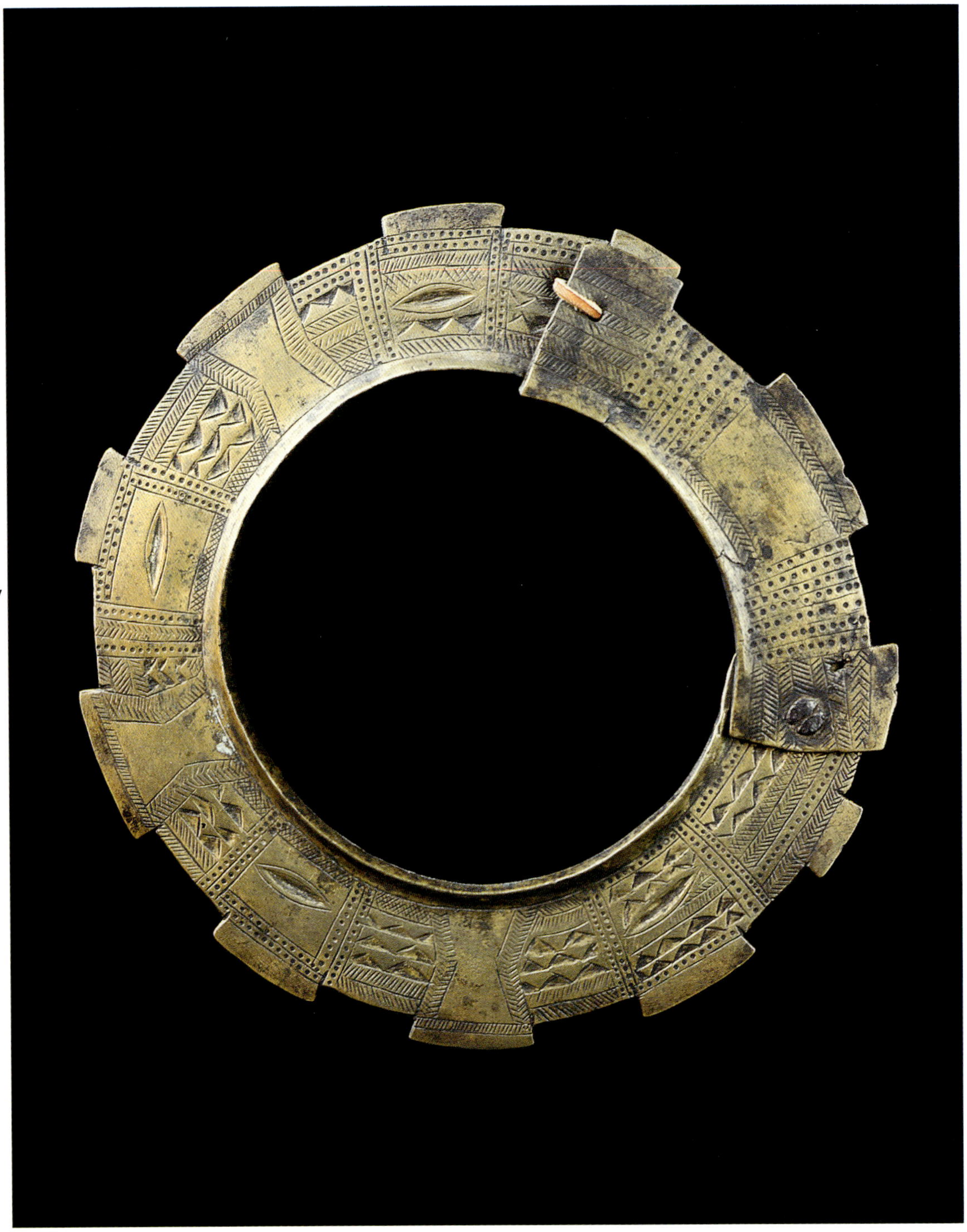

47

## Neck ornament (ikorwa)

Teke peoples, Democratic Republic of the Congo, copper alloy, h: 9 inches
Arthur Shone Collection

*Circular metal necklaces, engraved with geometric motifs, are worn by high-ranking chiefs as emblems of power. The notches and surface design symbolically refer to the extent of the chief's realm.*

48

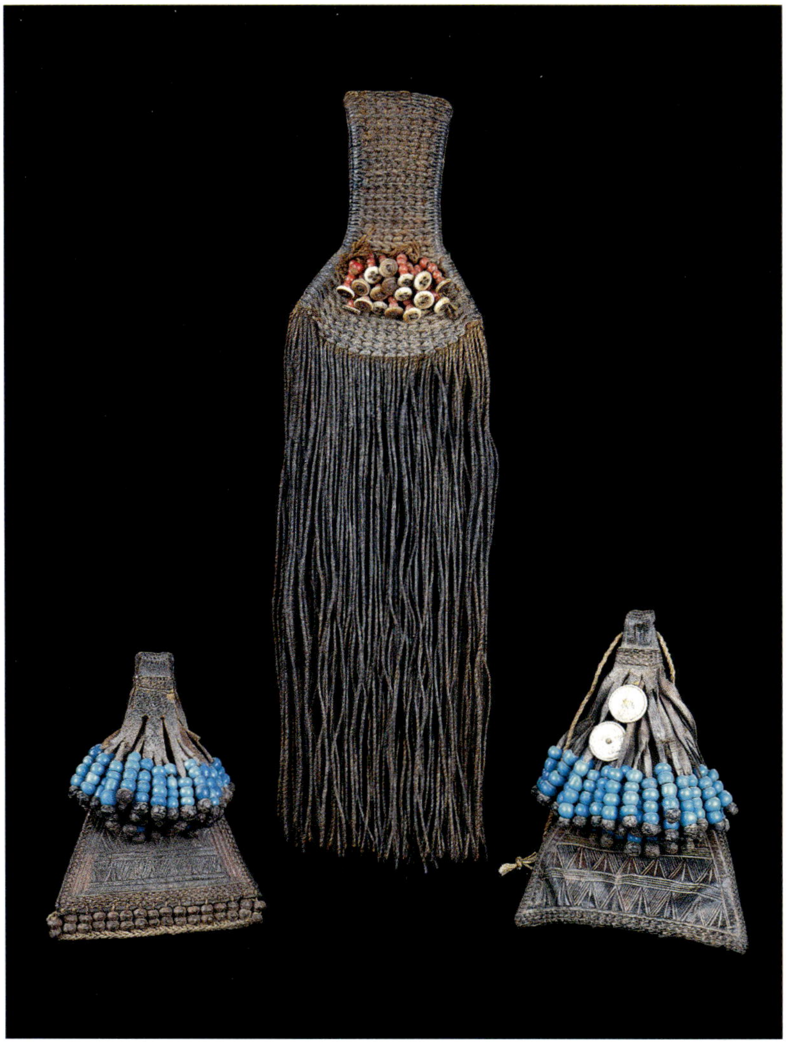

49

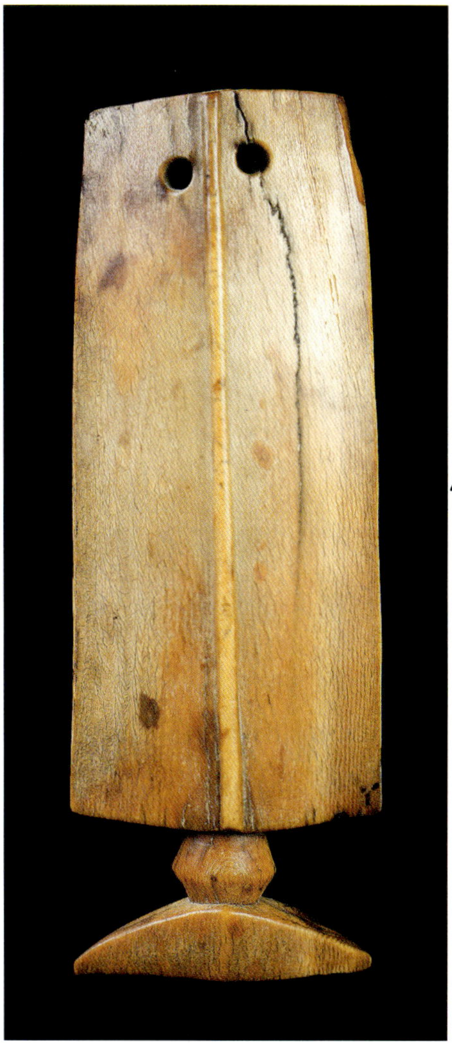

48

## Three cache sexe ornaments

Kirdi or Fulani peoples, Cameroon, hide, fiber, beads, buttons, cowrie shells, h: 18 inches
Arthur Shone Collection

*A married woman wore a cache sexe on special occasions. It was carefully folded over a hip belt to display the decorative elements on the front of the apron. On some examples, buttons were used in place of cowrie shells. Since Cameroon independence in 1960, regulations require women to be fully clothed, which made pubic aprons obsolete.*

49

## Pendant

Lobi peoples, Burkina Faso, Ghana or Côte d'Ivoire, ivory, h: 8 inches
LaVerne Shone Collection

*Throughout Africa, ivory is a prestige material available to those with sufficient wealth. The material complements the bold, yet elegant design of this pendant worn by men.*

50

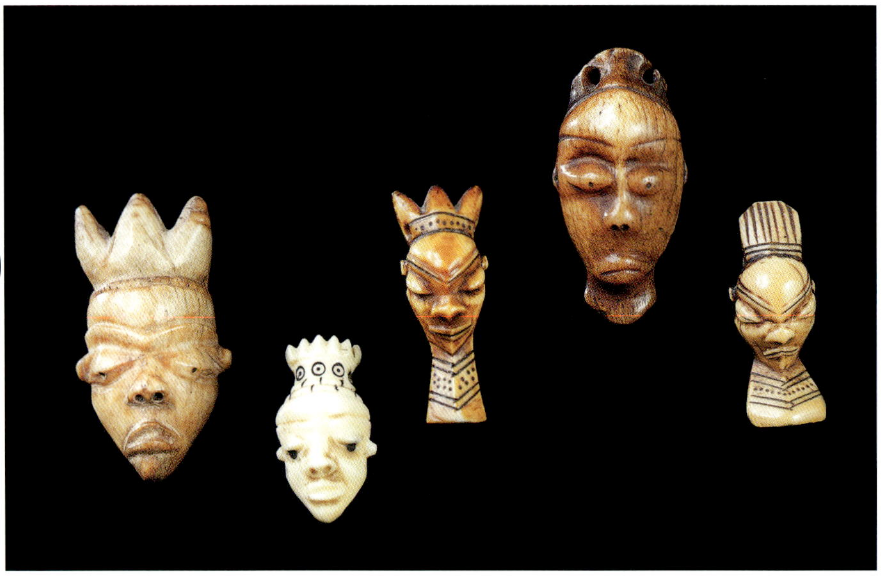

51

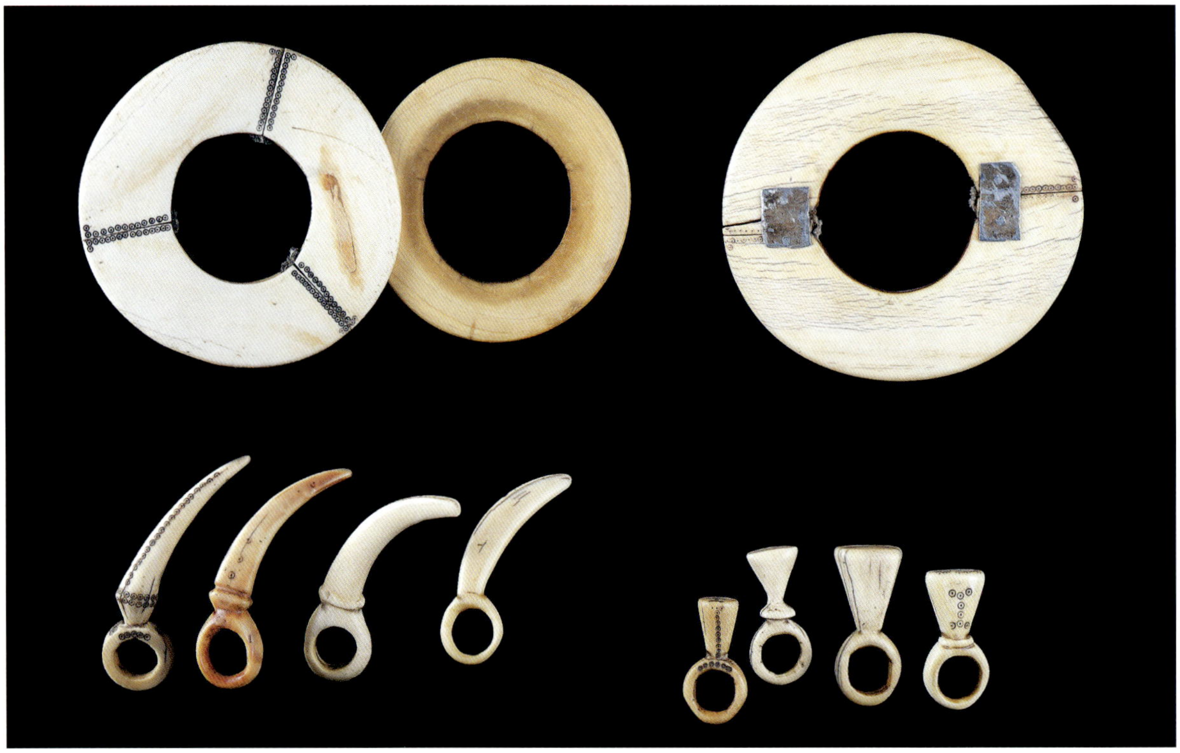

50

## Pendants (ikhoko)

Pende peoples, Democratic Republic of the Congo, ivory, h: 2 1/2 inches
Arthur Shone Collection

*These miniatures of mbuya wooden masks of various types are used as protective amulets. The dancer wearing a mask may carry an ikhoko to counterbalance the fearsome force of the mask. In addition, women, children and men carry these amulets as symbols of the ancestors' beneficial presence and for healing.*

51

## Finger rings, earrings and bracelets

Dinka peoples, Sudan, ivory, metal, h: 6 inches
LaVerne Shone Collection

*Among the pastoralists of eastern Africa, articles of personal adornment are important works of art. Ivory objects are some of the most sought after for their association with wealth and prestige.*

52

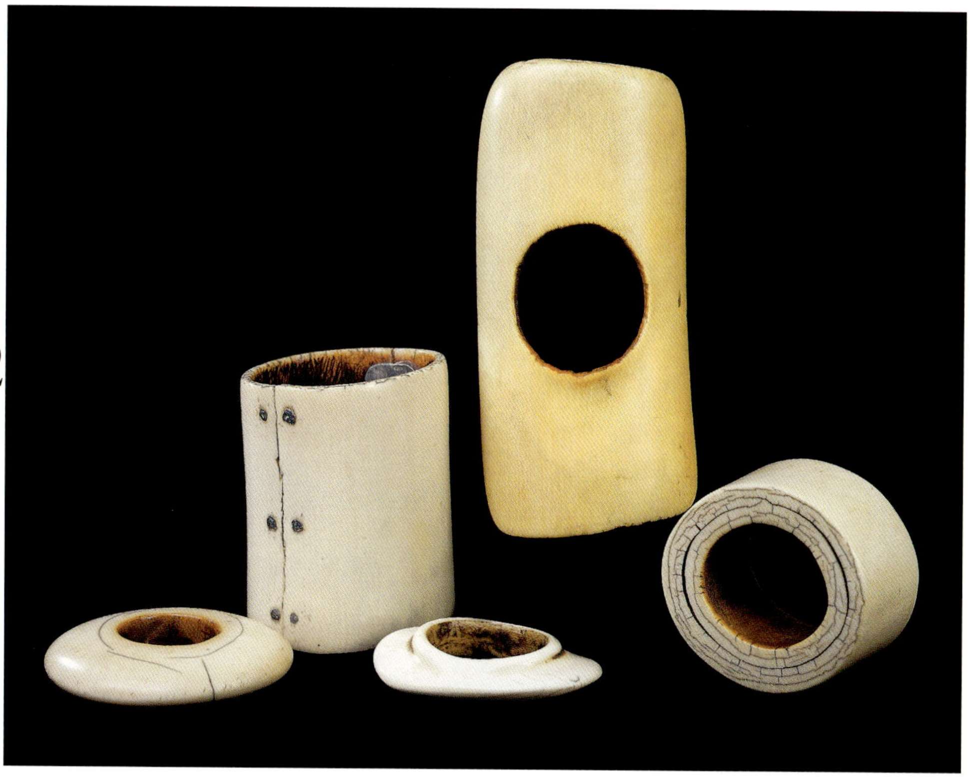

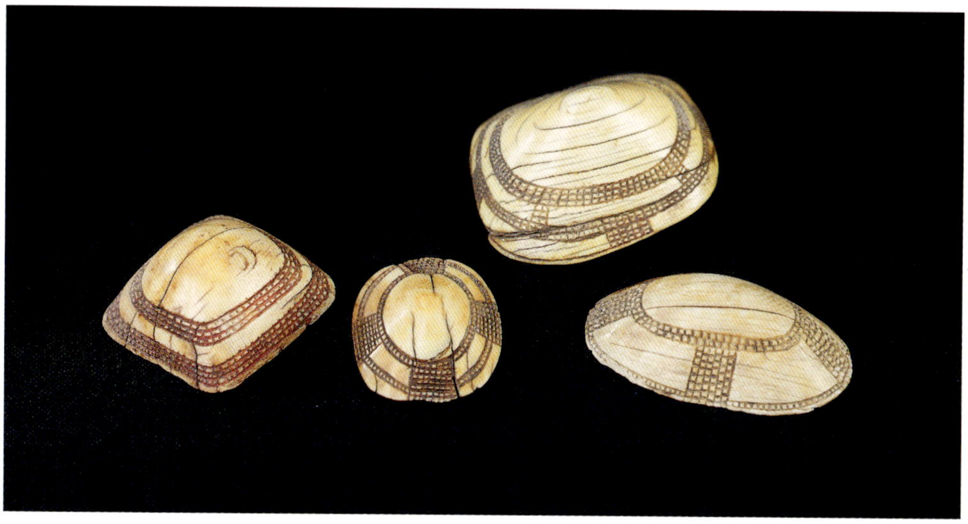

53

52

## Five armbands

Various peoples, ivory, h: 9 1/2 inches
Arthur Shone Collection

*Over most of Africa, wherever elephants roamed, objects made out of their tusks were the prerogative of high status. The hollow center of the tusks allowed bracelets to be made with a simple pair of cross cuts. However, the tallest armlet here is made from a section of the side of a tusk. It was worn on the upper arm in northern Ghana and Burkina Faso.*

53

## Ornaments

Ovambo peoples, Northern Namibia or Southern Angola, ivory, w: 3 1/2 inches
LaVerne Shone Collection

*Ovambo women attach these ivory ornaments resembling buttons to leather bandolier straps worn across the chest.*

54

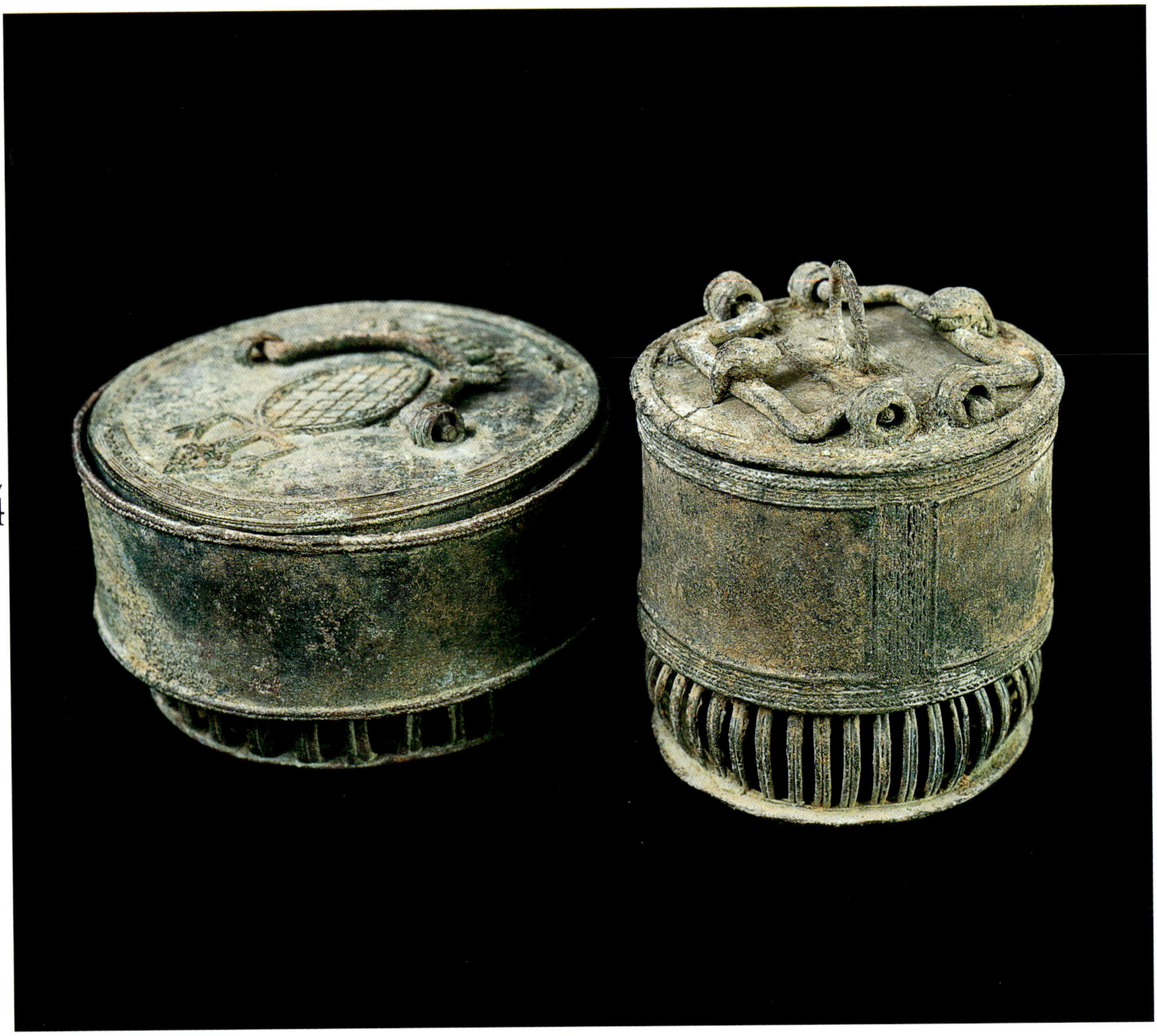

54

## Two containers (kuduo)

Asante peoples, Ghana, copper alloy, w: 5 3/4 inches
Donald and Sue Dugan Collection

*These cast boxes are used to store important personal wealth such as gold dust or beads. The form and geometric designs indicate Islamic influence on Asante art.*

55

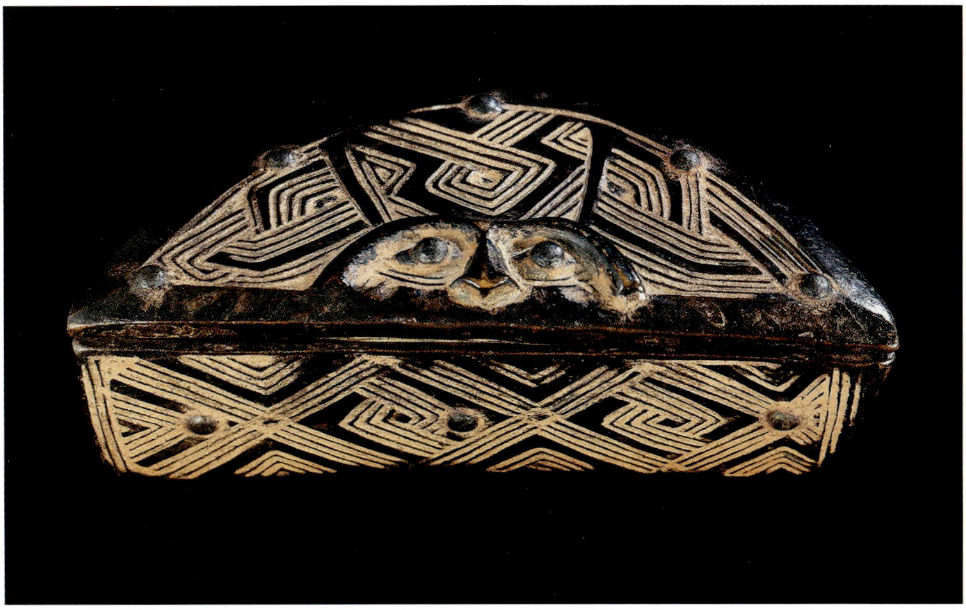

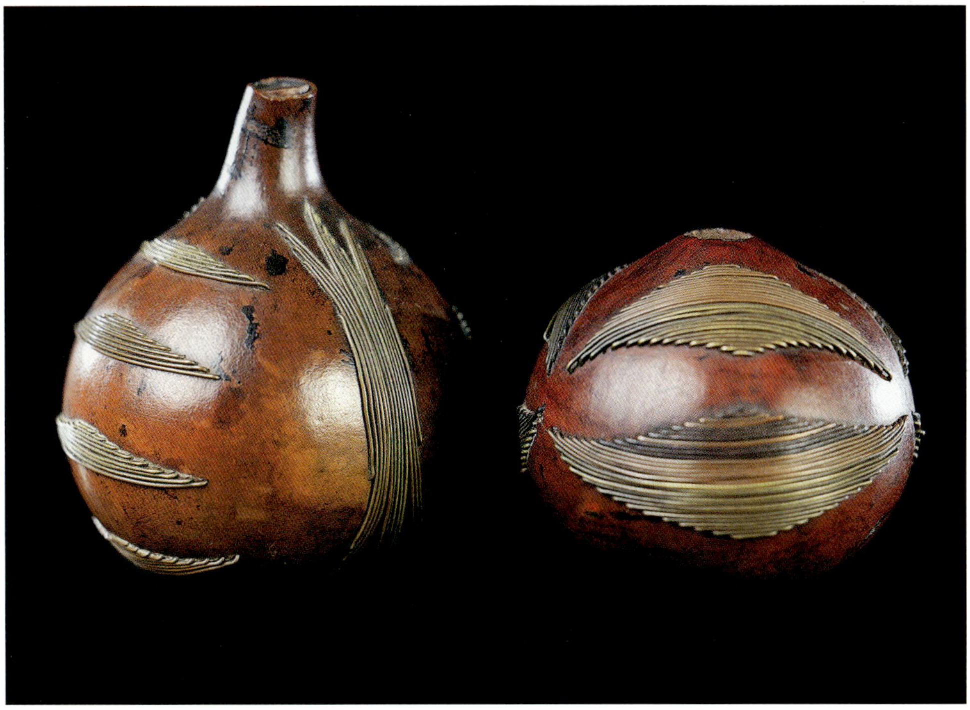

56

55

## Box

Kuba peoples, Democratic Republic of the Congo,
wood, pigment, w: 9 inches
Bonnie H. Bozorgi Collection

*Owned by men of high status, cosmetic boxes hold red tukula powder. They are decorated with carved geometric patterns resembling those on textiles.*

56

## Two snuff containers

Zulu peoples, South Africa,
calabash, metal, h: 3 inches
Arthur Shone Collection

*Europeans introduced tobacco to Africa more than 300 years ago. Snuff, a popular form, was carried in small containers of wood, horn and calabash. Some examples, such as these containers, have wire designs ornamenting the exterior.*

57

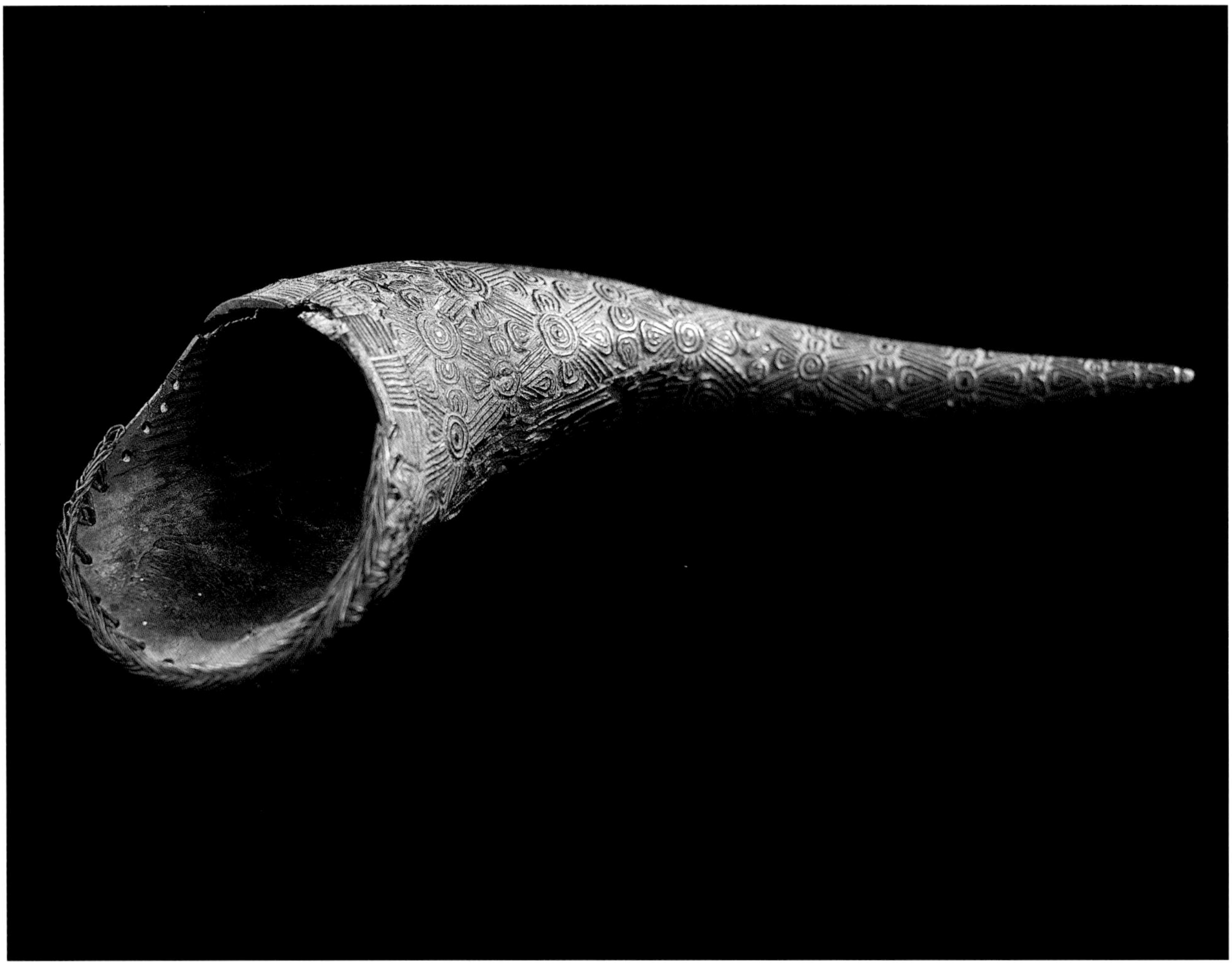

57

## Drinking horn

Western Grassfields, Cameroon, bushcow horn, l: 16 inches
Arthur Shone Collection

*Carved drinking horns are essential objects of regalia for Grassfields' Fons (chiefs). They are used for drinking palm wine during ceremonial and social occasions.*

# DRESS

Dress, jewelry and elaborate coiffures are important parts of the public persona of many Africans. Through materials and design, clothing carries rich symbolic messages that signify the individual's ethnic identity, social status and wealth.

58

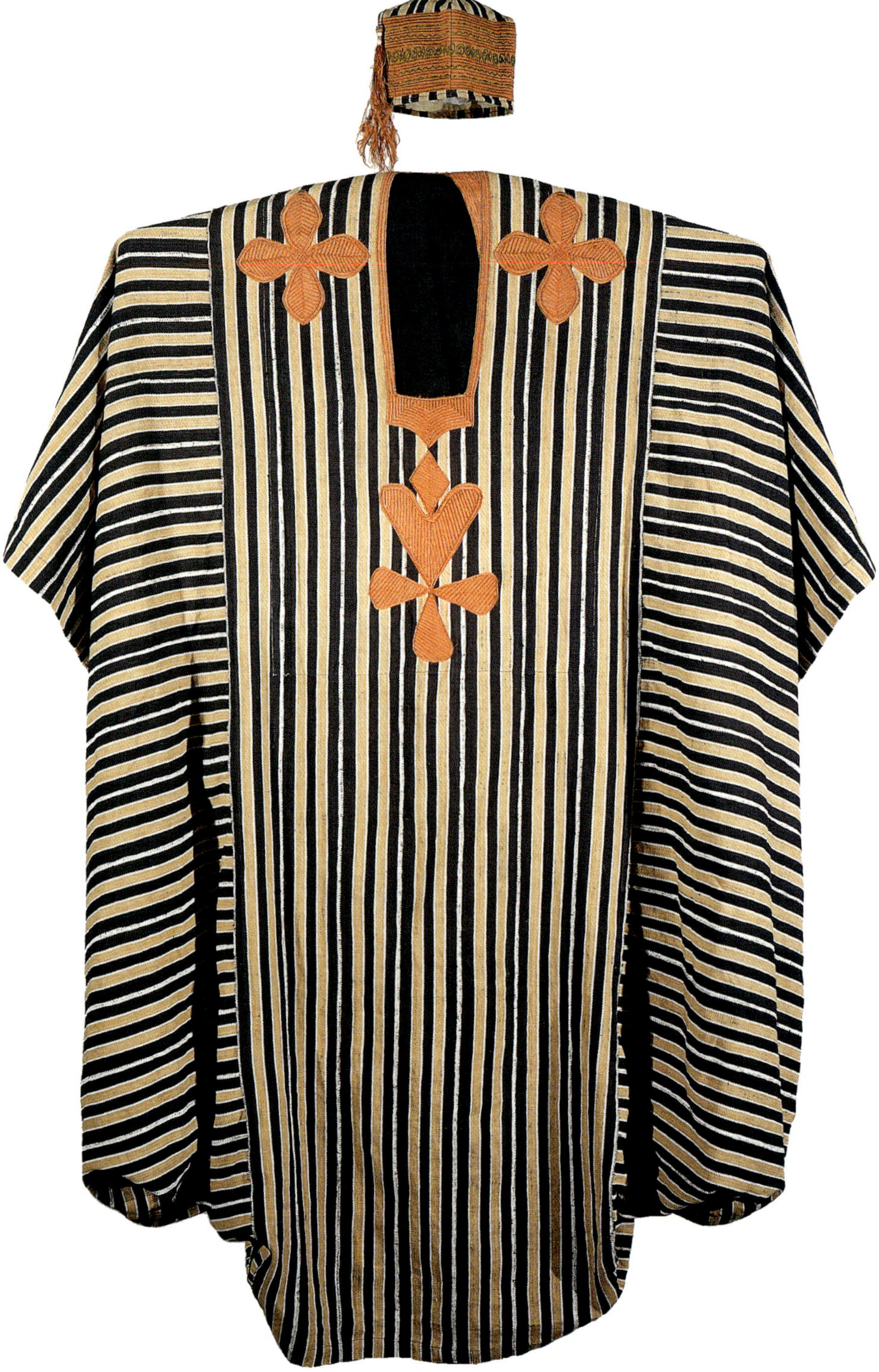

58

## Chief's coat

Dan peoples, cloth, indigo and kola dye, w: 71 inches
Mr. and Mrs. Irvin G. Bieser, Jr. Collection

*This chief's garment is made up of strips of fabric woven by men on a narrow, horizontal loom. The variations in the warp stripe patterns and hand embroidery on the shoulders and neckline enhance the appearance of the coat.*

59

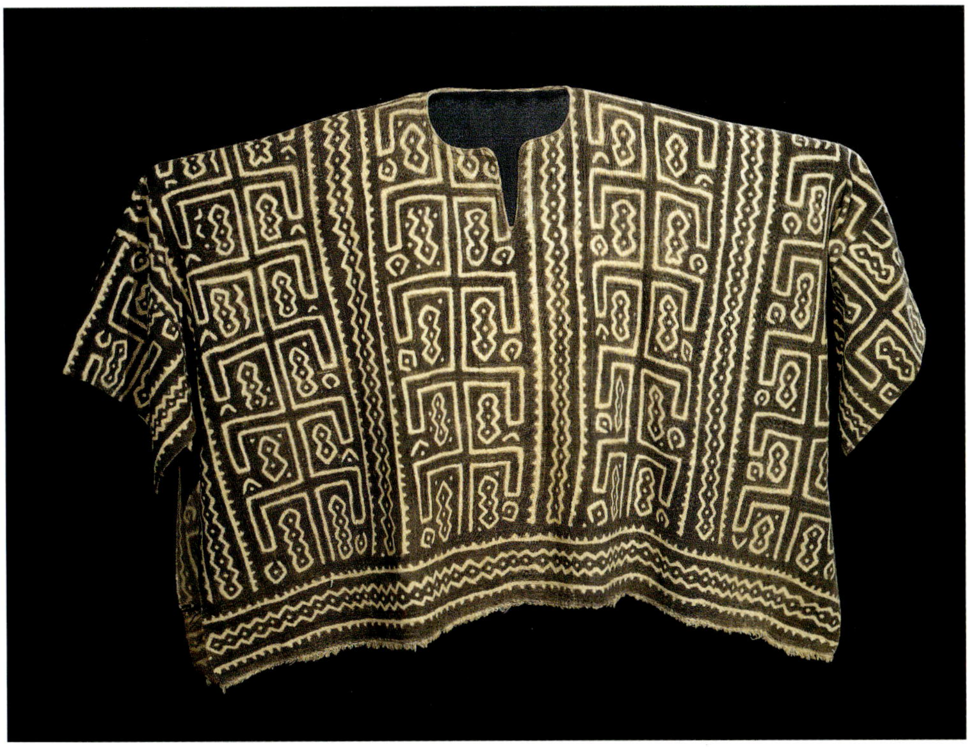

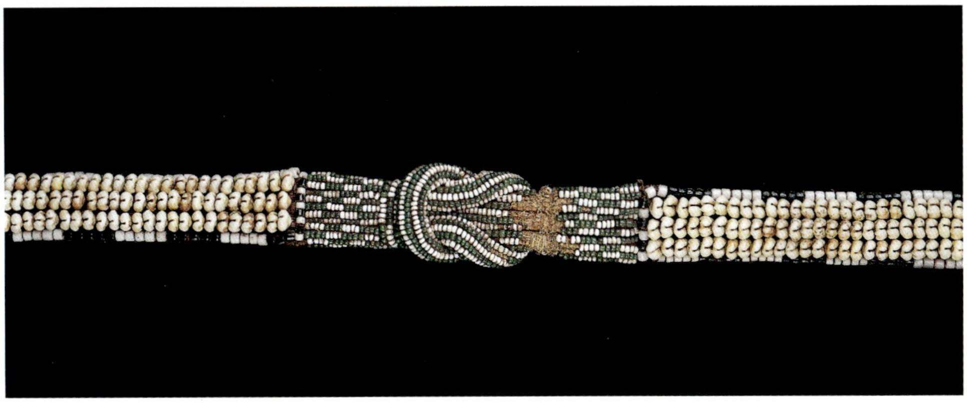

60

59

## Tunic

Bamana peoples, Mali, collected in Monrovia, Liberia, cloth, pigment, w: 56 inches
Dayton Society of Natural History/Boonshoft Museum of Discovery Collection
Gift of Mr. and Mrs. Irvin G. Bieser, Jr.

*The patterns on mud cloth or bogolanfini symbolize a variety of things including environmental features such as rivers and plants, social symbols or historical events.*

60

## Belt

[Detail]

Kuba peoples, Democratic Republic of the Congo, beads, fiber, cowrie shells, leather, l: 39 inches
Willis Bing and Audrey Davis Collection

*Among the Kuba and kingdoms of the Cameroon Grassfields, beaded ornaments are the prerogative of royalty. The knot is a reference to leadership, symbolizing continuity and strength.*

61

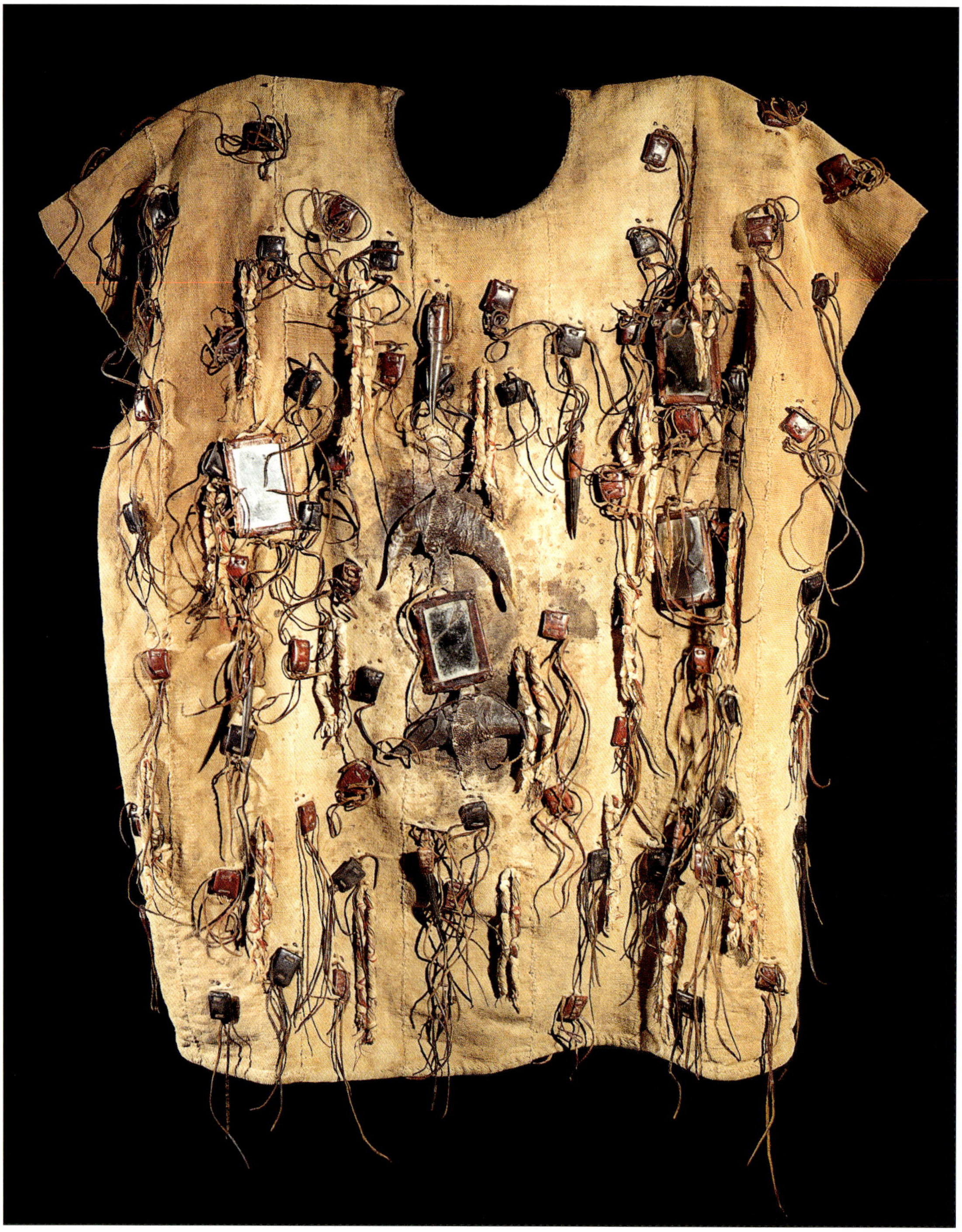

61

## Hunter's tunic

Bamana peoples, Mali, cloth, fiber, metal, horns, mirror, pigment, h: 36 inches
Arthur Shone Collection

*Hunters or warriors wear these garments. The additive material such as horns, animal claws, teeth, mirrors and amulets containing verses from the Koran are power symbols intended to protect the individual from harm.*

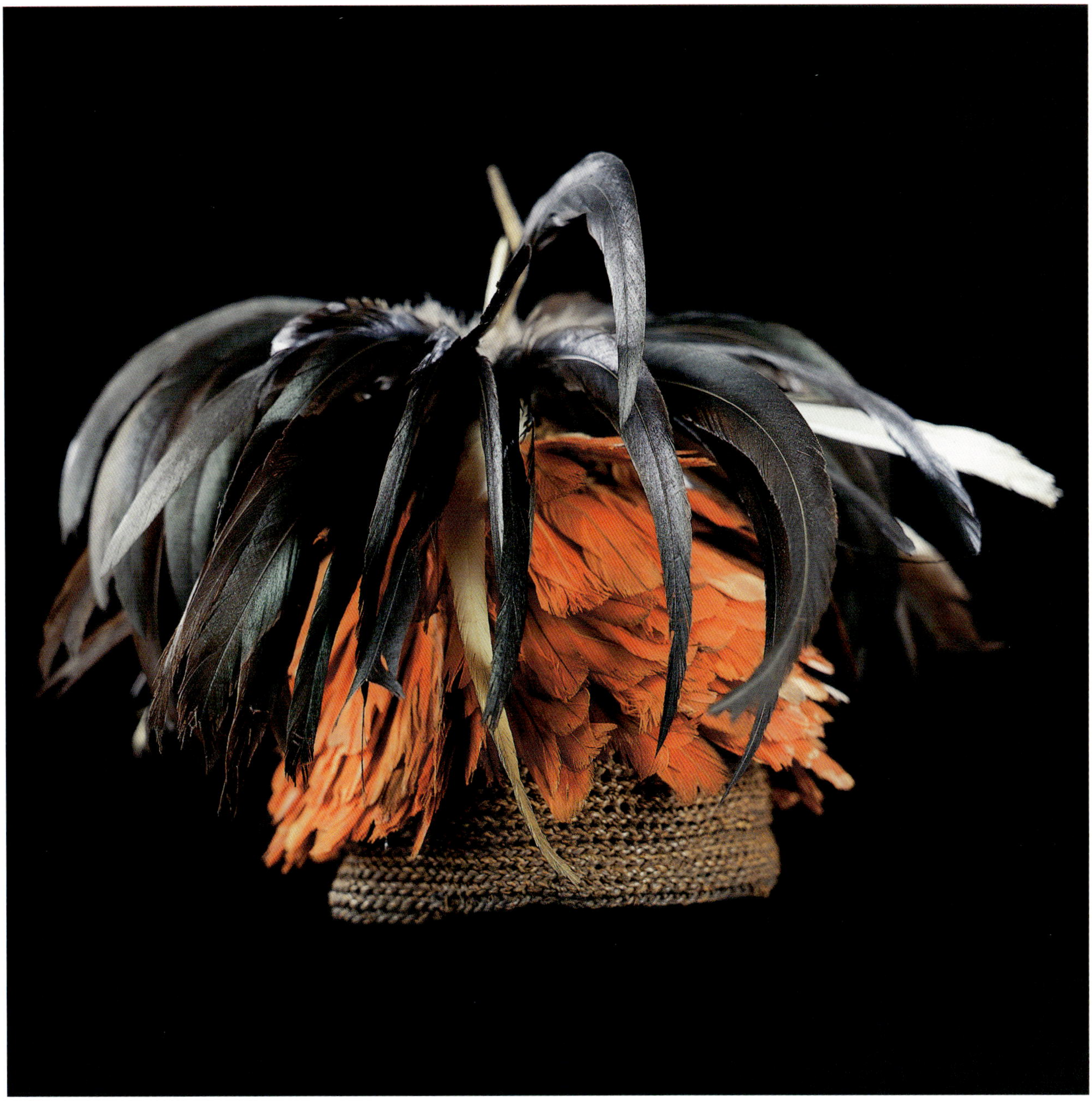

62

62

## Hat

Western Grassfields, Cameroon, feathers, fiber, w: 16 1/2 inches
Arthur Shone Collection

*The ingenious design of this hat enabled the owner to carefully roll the feathers inside the cap to carry or store it when it was not being worn.*

63

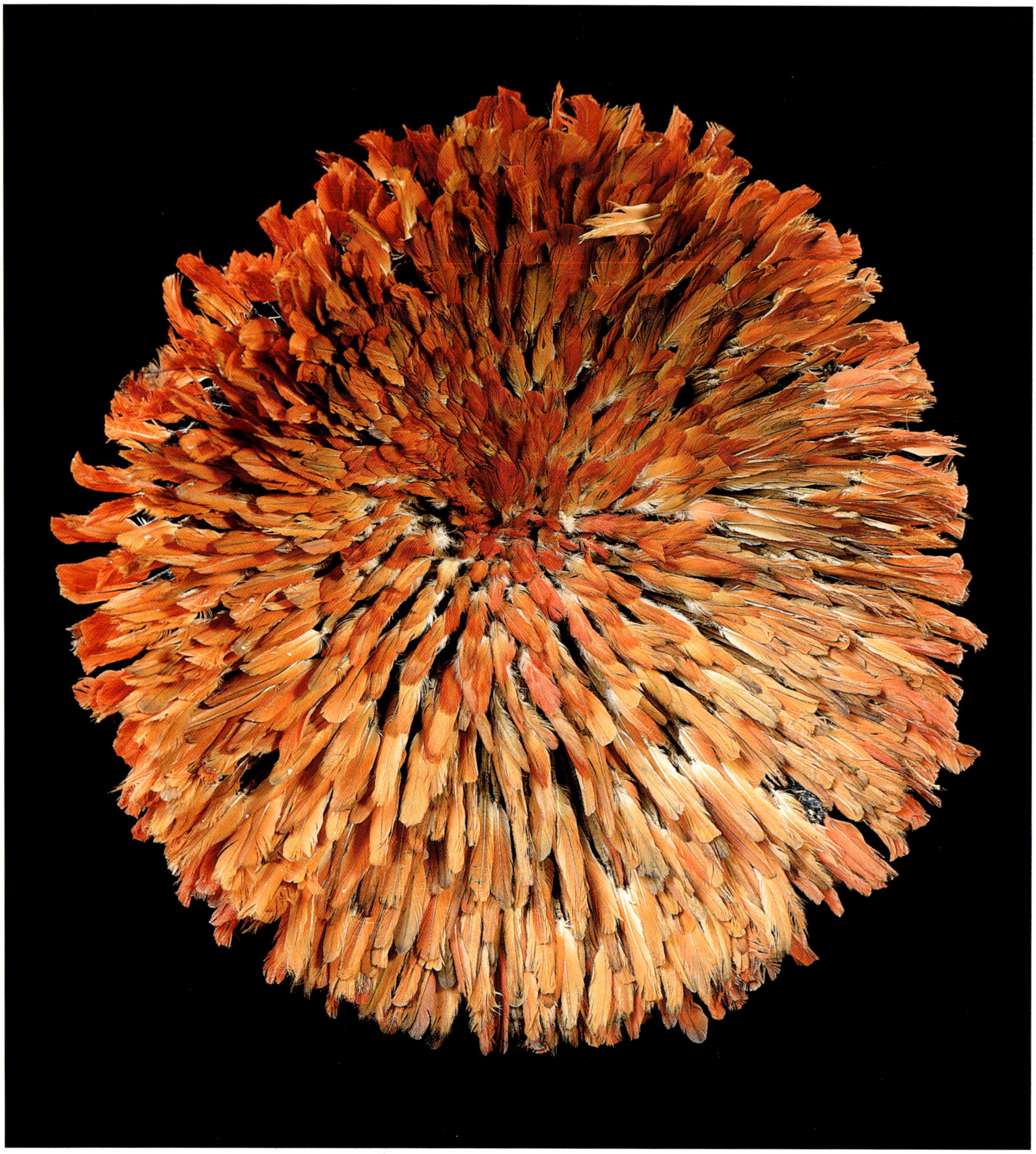

63

## Hat

Tikar or Western Grassfields, Cameroon, feathers, fiber, h: 25 inches
LaVerne Shone Collection

*Colorful dyed feathers indicate that this hat may have been worn by royals or by a dancer at palace celebrations or funerals.*

# TEXTILES

Textiles are a popular art form made by both men and women in sub-Saharan Africa. The demands of royalty, necessity and an interest in display fuel the production of textiles in many cultures. Cloth is an excellent matrix to exhibit vibrant color, intricate designs and originality.

64

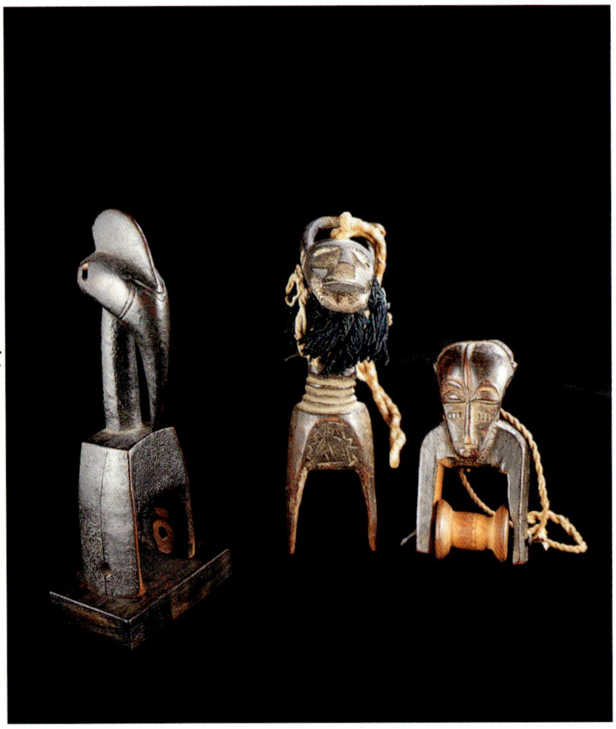

65

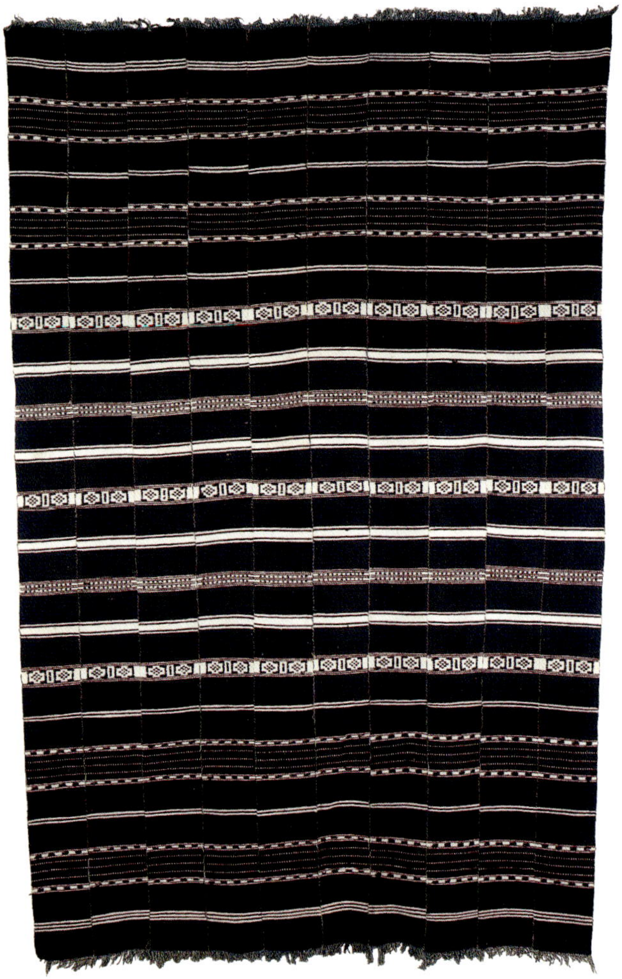

64

## Heddle pulley

Guro peoples, Côte d'Ivoire
wood, h: 8 inches
Arthur Shone Collection

## Two heddle pulleys

Senufo peoples, Côte d'Ivoire or Mali
wood, fiber, pigment, h: 7 inches
Mr. and Mrs. Irvin G. Bieser, Jr. Collection

*Many African horizontal men's looms have double heddles. The double heddle is an appliance that raises and lowers the warp threads to create a shed or tent for the shuttle that holds the weft threads. In some cultures, such as the Baule and Senufo, heddle pulleys have carved figural decoration.*

65

## Blanket

Fulani peoples, Mali, cotton, dye, w: 55 inches
Mr. and Mrs. Irvin G. Bieser, Jr. Collection

*This cotton cover is made of ten long strips sewn together. The horizontal white bands have intricate patterns of crosses, bars and bead-like forms. Similar cloths reported to be made by the Fulani in the Mali region of Macina, are offered for sale over much of west Africa, including Burkina Faso where this example was collected.*

66 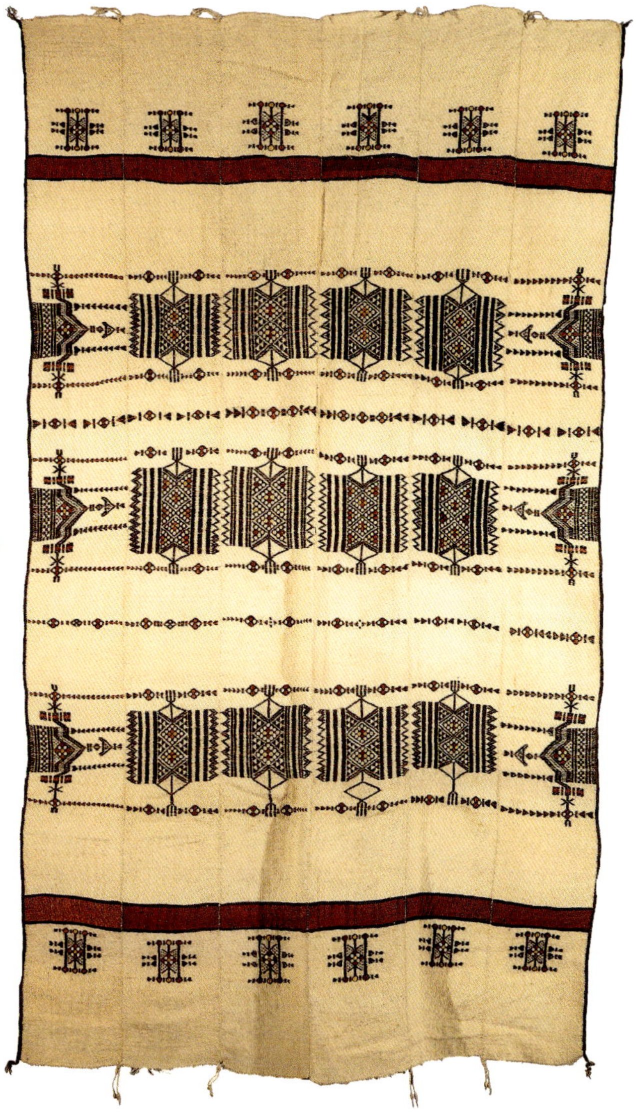

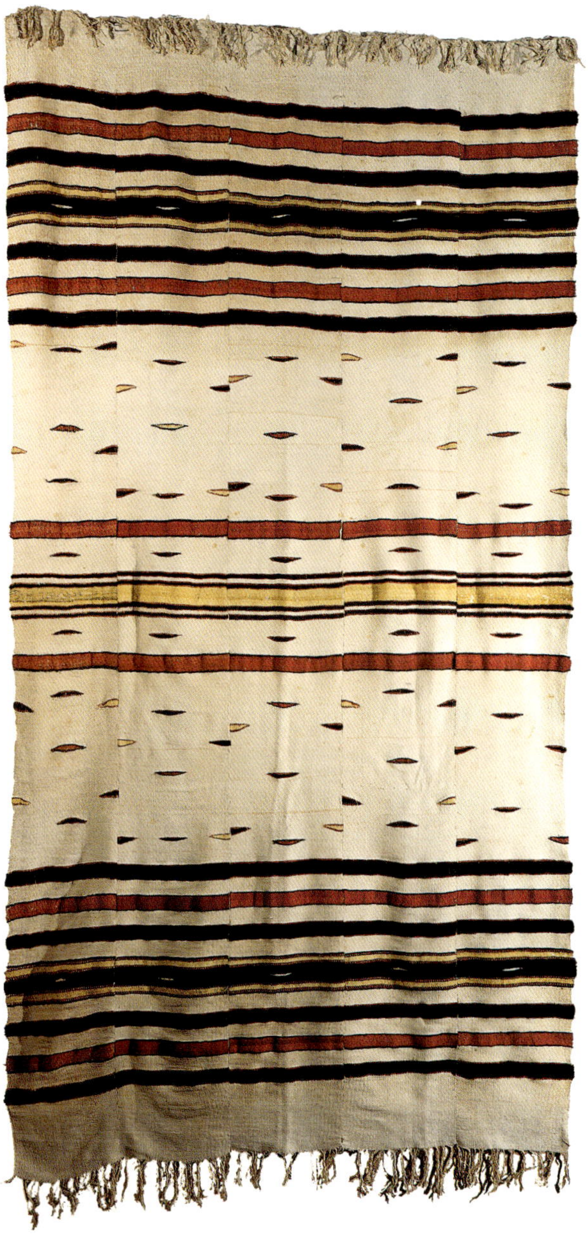 67

66

## Blanket

Fulani (Peul) peoples, Mali, wool, dye, w: 50 1/2 inches
Mr. and Mrs. Irvin G. Bieser, Jr. Collection

*The Fulani people of the western Sudan have a long tradition of weaving cloth that is now found at major markets in Mopti and Bamako in Mali. The pattern has its origin in north African textiles.*

67

## Cloth

Mossi or Dyula peoples, Burkina Faso, cotton, dye, w: 51 inches
Mr. and Mrs. Irvin G. Bieser, Jr. Collection

*Colored weft stripes are commonly found in both broad and strip cloths. Different colors of warp and weft yarns are combined at specific intervals to create the random small colorful spots on this blanket.*

68

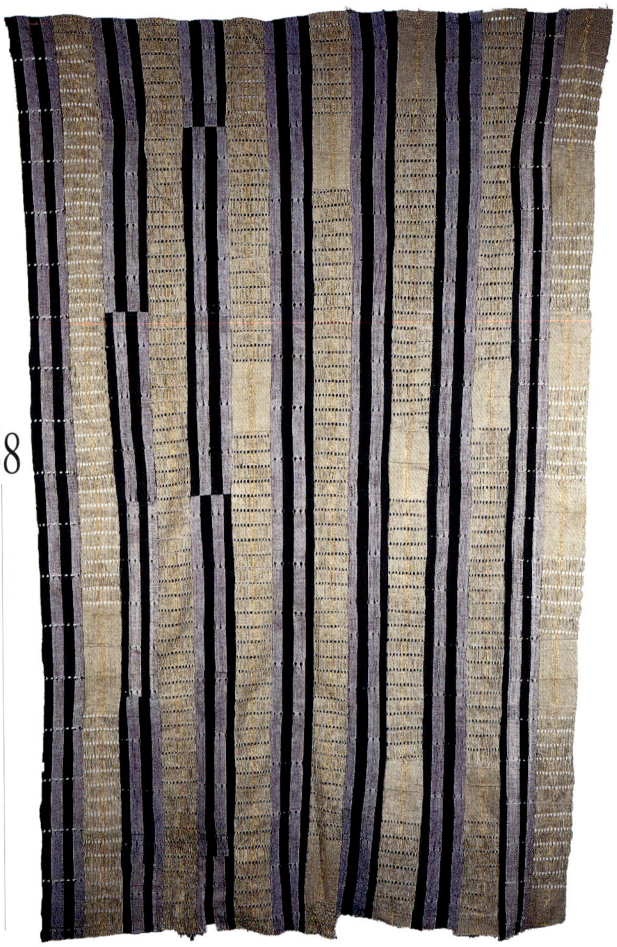

68

## Cloth (asoke)

Yoruba peoples, Nigeria
cotton, dye, w: 54 inches
Willis Bing and Audrey Davis Collection

*Small looms are used to produce long narrow strips of cloth, which may be cut and sewn together to create large square or rectangular cloths. The open-work elements in Yoruba weaving are exceptionally labor intensive.*

69

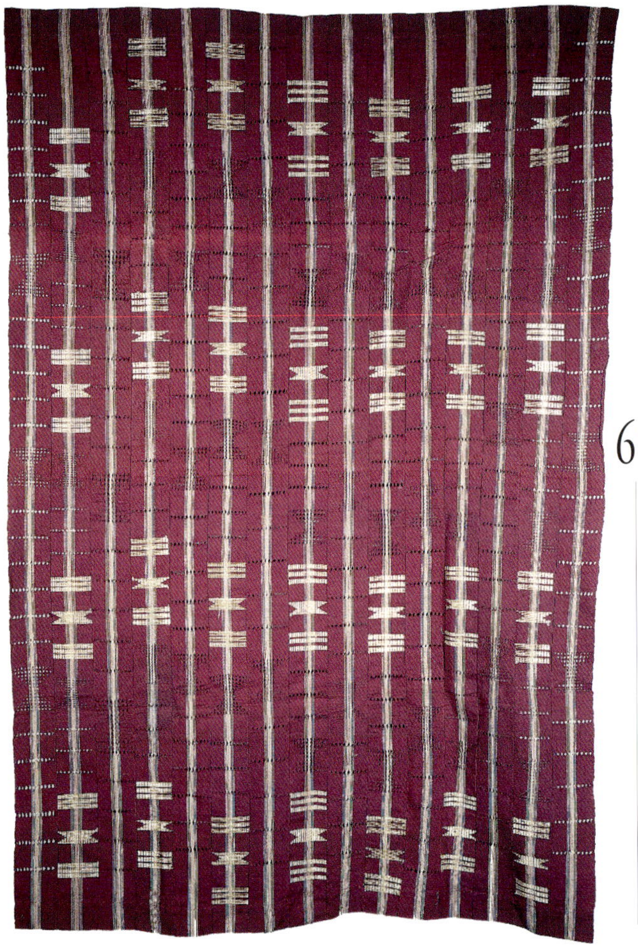

69

## Cloth (asoke)

Yoruba peoples, Nigeria
cotton, dye, w: 56 inches
Willis Bing and Audrey Davis Collection

*One of the appealing elements of Yoruba textiles is the unexpected placement of design elements. The asymmetrical patterns make the cloth visually interesting.*

70

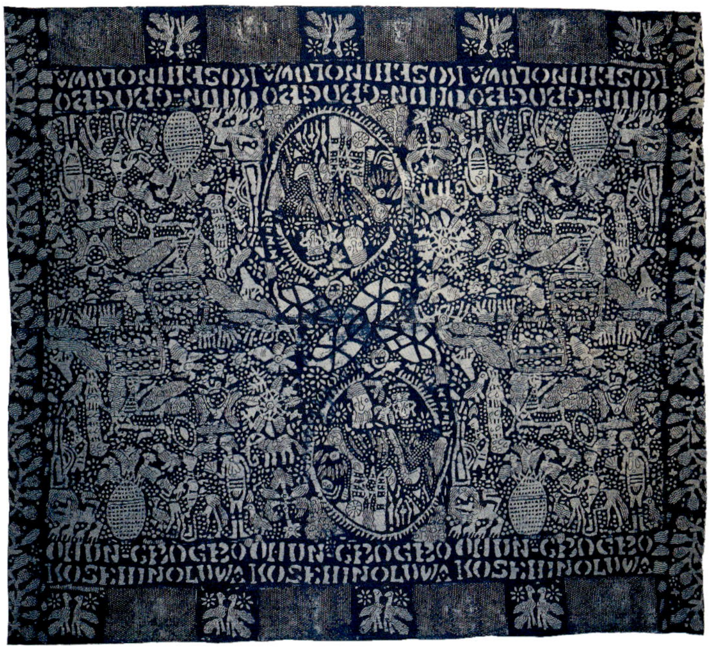

70

## Cloth (adire)

Yoruba peoples, Nigeria, cloth, indigo dye, w: 78 inches
Willis Bing and Audrey Davis Collection

*Resist dyeing is a major textile technique among Yoruba women. This example is decorated with a popular stenciled design. Cassava paste blocks the indigo dye from the cloth creating the white designs. The central section of each half is the highly stylized celebratory medallion of an English king and queen, hence the name Jubilee or Coronation.*

71

## Cloth

Liberia, cotton, indigo and kola dyes, w: 44 1/2 inches
Mr. and Mrs. Irvin G. Bieser, Jr. Collection

*Dyers use a variety of natural pigments and techniques to color cloth. A frequently used method involves folding, stitching or tying an area of the cloth to prevent the dye from penetrating.*

72

## Cloth (adinkra)

[Detail]

Asante peoples, Ghana, cloth, dye, w: 120 inches
Willis Bing and Audrey Davis Collection

*In the past, Asante royals wore adinkra cloth for mourning, but today it is seen at a variety of festivals and ceremonies. The surface decoration is applied using carved wooden or calabash stamps.*

71

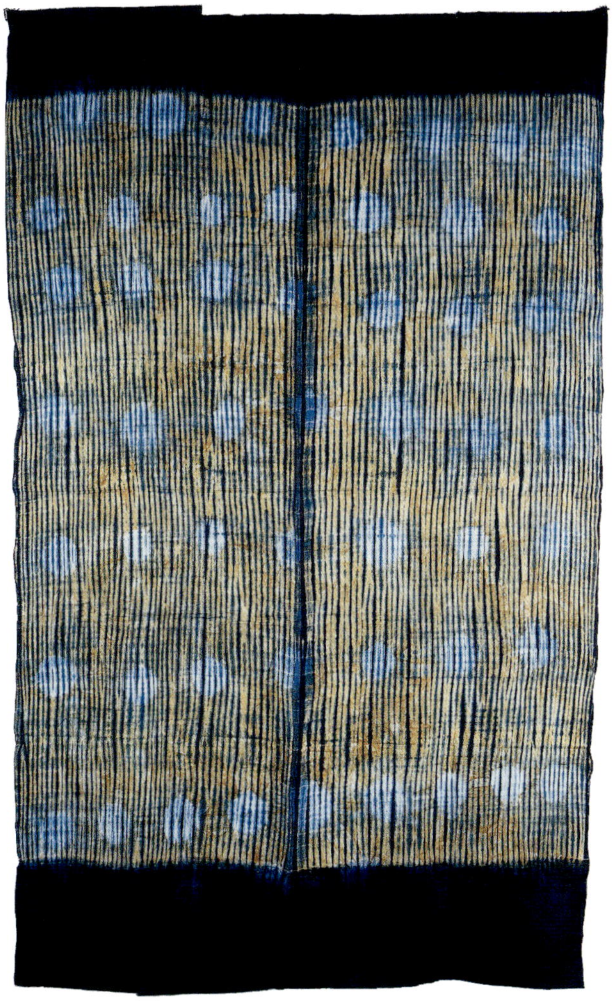

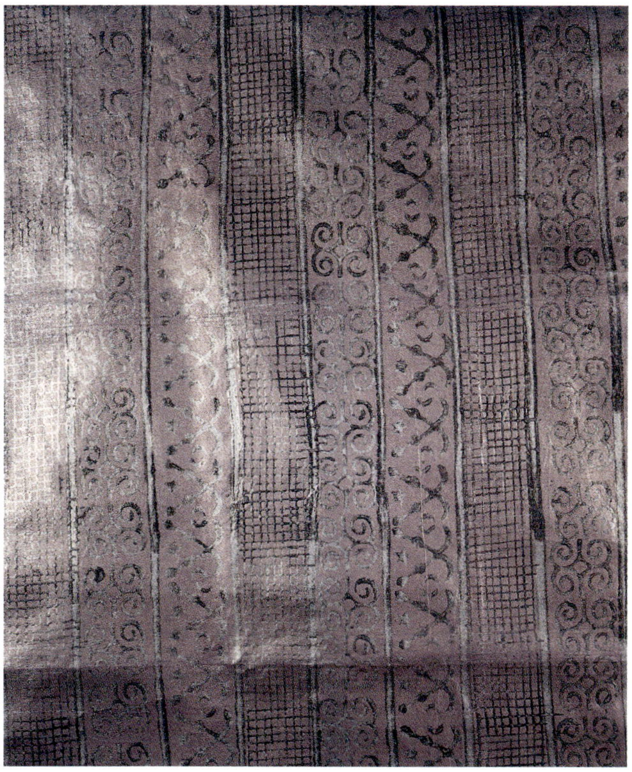

72

73

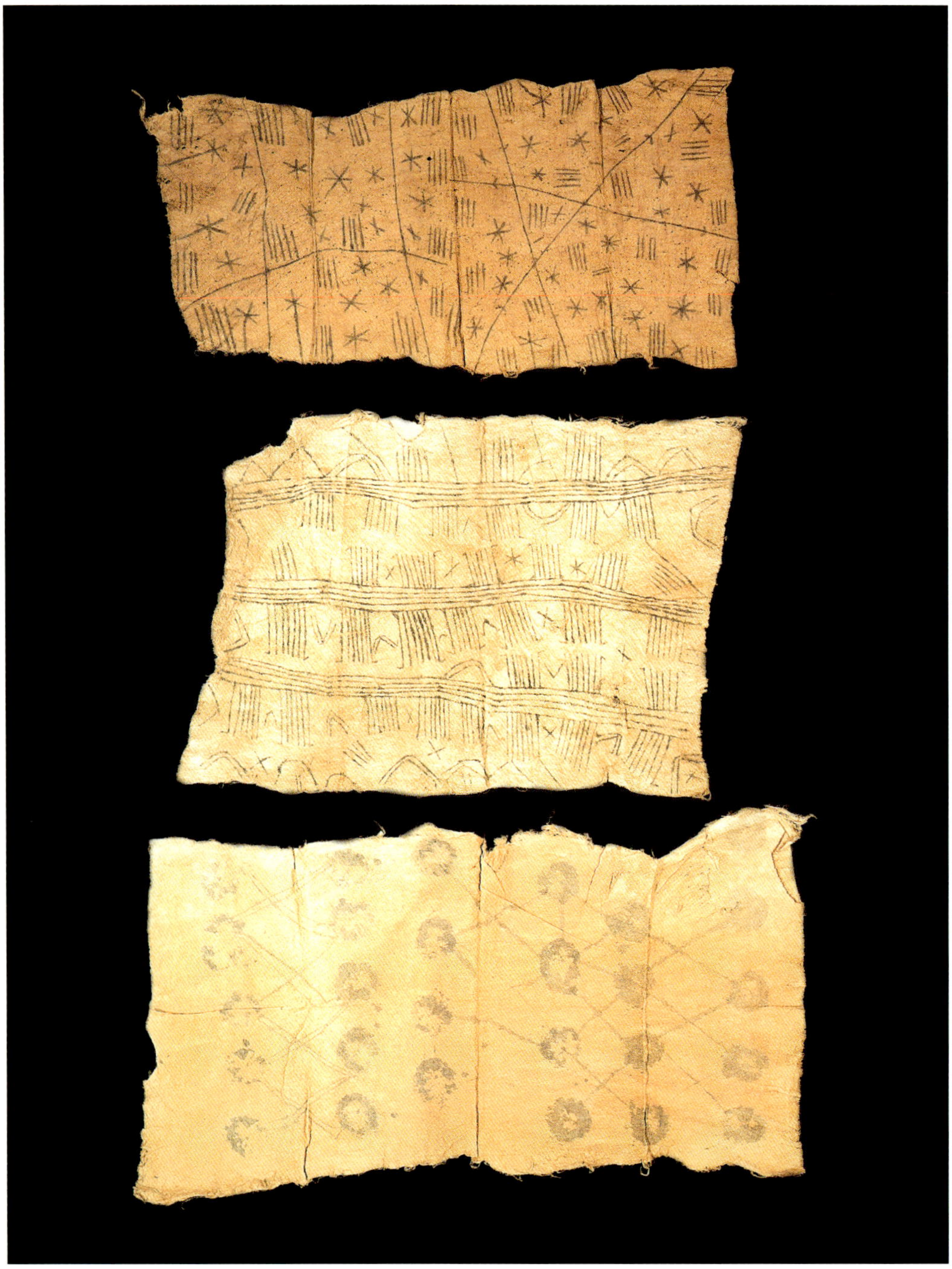

73

## Two cloths (morumba)

Mbuti peoples, Democratic Republic of the Congo, barkcloth, pigment
LaVerne Shone Collection

*Barkcloth panels are made and painted by Mbuti women. A woman's skill in two-dimensional design is highly praised in Mbuti society as an indication of her intelligence and creativity.*

## Cloth (morumba)

Mbuti peoples, Democratic Republic of the Congo, barkcloth, pigment, w: 30 inches
Bonnie H. Bozorgi Collection

*Barkcloths are painted with a variety of motifs that represent rope, stars, combs and arrows. Consistent with other sub-Saharan peoples, the rhythm of the patterns has been intentionally broken to enhance the visual appeal of the cloth.*

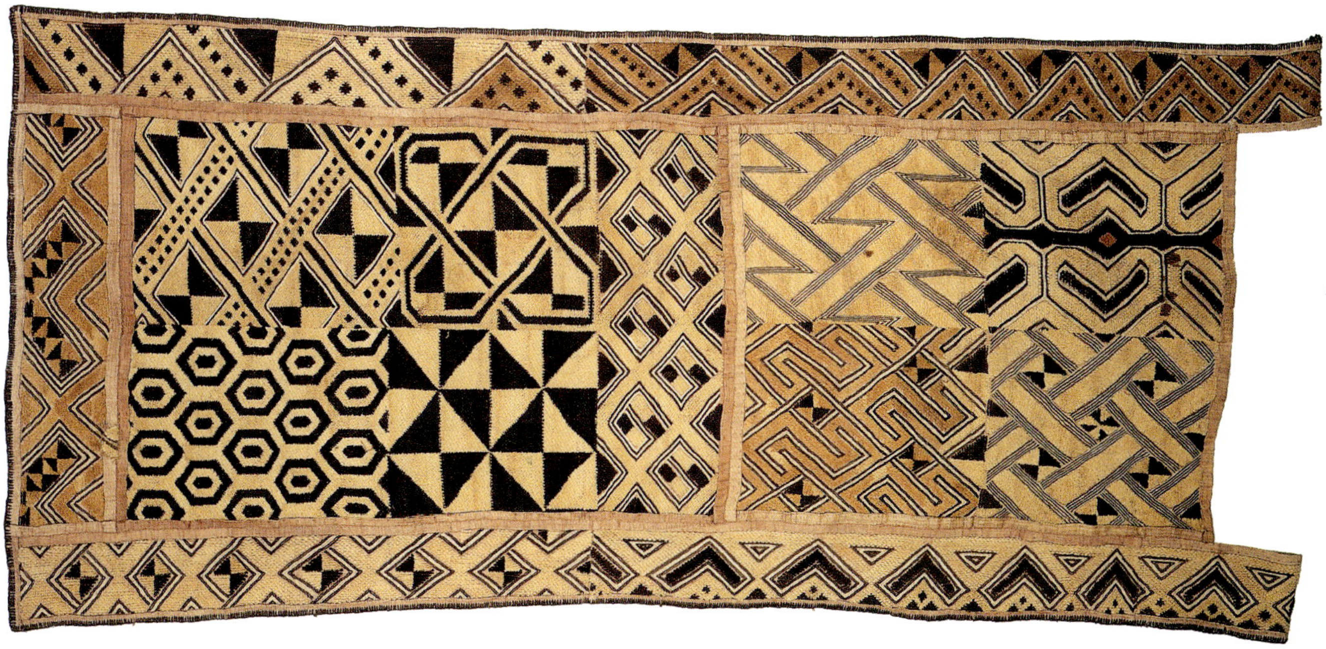

74

74

## Woman's skirt

Kuba peoples, Democratic Republic of the Congo, raffia, dye, w: 67 inches
Dianne Komminsk Collection

*Kuba cloth of this type, often called "Kuba velvets," are produced in a slow and labor-intensive method. Men weave the basic textile; then women embroider raffia threads through the top fibers of the woven cloth and each thread is carefully clipped, creating the look and feel of velvet.*

75

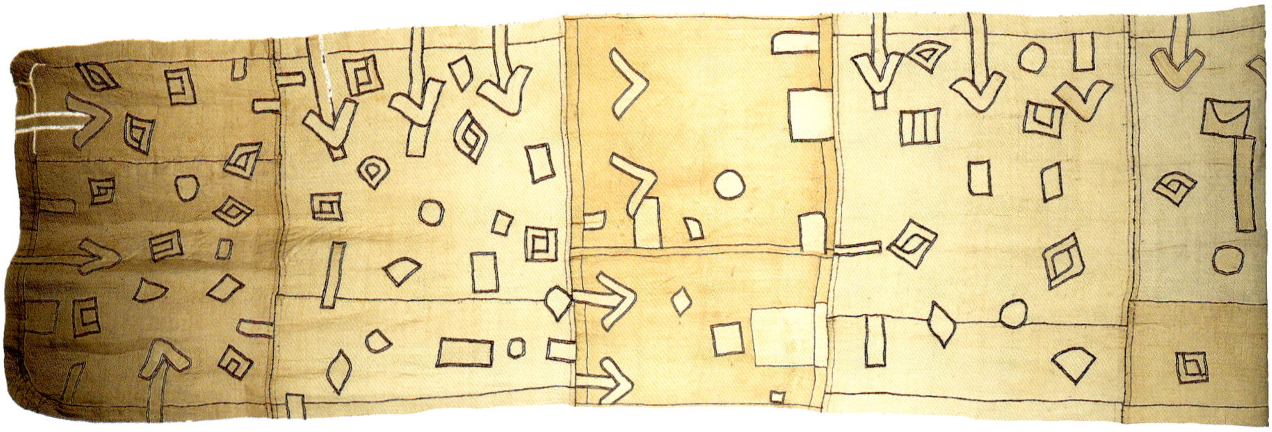

75

## Woman's skirt

Kuba peoples, Democratic Republic of the Congo, raffia, dye, w: 98 inches
Dianne Komminsk Collection

*Large raffia fabrics are made up of complex appliqués and are probably created by a number of women of the same family. They were worn, wrapped many times around the waist, at funerals and other ceremonial occasions.*

## Woman's skirt

[Detail]

Kuba peoples, Democratic Republic of the Congo, raffia, dye, w: 155 inches
Dianne Komminsk Collection

*Kuba textiles are some of best-known textiles produced in Africa. In the past, textiles were traded as currency because of their beauty and value.*

# CURRENCY

Many types of objects used as currency have been made in Africa for centuries before the introduction of coinage by foreigners. It originally came in a variety of materials and forms, including cowrie shells, stone and glass beads, and textiles. Others of iron and copper were, at times, based on functional items such as spear blades, knives or farm implements.

76

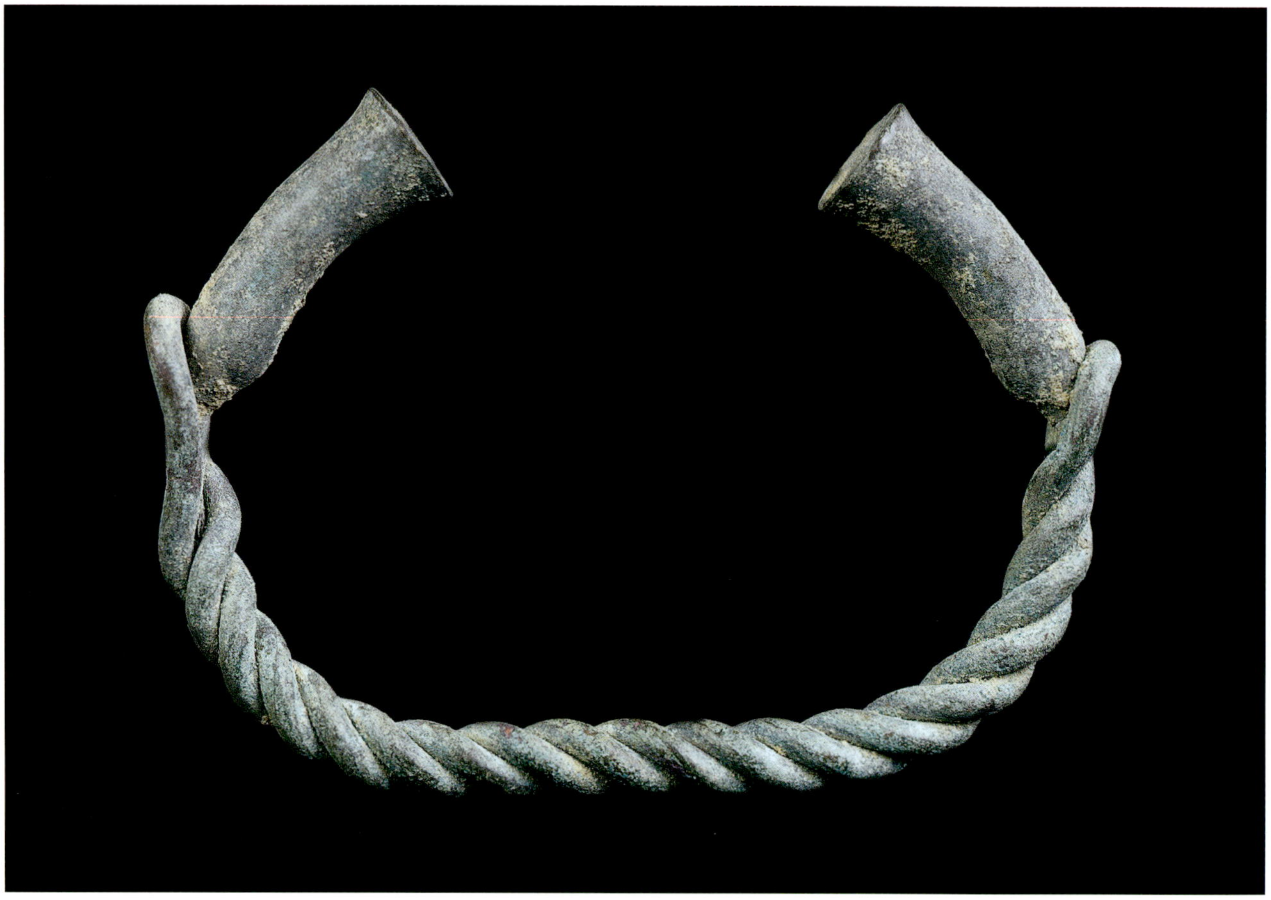

77

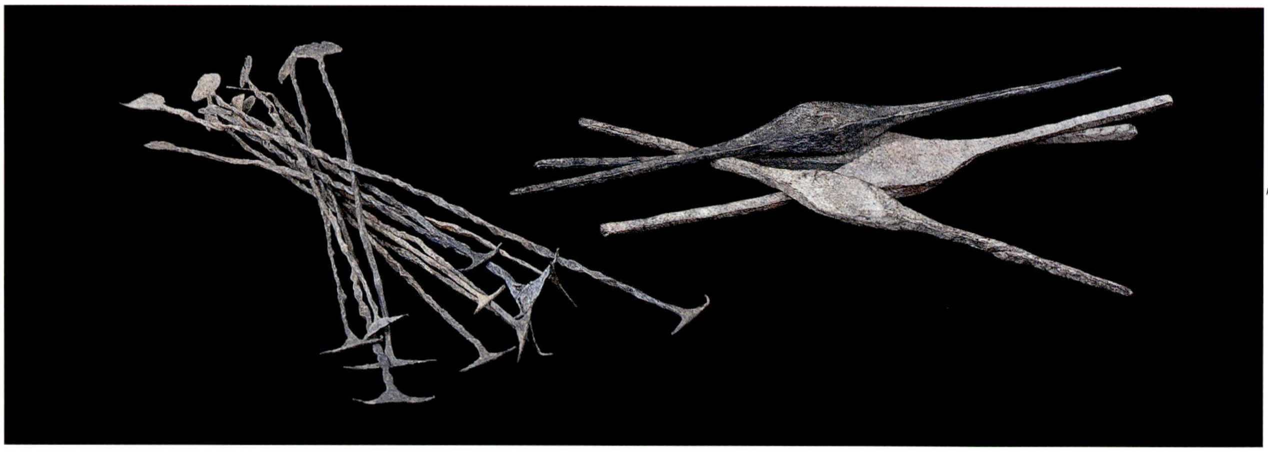

76

## Manilla

Cross-River, Nigeria, copper alloy, w: 9 inches
Dianne Komminsk Collection

*Currency in the form of bracelets, called manillas, has been found among many west African coastal groups. Large examples from Nigeria have been called king or queen manillas.*

77

## Currency

Kissi peoples, Liberia, iron
LaVerne Shone Collection

*Individually of small value, "Kissi pennies" were usually traded in bundles.*

## Currency

Igbo peoples, Nigeria, iron, l: 16 inches
Dianne Komminsk Collection

78

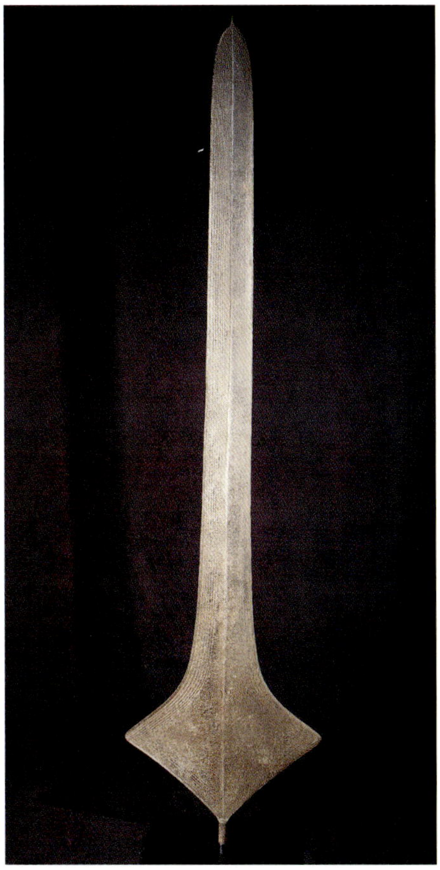

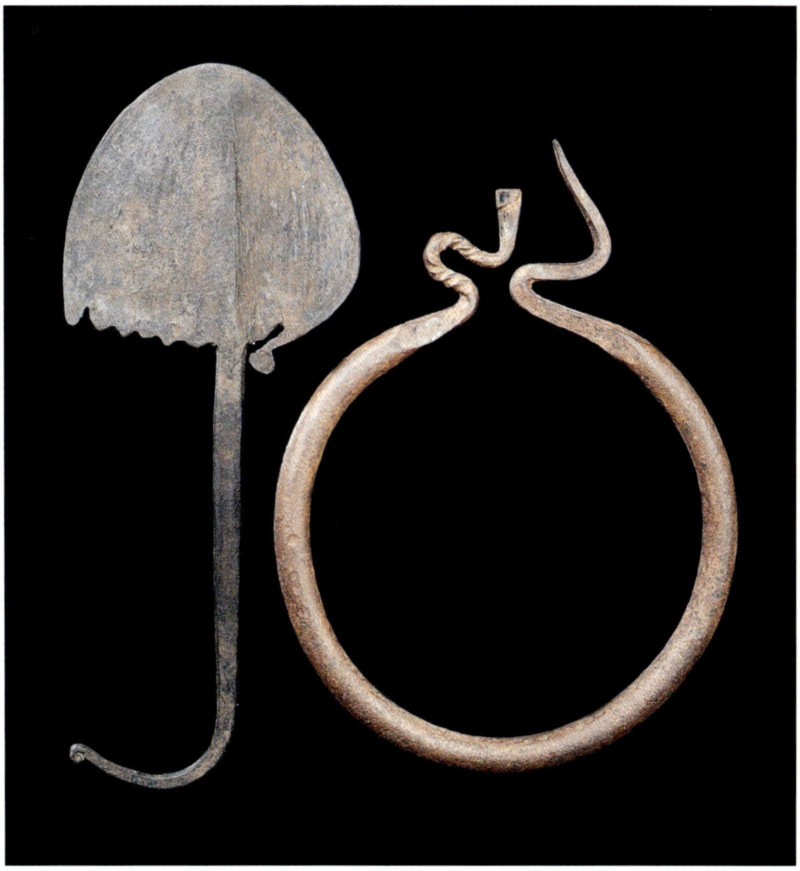

79

80

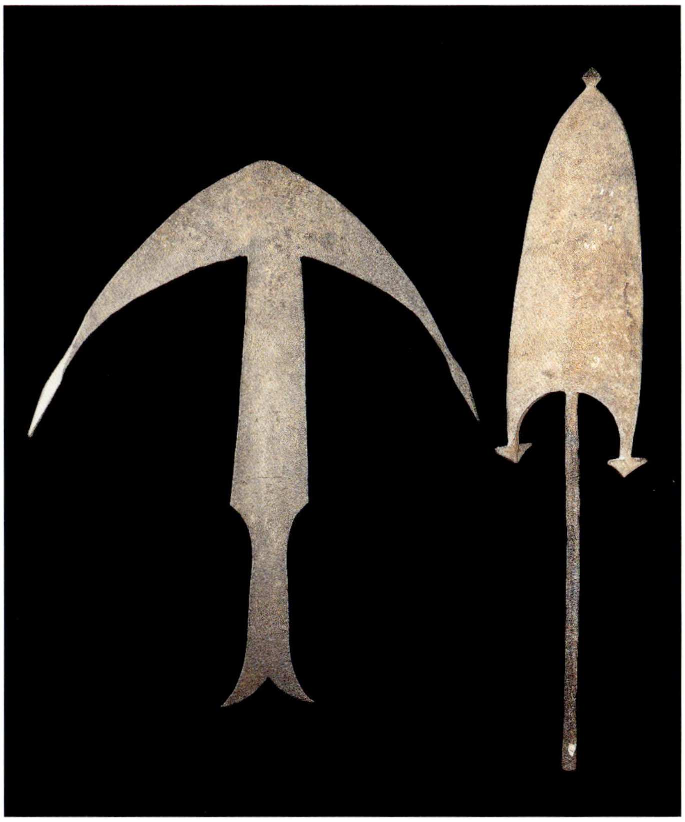

78

## Currency

Lokele or Topoke peoples, Democratic Republic of the Congo
iron, h: 67 inches
Arthur Shone Collection

*Groups of spear points in various sizes were tied together as part of the cost of obtaining a wife.*

79

## Currency

Chamba peoples, Nigeria, iron, h: 19 inches
Dianne Komminsk Collection

## Currency

Kirdi peoples, Cameroon, metal
Dianne Komminsk Collection

*This example may be of ritual significance instead of or in addition to its role as currency.*

80

## Currency

Kwele peoples, Gabon, iron, h: 25 inches
Arthur Shone Collection

## Currency

Ngbaka peoples, Democratic Republic of the Congo, metal
Arthur Shone Collection

*The form of this currency is derived from a hoe.*

81

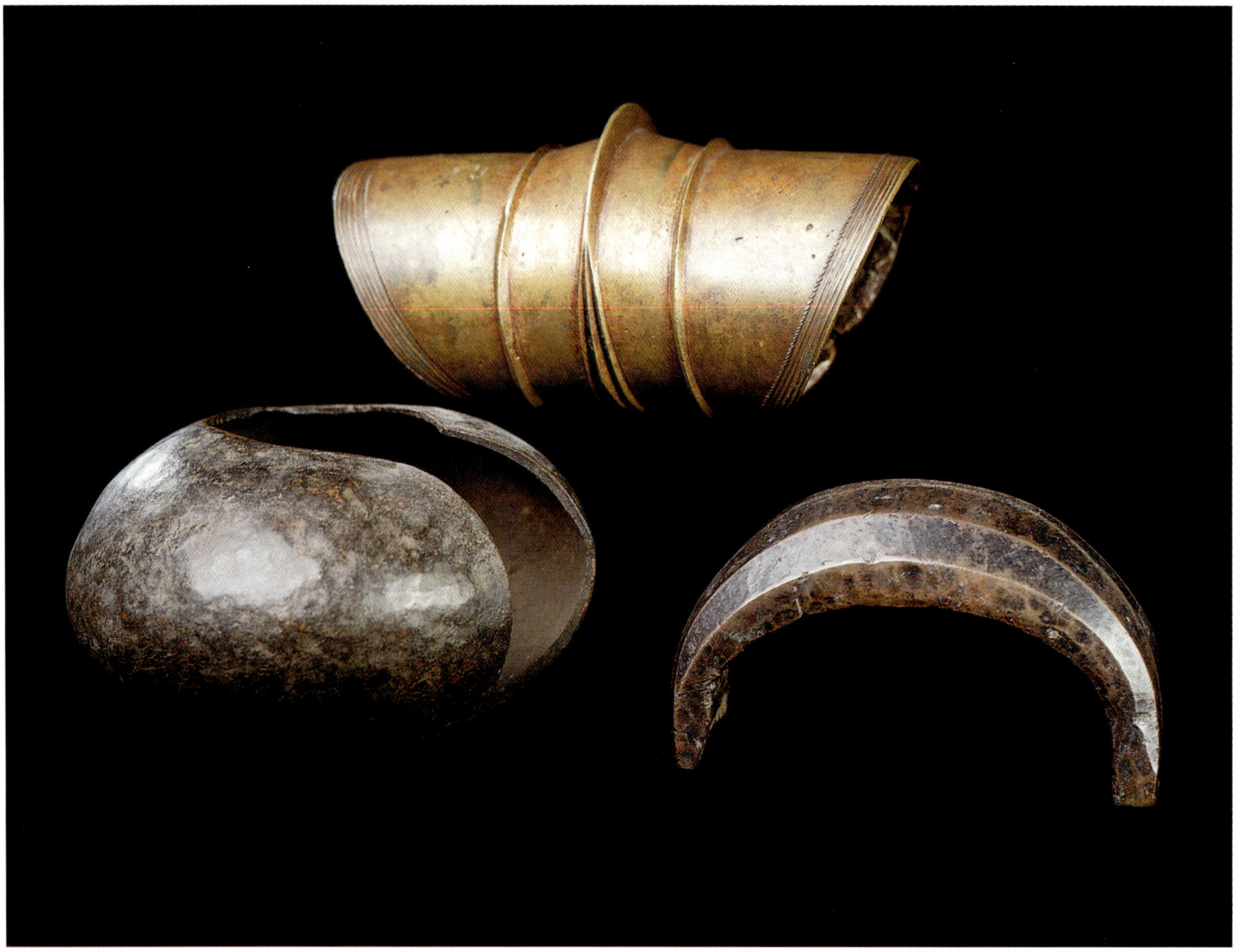

81

## Currency

Ngonde or Ekonda peoples, Democratic Republic of the Congo, copper alloy, w: 10 1/2 inches
Dianne Komminsk Collection

*Worn as an anklet, this large, heavy ornament served to reflect the high status and wealth of the woman who wore it.*

## Currency

Mbole peoples, Democratic Republic of the Congo, copper alloy
LaVerne Shone Collection

## Currency

Mbole peoples, Democratic Republic of the Congo, copper alloy
LaVerne Shone Collection

# WEAPONS

Blacksmiths have long created a variety of weapons for warfare. Some weapons must be imbued with power by a religious specialist to function properly. Many weapons have been adapted for ceremonial use; when displayed, they symbolize the prestige and status of their owners. At times, they have served as currency.

82 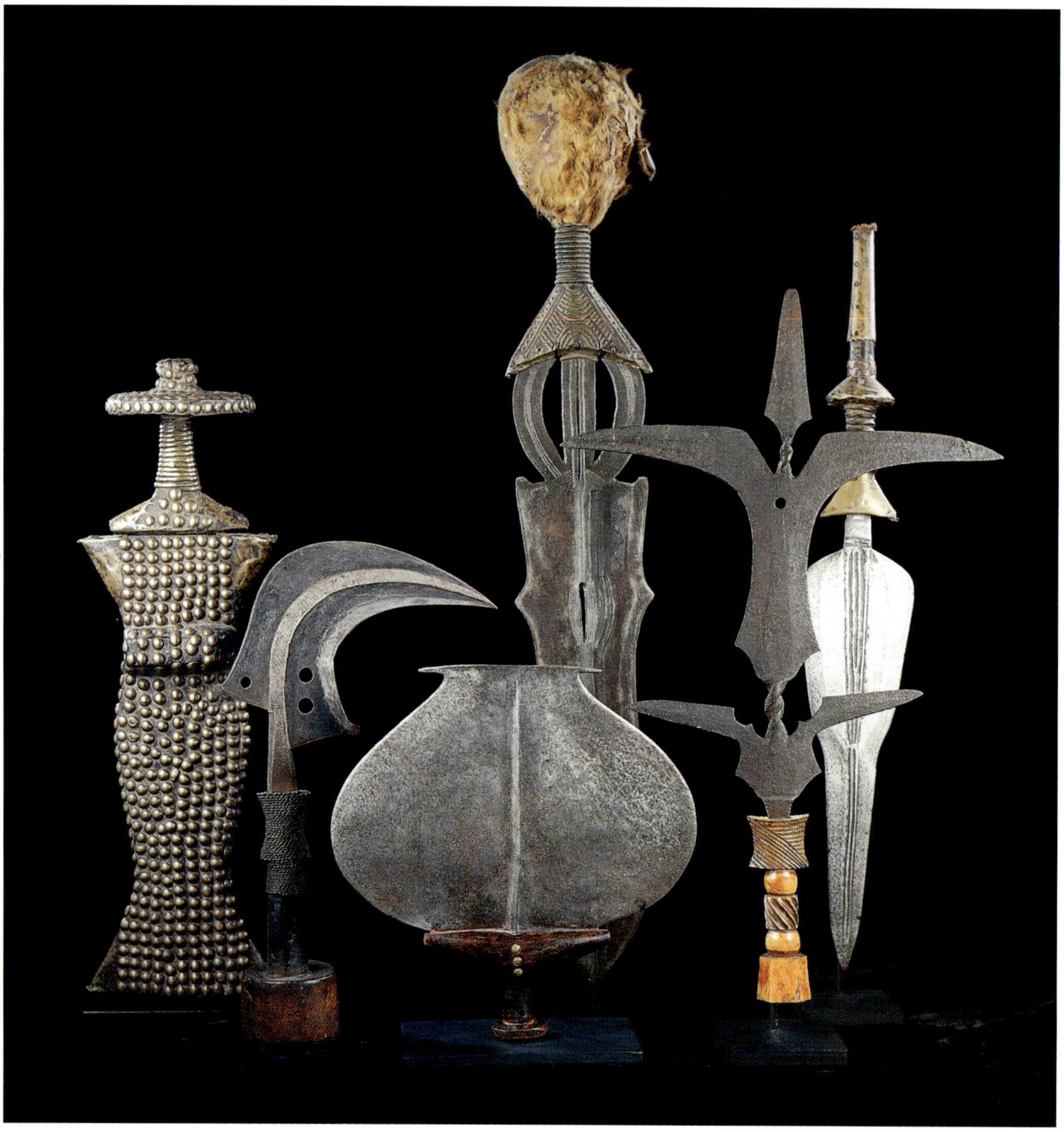

82

## Ceremonial knife

Konda or Nkundu peoples, Democratic Republic of the Congo
wood, leather, iron, copper nails
Arthur Shone Collection

*Some types of weapons were borrowed or used by more than one ethnic group.*

## Ceremonial knife

Mangbetu peoples, Democratic Republic of the Congo
iron, wood
Arthur Shone Collection

*Based on a European form, this weapon is termed a falchion.*

## Ceremonial knife

Dzing, Mbuun, Yanzi or Ngul peoples, Democratic Republic of the Congo
iron, wood, copper nails
Arthur Shone Collection

*This example is one of several unusual sword or knife forms found in central Democratic Republic of the Congo.*

## Ceremonial knife

Poto peoples, Democratic Republic of the Congo
iron, wood, hide, h: 26 inches
Arthur Shone Collection

*Usually described as anthropomorphic in form, the resemblance is probably a Western notion and not African.*

## Ceremonial knife

Konda peoples, Democratic Republic of the Congo
iron, ivory
Arthur Shone Collection

*A number of non-functional display forms is found among the Konda.*

## Ceremonial knife

Kusu, Saka or Tetela peoples, Democratic Republic of the Congo
metal, wood
Arthur Shone Collection

*This knife is another form shared among central African peoples.*

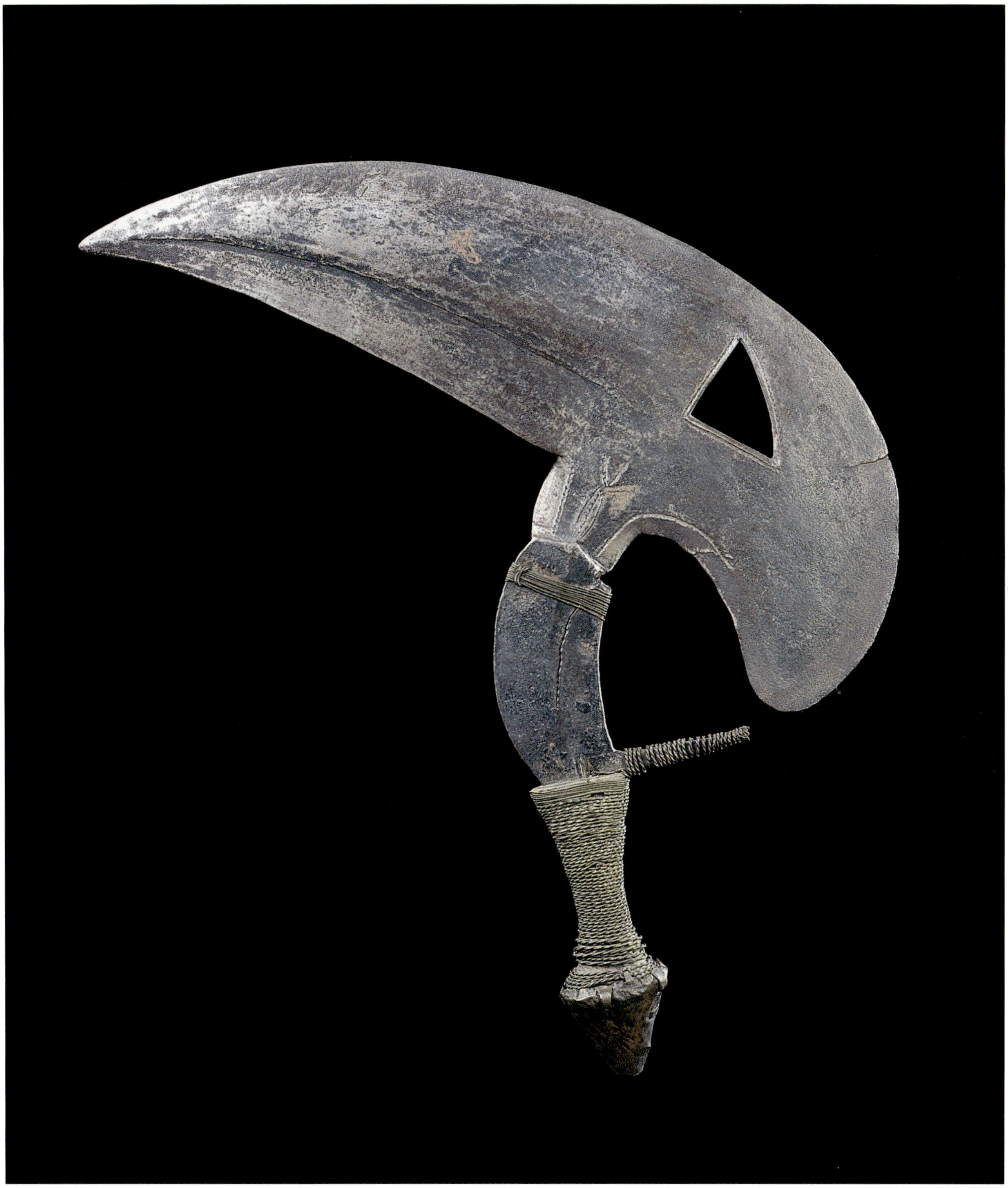

83

83

## Ceremonial knife

Kota peoples, Gabon, metal, h: 14 inches
Vincent and Elana Bolling Collection

*A throwing knife, this is one of the best known and most desirable African weapon forms among collectors.*

84

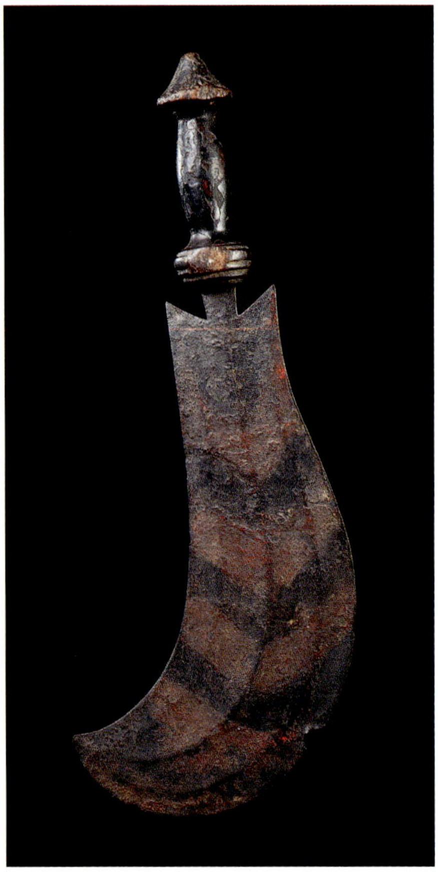

85

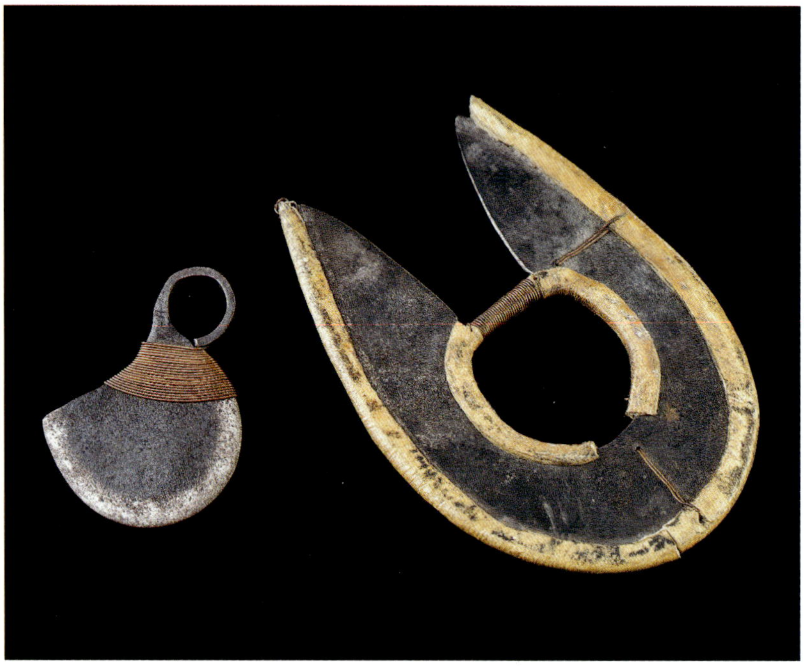

84

## Ceremonial sword

Loma or Kpelle peoples, Liberia
metal, wood, pigment, h: 19 1/2 inches
Mr. and Mrs. Irvin G. Bieser, Jr. Collection

85

## Wrist and ring knives

Turkana peoples, Tanzania
metal, leather, h: 7 inches
Dayton Society of Natural History/
Boonshoft Museum of Discovery Collection

*These unusual forms are also found among the Karamojong.*

86

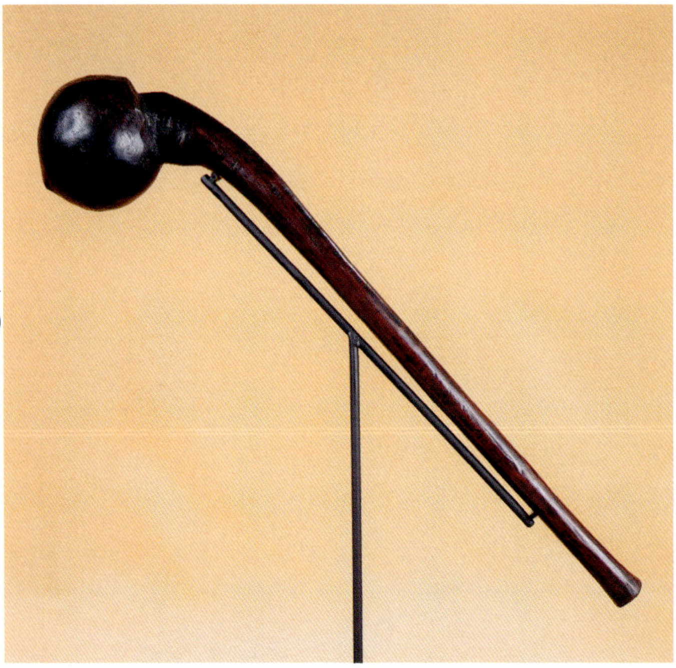

86

## Club (knobkerrie)

San peoples, South Africa or Namibia
wood, h: 19 1/4 inches
Dr. and Mrs. William E. Rogers Collection

*The 19th century publications, such as Ratzel, credit clubs like this to the "Bushmen," now more accurately called San.*

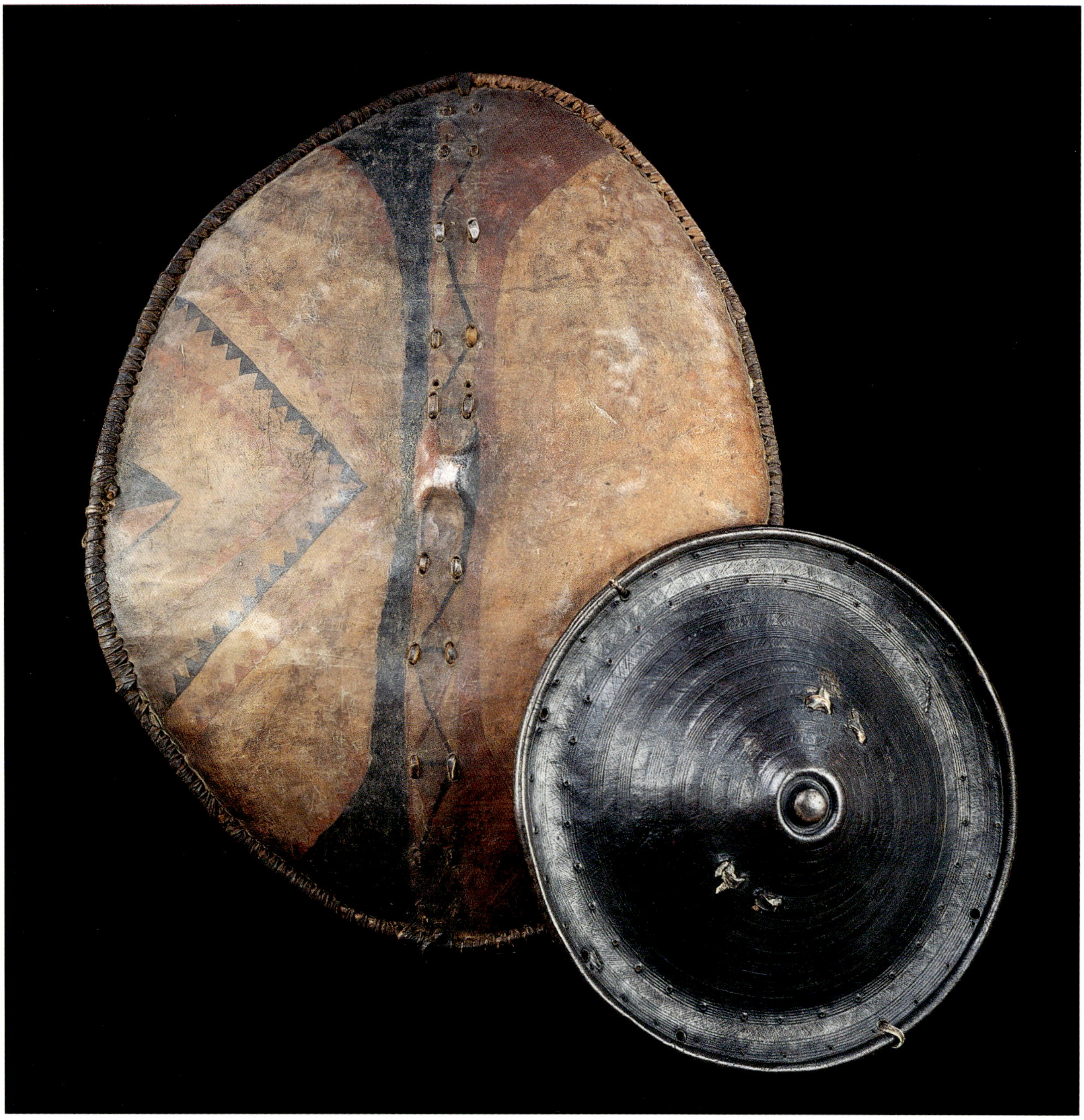

87

87

## Shield

Maasai peoples, Kenya, leather, wood, pigment, fur, h: 37 inches
Dayton Society of Natural History/Boonshoft Museum of Discovery Collection

*A classic example, the designs on this shield probably refer to a particular clan.*

## Shield (gondale)

Dorze peoples, Ethiopia, leather
Dayton Society of Natural History/Boonshoft Museum of Discovery Collection

88

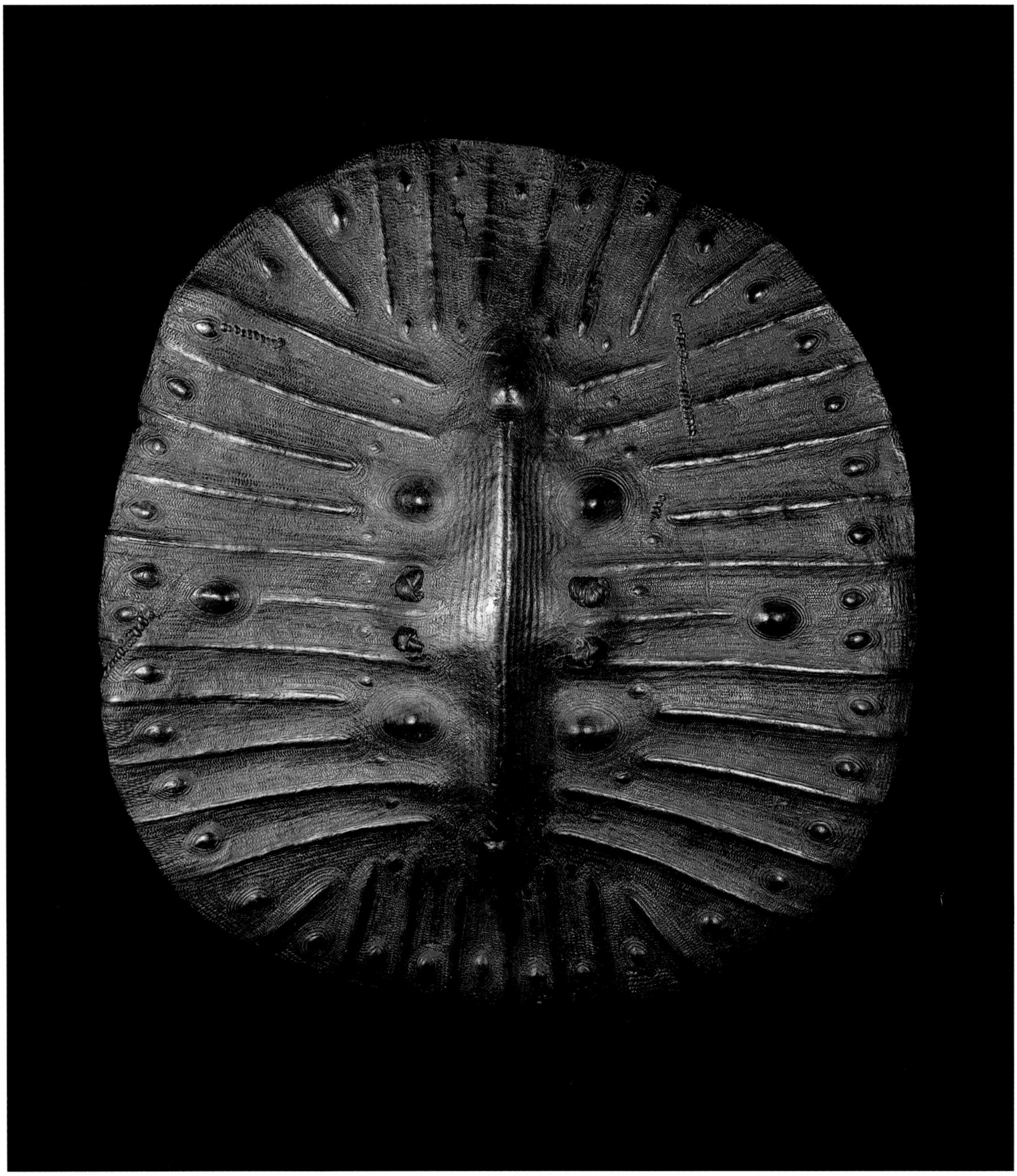

88

## Shield

Arusi peoples, Ethiopia, leather, fiber, h: 28 inches
Dr. and Mrs. William E. Rogers Collection

*Various peoples in central and southern Ethiopia use circular shields made from buffalo, ox or, at times, hippopotamus hide.*

# MUSIC

Music, like dance, is a significant part of life, both secular and sacred. It makes mundane tasks more enjoyable. Drums, side-blown trumpets, flutes and string instruments are found throughout the continent. They vary in style and form depending on region and ethnic group.

89

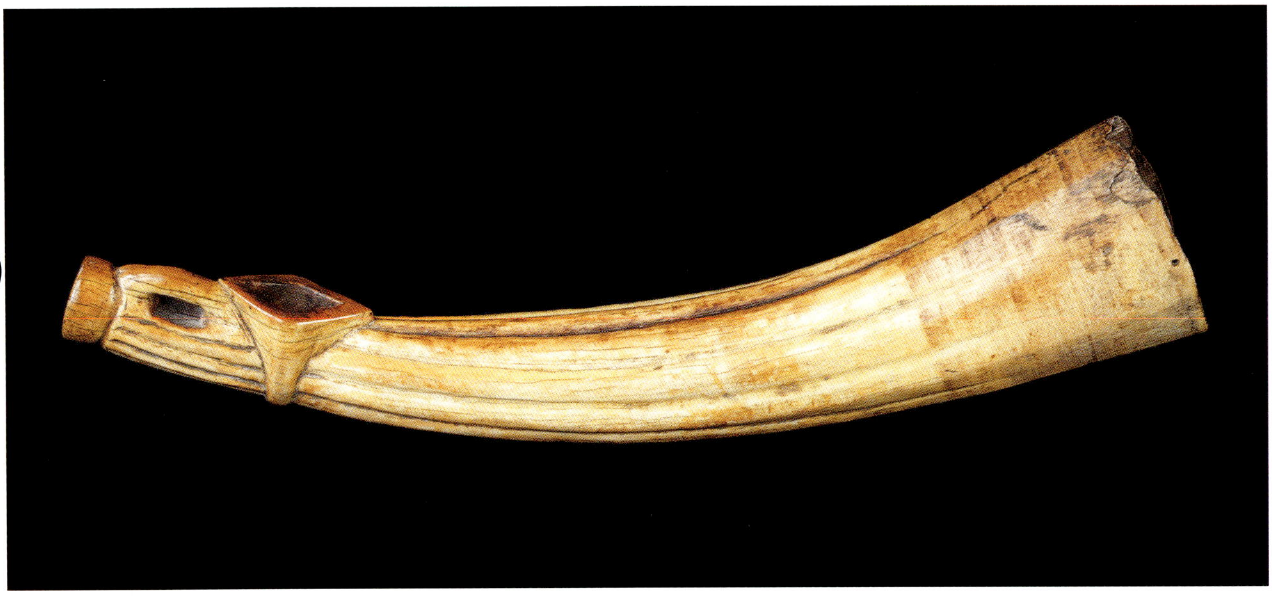

90

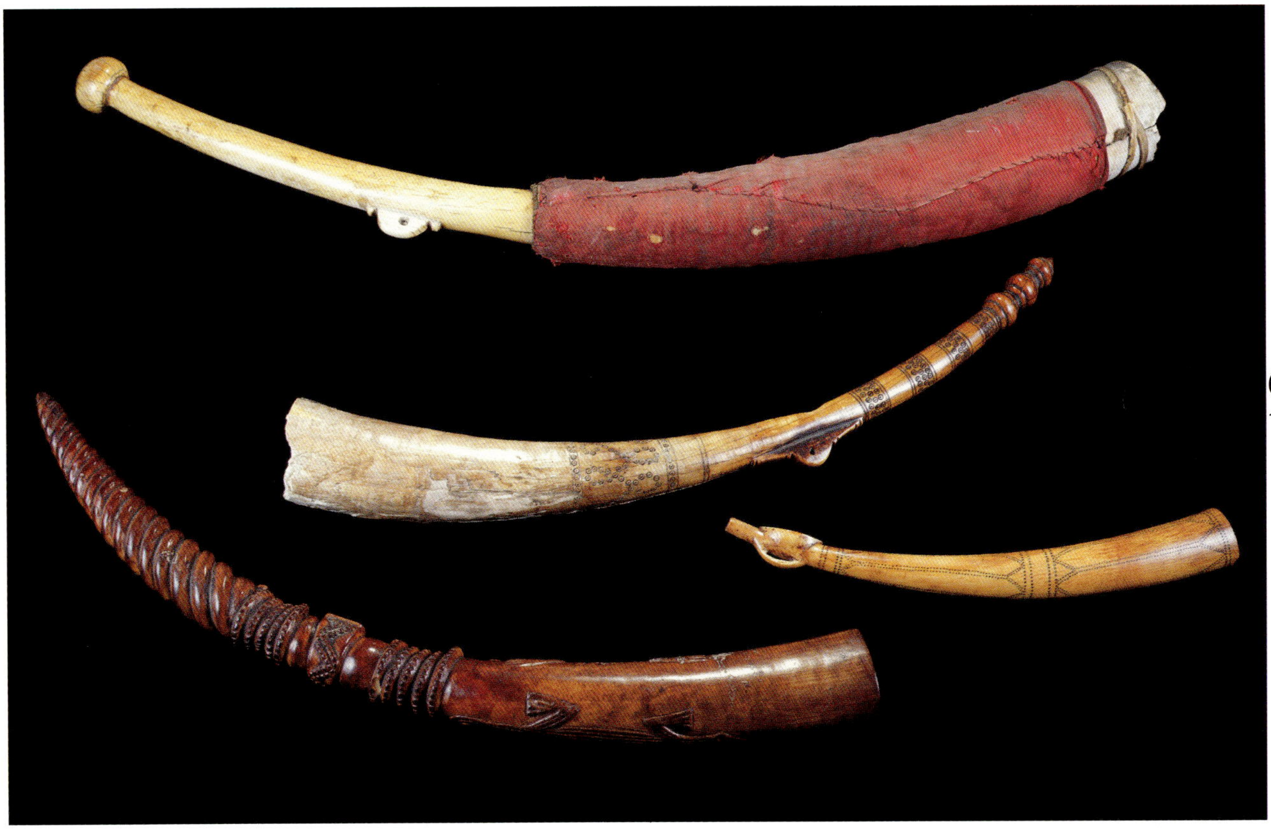

89

## Side-blown trumpet

Sierra Leone, ivory, l: 27 inches
LaVerne Shone Collection

*Side-blown trumpets are an ancient form that is still found throughout the continent. Trumpet playing musicians often accompany chiefs when they appear for public ceremonies.*

90

## Four side-blown trumpets

Democratic Republic of the Congo, ivory, cloth, l: 37 inches
LaVerne Shone Collection

*These instruments, termed oliphants, were royal or chiefly emblems. They would accompany the chief's orchestra. They were blown to announce a presence of a chief at major festivals, collective hunts or fishing parties. They would also be used like a bugle in battle.*

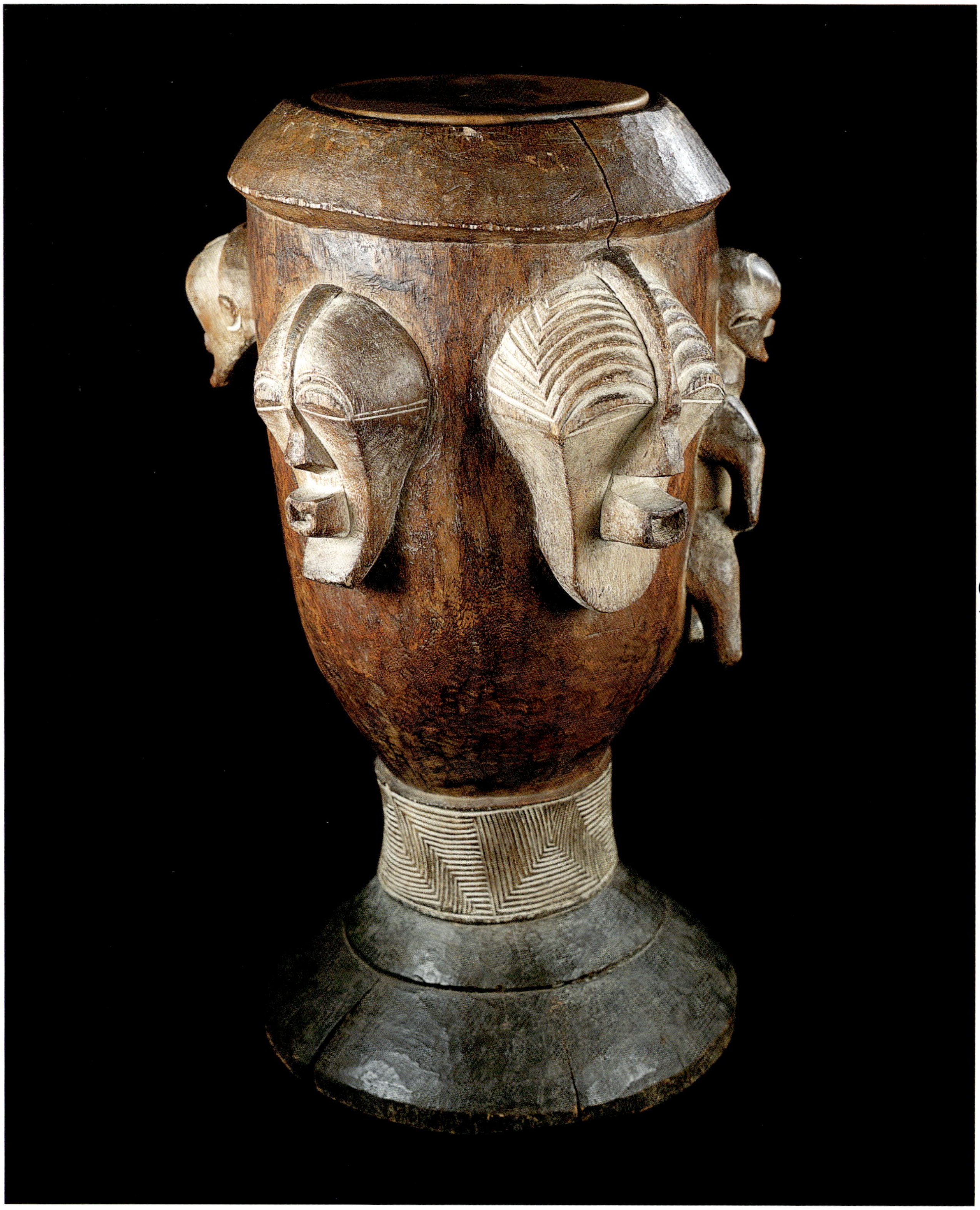

91

91

## Drum

Songye peoples, Democratic Republic of the Congo, wood, hide, h: 28 inches
Dianne Komminsk Collection

*This unusual Songye chief's drum is decorated with male and female figures and three masks. The figures represent the primordial couple and express the notion of balance and harmony between opposing forces. The masks represent father, mother and child, which symbolically comprise the ancestral family.*

92

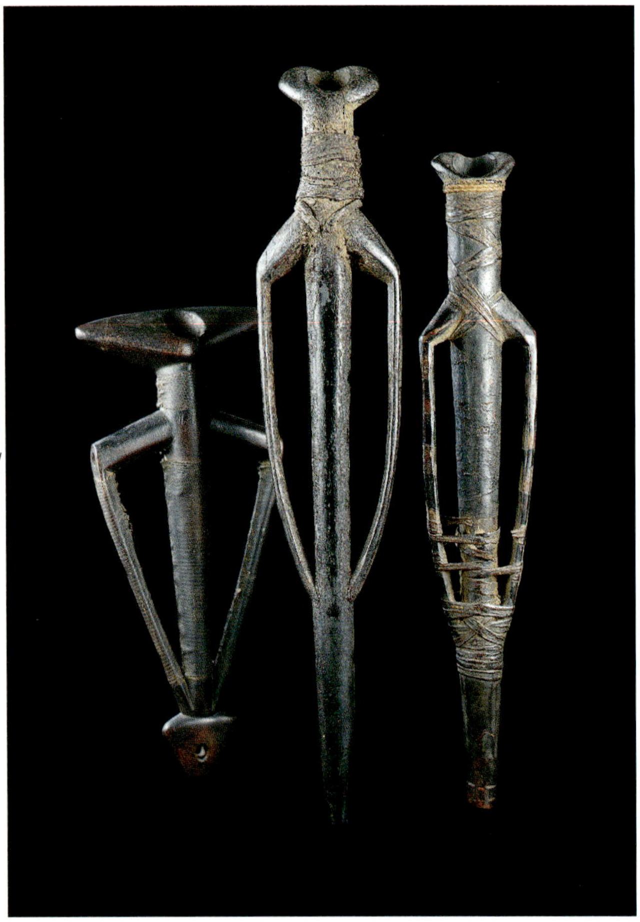

92

## Flutes

Mossi peoples, Burkina Faso, wood, leather, h: 20 inches
Arthur Shone Collection

*The Mossi and a number of other groups in Burkina Faso use flutes of this type. The instruments are designed to be functional; however, the artist has incorporated aesthetic choices such as symmetry and balance.*

93

## Rattle/chimes

Kirdi peoples, Cameroon Nigeria border
iron, l: 23 inches
Dianne Komminsk Collection

*This example and similar percussive instruments have been wrongly identified as currency.*

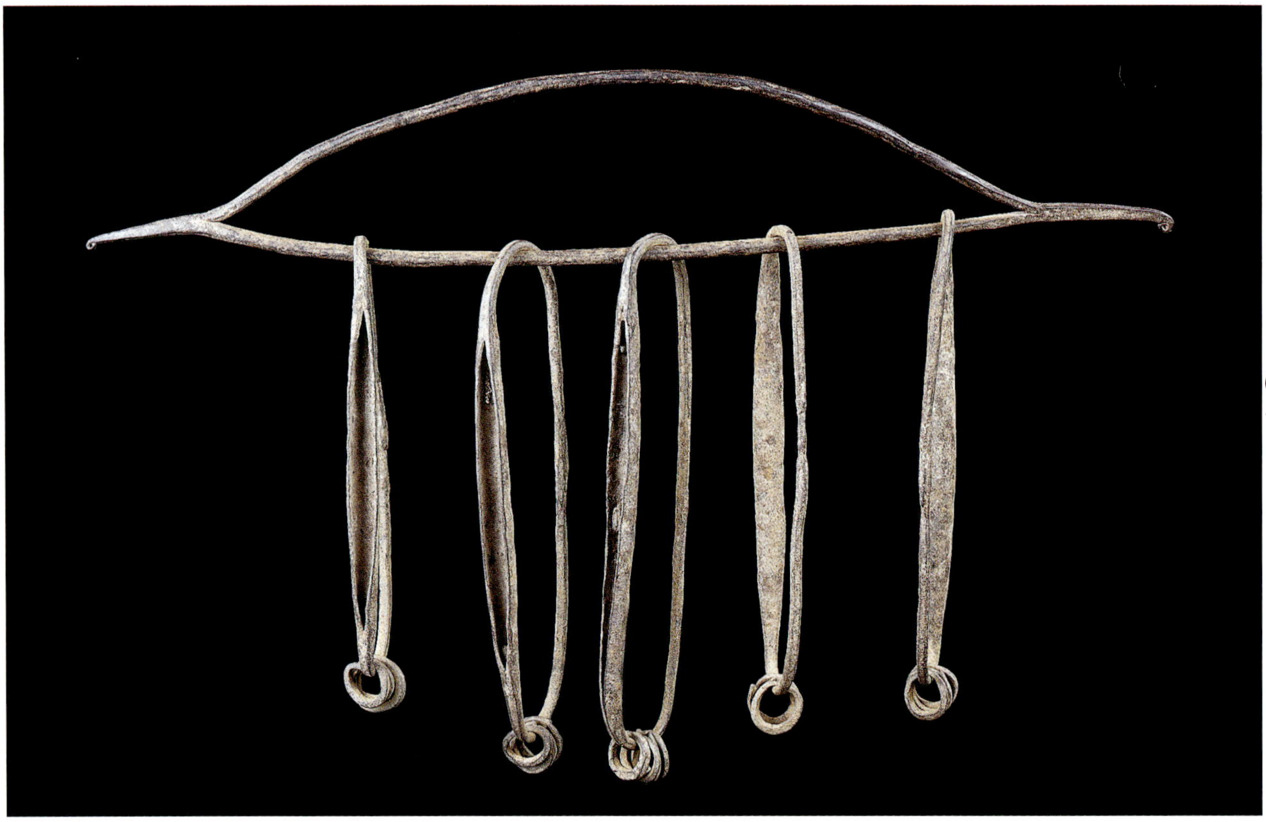

93

# FURNITURE AND HOUSEHOLD OBJECTS

African households contain a variety of domestic items such as furniture, kitchen utensils and game boards designed for comfort, convenience and entertainment. Most types of furniture are exclusively personal rather than shared property in the home. An individual will use and maintain his stool, headrest or chair as a prized possession throughout his or her life. These objects are important symbols of status, ethnic affiliation, gender and authority. They may identify the owner as an elder, leader or person of some financial means. Moreover, stools, headrests and some kitchen utensils, such as meat trays, have a spiritual component, providing vital links to the ancestors and the spirit world.

94

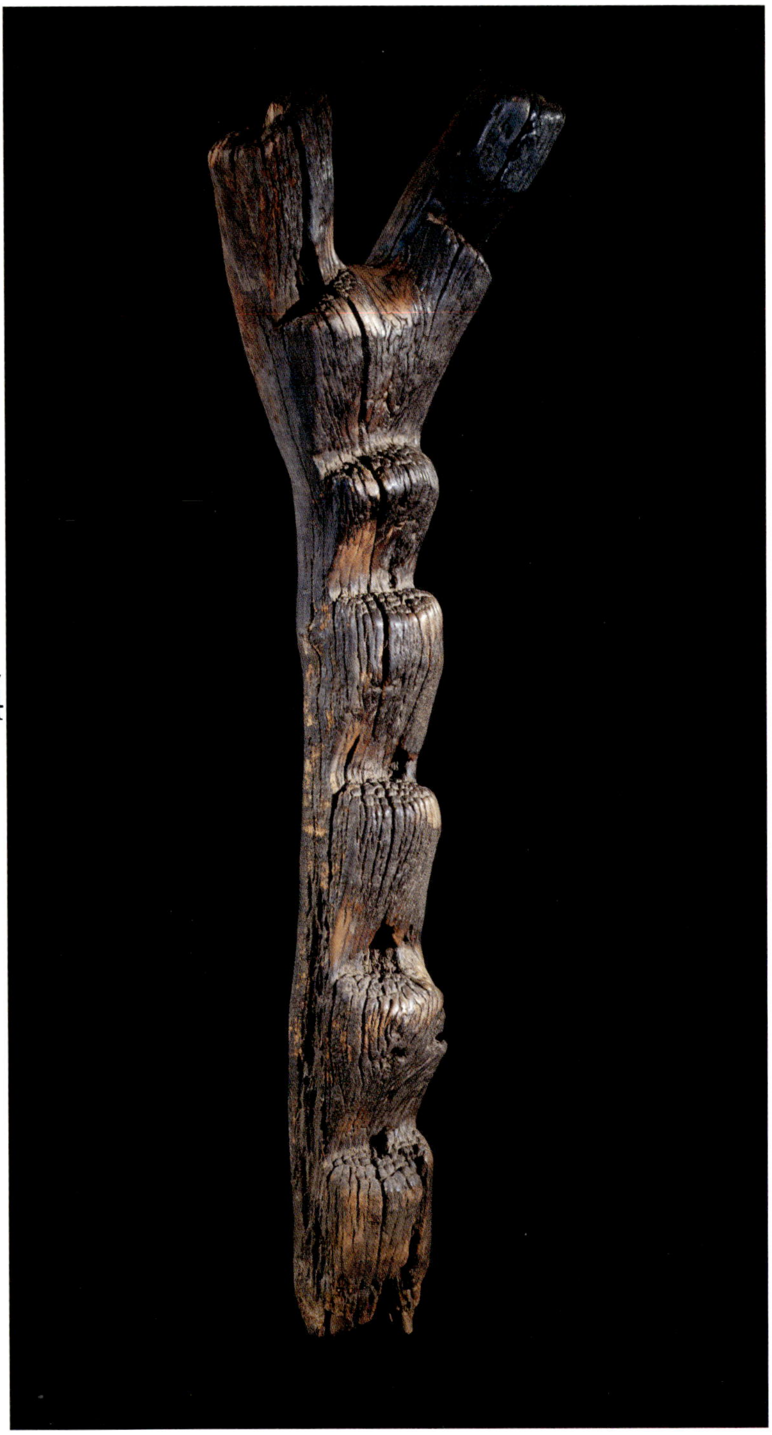

94

## Ladder

Dogon peoples, Mali, wood, h: 64 inches
Dianne Komminsk Collection

*Y-shaped ladders are found among a number of groups in the western Sudan. This example has a rich patina caused by bare feet and long communal use.*

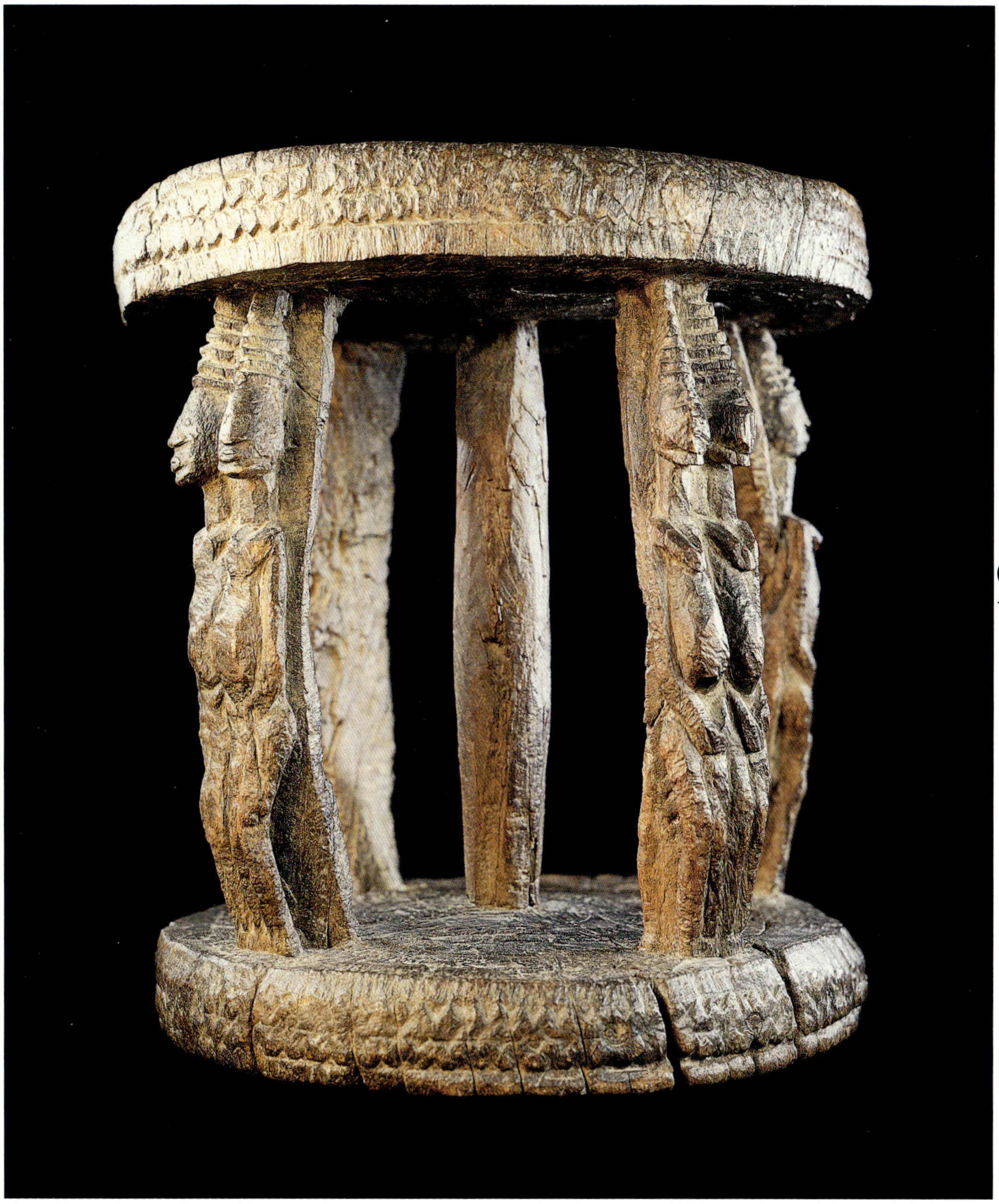

95

95

## Stool

Dogon peoples, Mali, wood, h: 16 inches
Arthur Shone Collection

*Stools are used in the daily lives of most Dogon people. This round caryatid example illustrates the Dogon sense of balance and symmetry. It was probably the property of a Hogan (chief).*

96

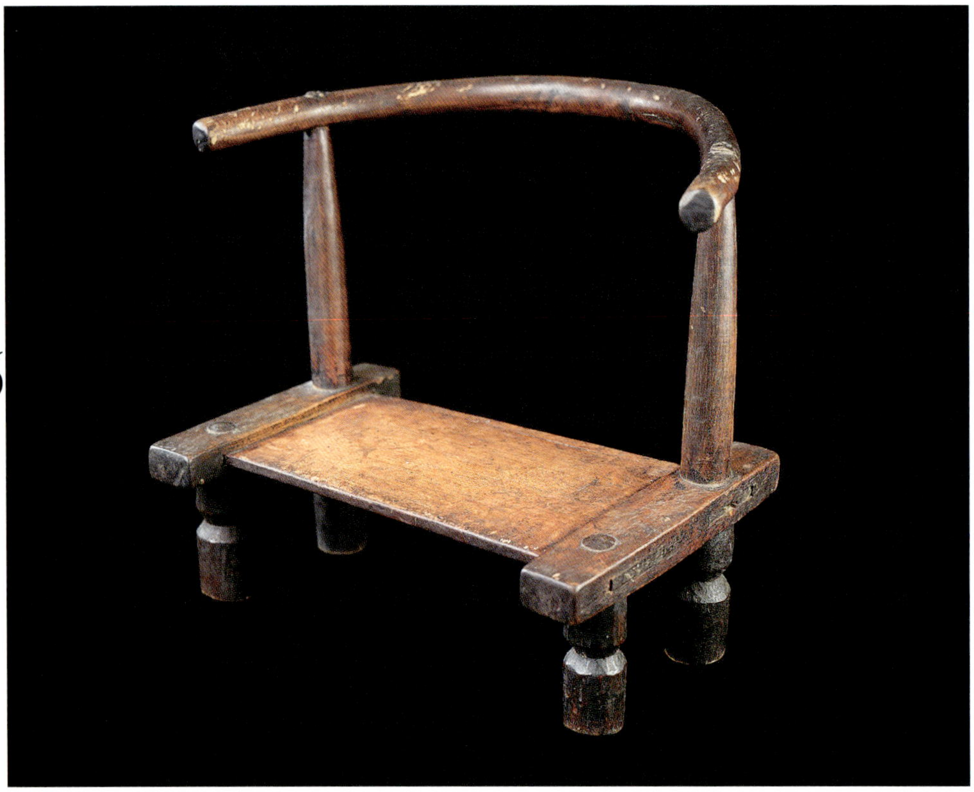

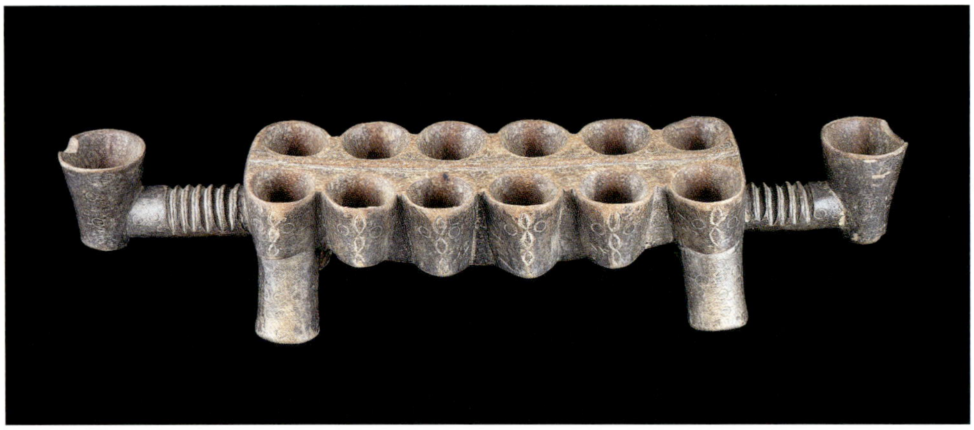

97

96

## Chair

Loma or Kpelle peoples, Liberia, wood, w: 16 1/2 inches
Mr. and Mrs. Irvin G. Bieser, Jr. Collection

*This chair is both functional and a prestige object owned by an elder. The type has been called a "grandfather chair" because young women carry them during coming of age ceremonial dances to honor their grandfathers.*

97

## Game board

Dan peoples, Liberia, wood, l: 30 inches
Mr. and Mrs. Irvin G. Bieser, Jr. Collection

*Similar game boards are found all over the continent, although the number of holes, the name and the rules vary from region to region. It is a game of strategy where one player attempts to capture his opponent's pieces.*

98

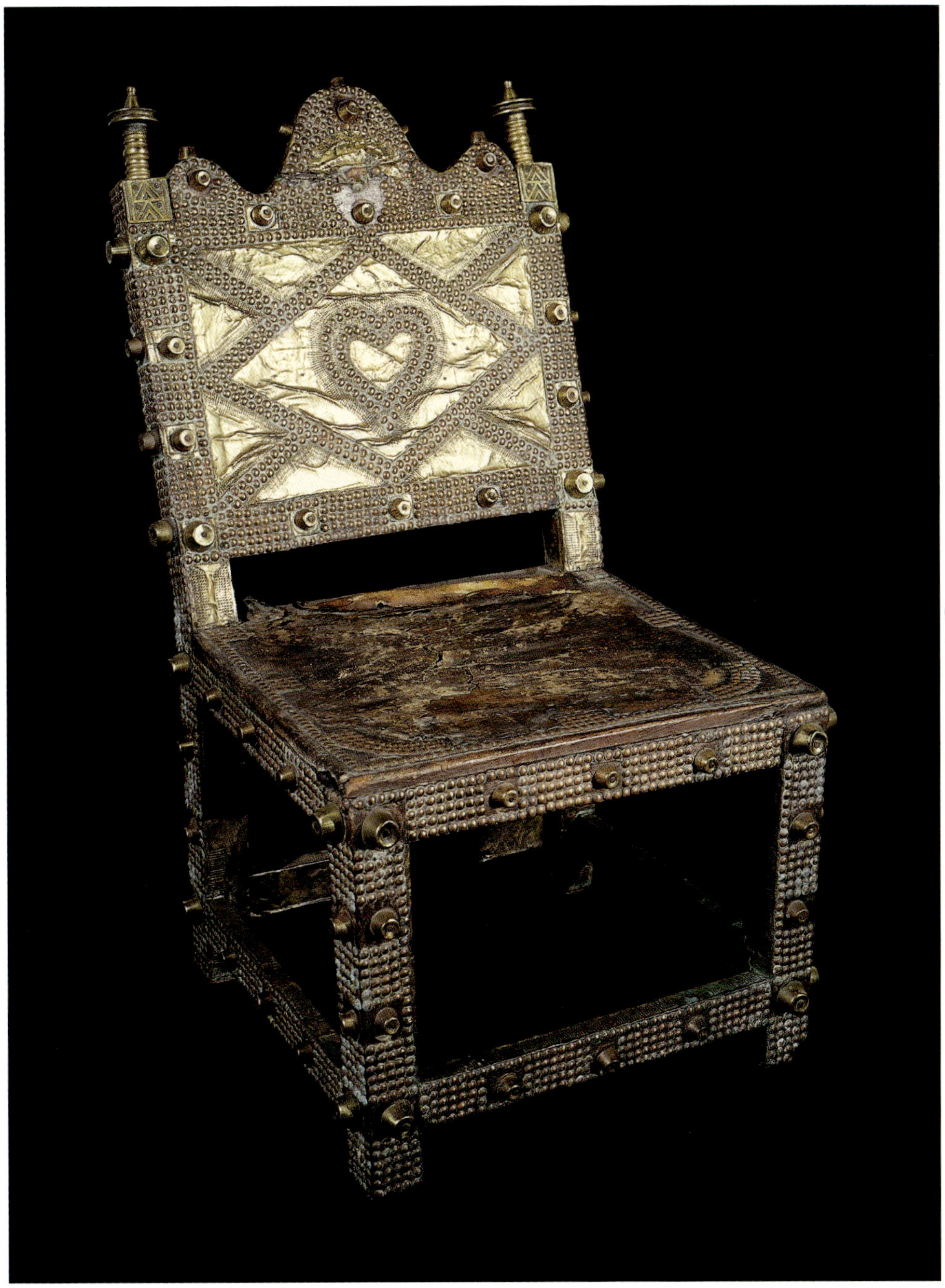

98

## Chair (asipim)

Asante peoples, Ghana, wood, copper alloy, brass tacks, leather, h: 32 1/2 inches
Mr. and Mrs. Irvin G. Bieser, Jr. Collection

*Unlike stools in Asante culture, asipim ("I stand firm") chairs have no spiritual function, but serve as important symbols of wealth and status. They are based on European chairs of the 17th century introduced as gifts by early travelers.*

99

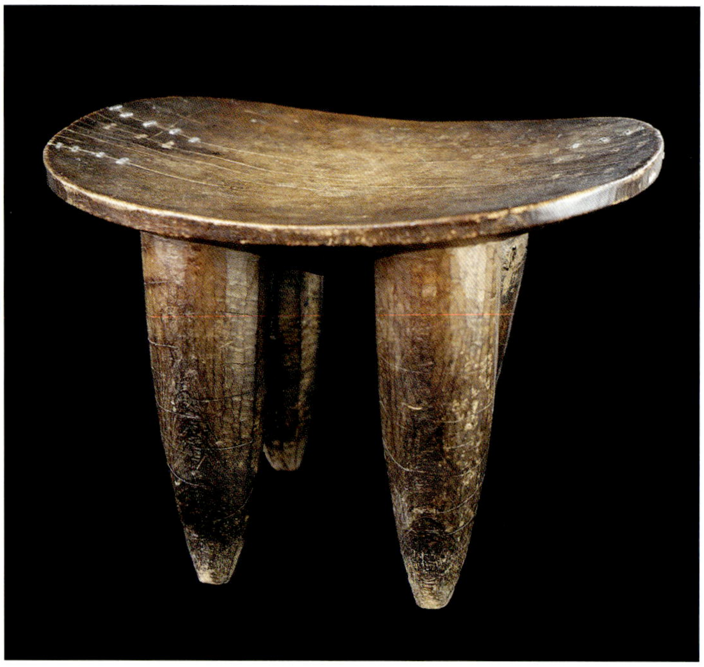

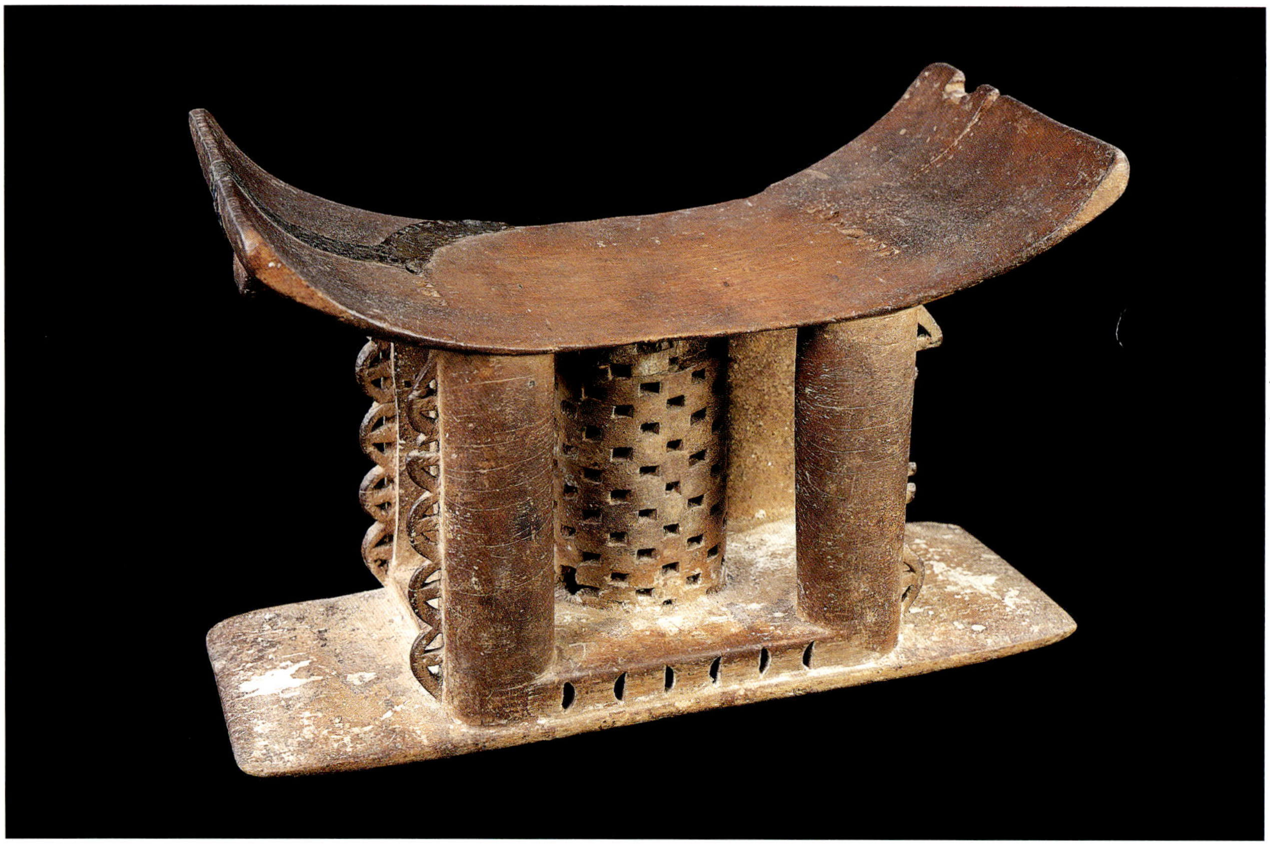

100

99

## Laundry stool

Senufo peoples, Côte d'Ivoire, wood, w: 21 inches
LaVerne Shone Collection

*This sturdy stool, carved from a single block of wood, is often called a laundry stool. Senufo women used it as a scrubbing surface when washing clothes in the river.*

100

## Stool

Asante peoples, Ghana, wood, metal, h: 10 1/2 inches
Mr. and Mrs. Irvin G. Bieser, Jr. Collection

*Asante stools have a utilitarian and spiritual function. The stool is believed to contain the spirit or life force of the owner and is kept throughout the individuals life. The central hollow pillar held protective amulets.*

101

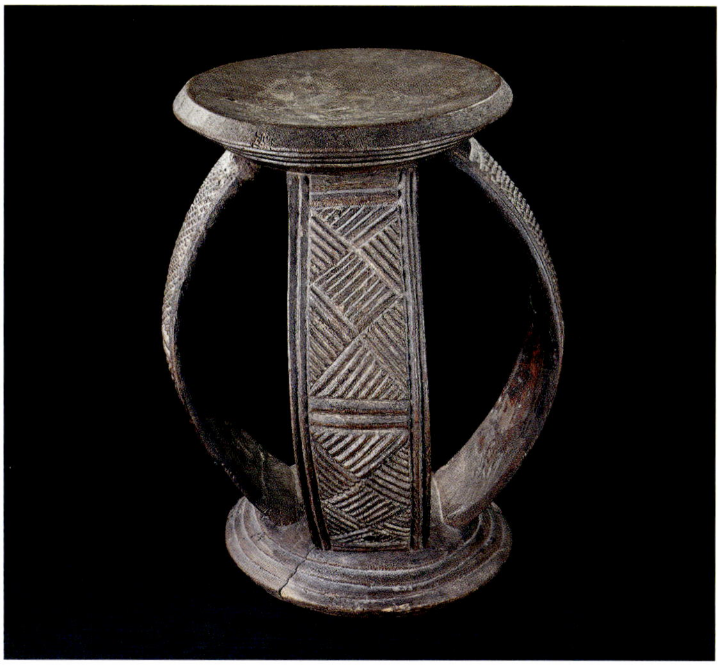

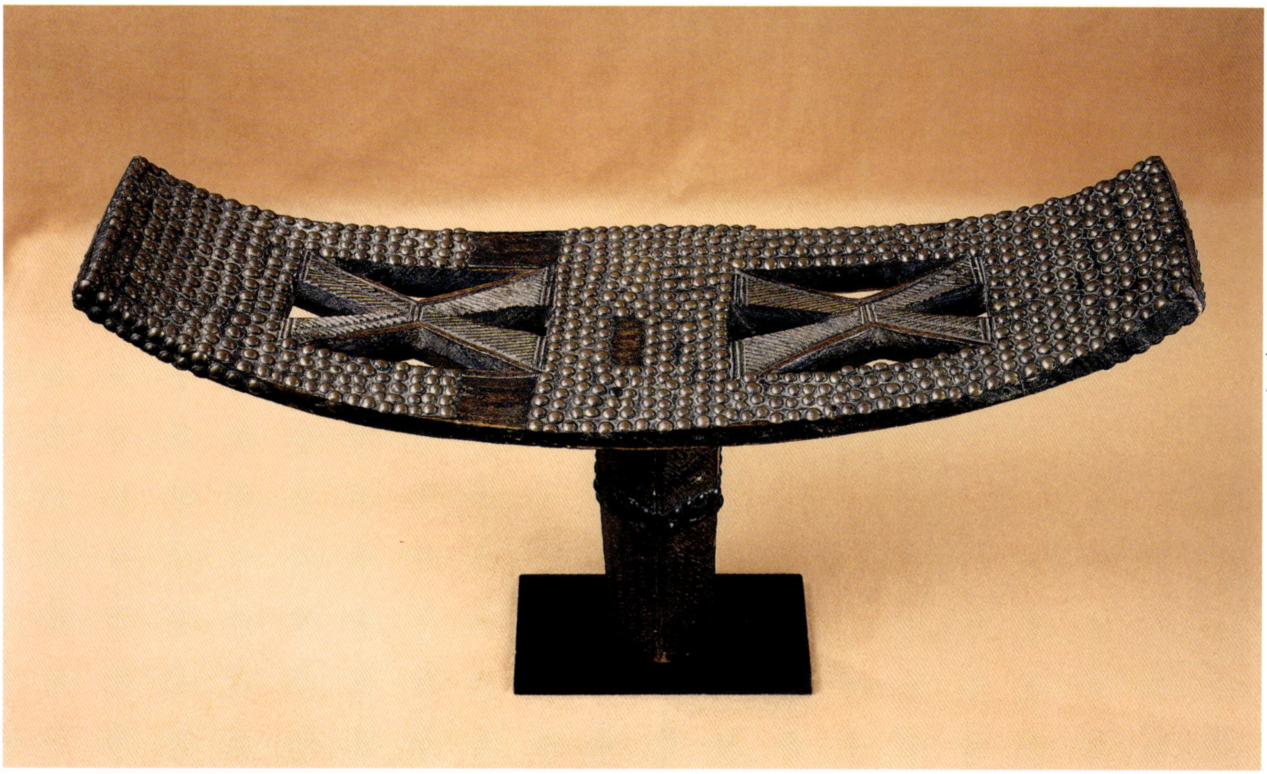

102

101

## Stool

Luba peoples, Democratic Republic of the Congo
wood, h: 16 1/2 inches
LaVerne Shone Collection

*Non-figurative Luba stools, although less well known than the caryatid royal stools, may well echo a more ancient form. The deeply carved supports represent paths leading to the seat, symbolic of the center of political and sacred power.*

102

## Tip stool

Jonga peoples, Democratic Republic of the Congo
wood, brass tacks, w: 25 inches
Dianne Komminsk Collection

*Decorated with engraved motifs and brass tacks, this object can be sat upon as a stool or used as a back rest. It served as an emblem of rank for dignitaries in a wide area in central Democratic Republic of the Congo including the Jonga and Kuba.*

103

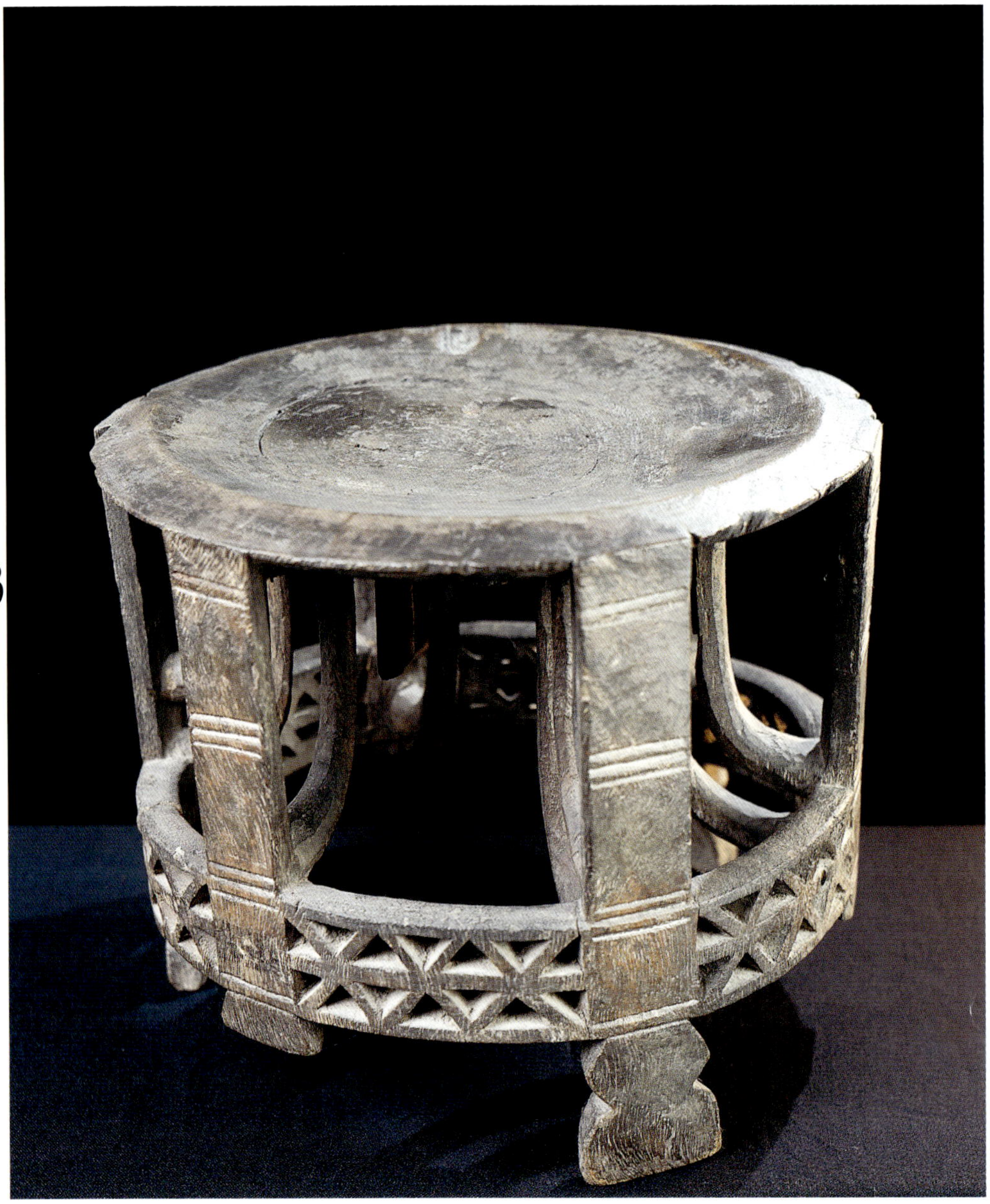

103

## Stool

Kwere or Zaramo peoples, Tanzania, wood, d. 18 1/2 inches
LaVerne Shone Collection

*Among the Kwere and Zaramo, men use circular stool types such as this; women's stools have woven fiber seats. This example displays chip-carving in a style called Swahili and shows coastal Arabic influence.*

104

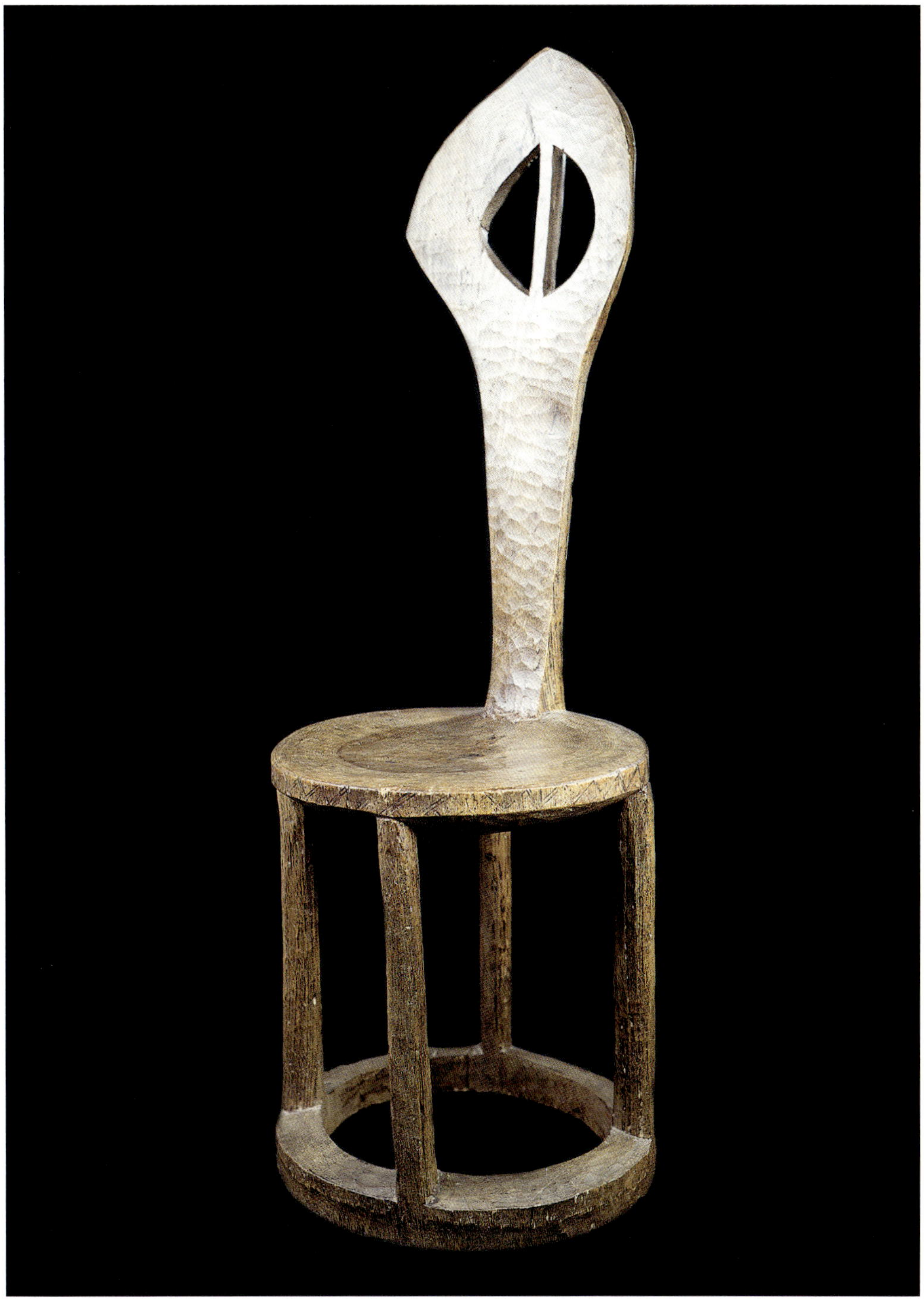

104

## Chair

Somali peoples, Ethiopia, wood, h: 49 inches
LaVerne Shone Collection

*Because they were disseminated widely through the region along early caravan trade routes, high-backed stools are found throughout eastern Africa.*

105

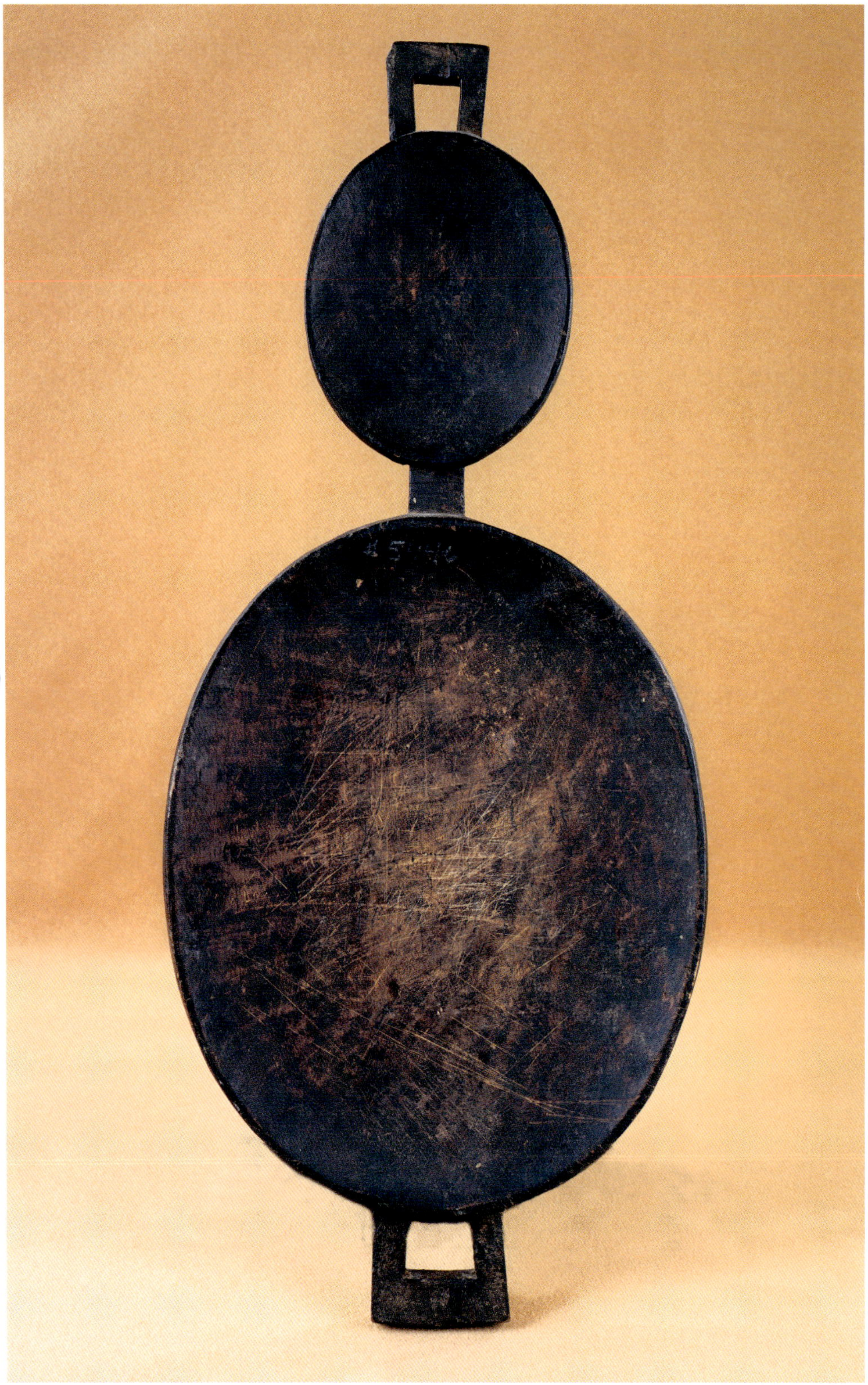

105

## Meat tray

Zulu peoples, South Africa, wood, h: 25 inches
Dianne Komminsk Collection

*In Zulu culture, meat trays used by men vary in size. Some are large enough for communal purposes. On special occasions elder men serve the roasted meats of ritually slaughtered animals, specifically beef and goat.*

106

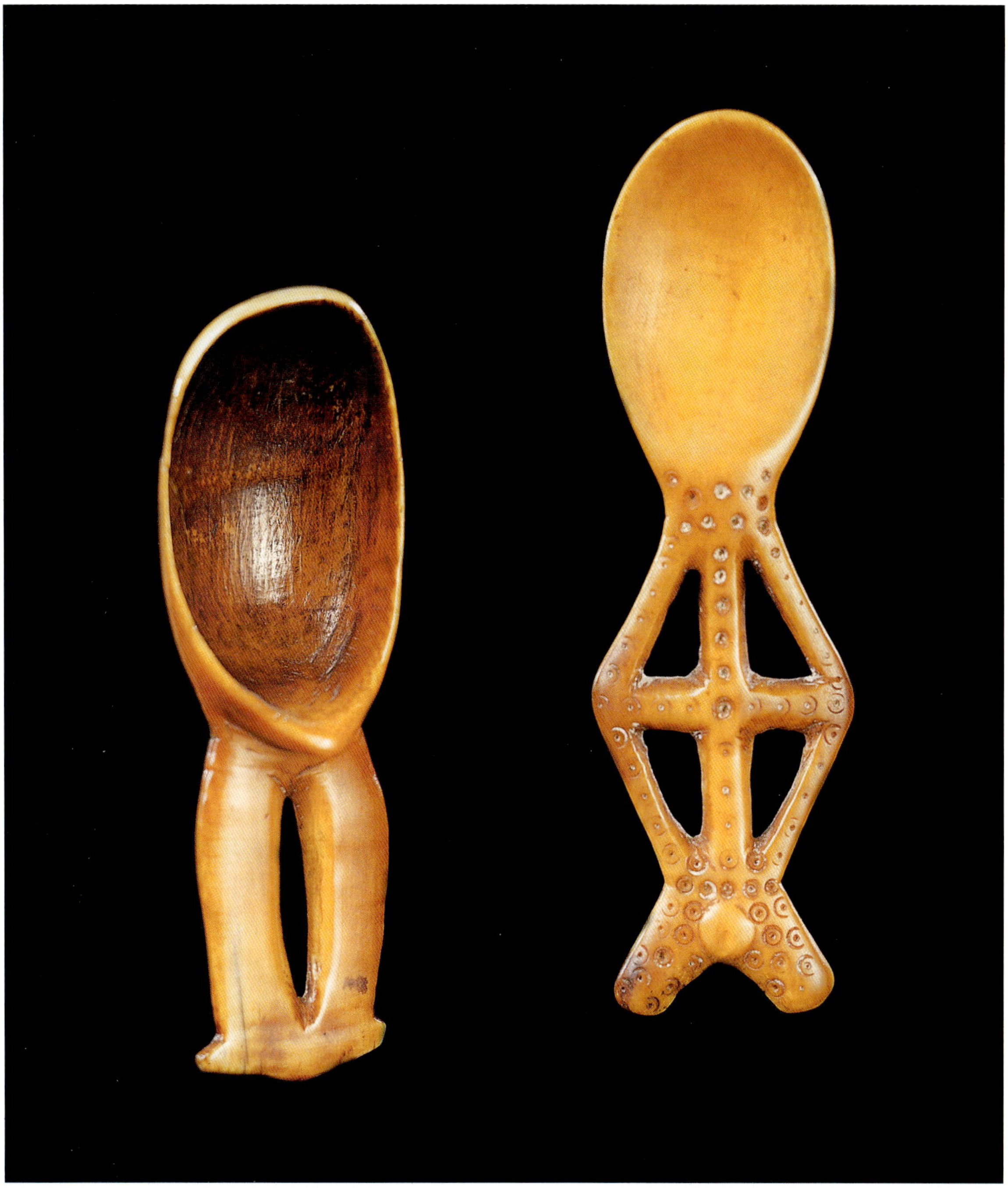

106

## Two Spoons

Boa and Lega or neighboring peoples, Democratic Republic of the Congo, ivory, h: 6 inches
Arthur Shone Collection

*Spoons in ivory or bone are used by a number of peoples in central Africa. Among the Lega, Bwami members who have reached the highest grade (kindi) hold the spoons while dancing, when feeding the masks or elders and during poison ordeals.*

107

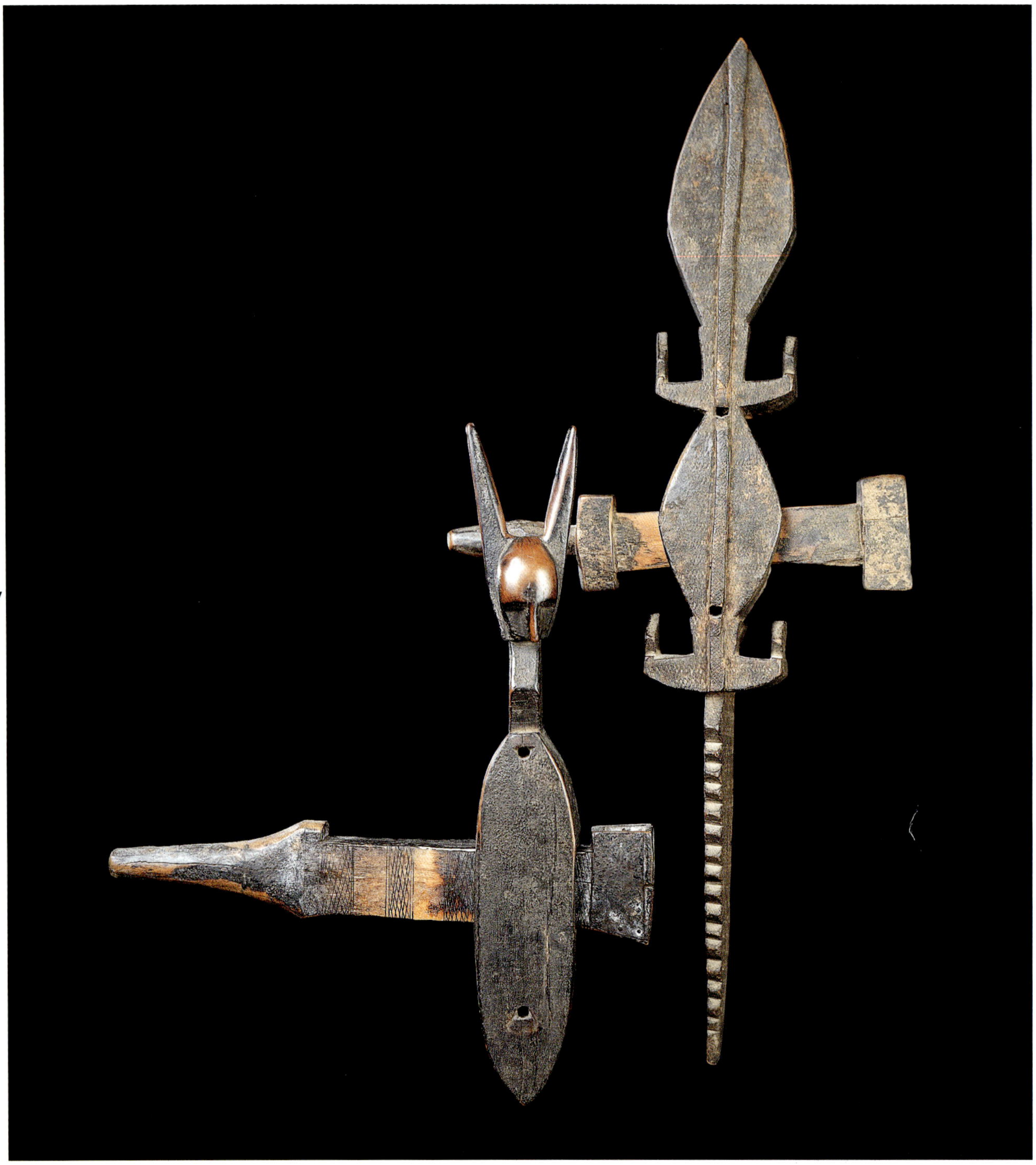

107

## Door lock

Bamana peoples, Mali, wood, metal
Dianne Komminsk Collection

## Door lock

Bamana peoples, Mali, wood, metal, h: 31 inches
Arthur Shone Collection

*Functional door locks of this type are derived from north African prototypes and are used by a number of ethnic groups south of the Sahara. They often are embellished with abstract, figurative or animal designs. The crocodile form of the lock on the right symbolizes power and authority in Bamana culture.*

# CERAMICS

The potter's wheel has existed in north Africa since ancient Egyptian times. However, it did not appear south of the Sahara until the mid-20th century. Hand-built pottery continues to be made using a variety of techniques. Women artists dominate the medium, producing vessels for cooking, storage, shrines and sale in local markets.

108
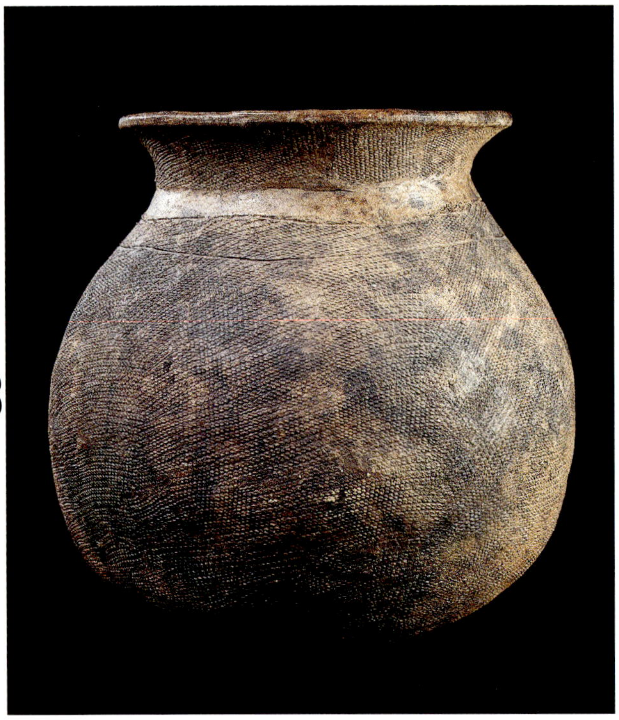

109
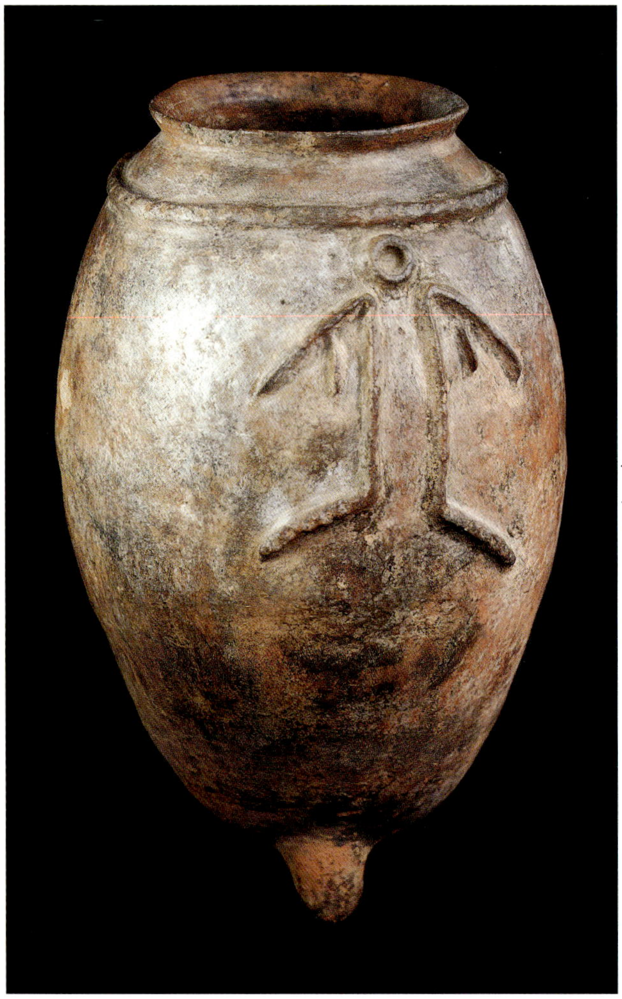

110
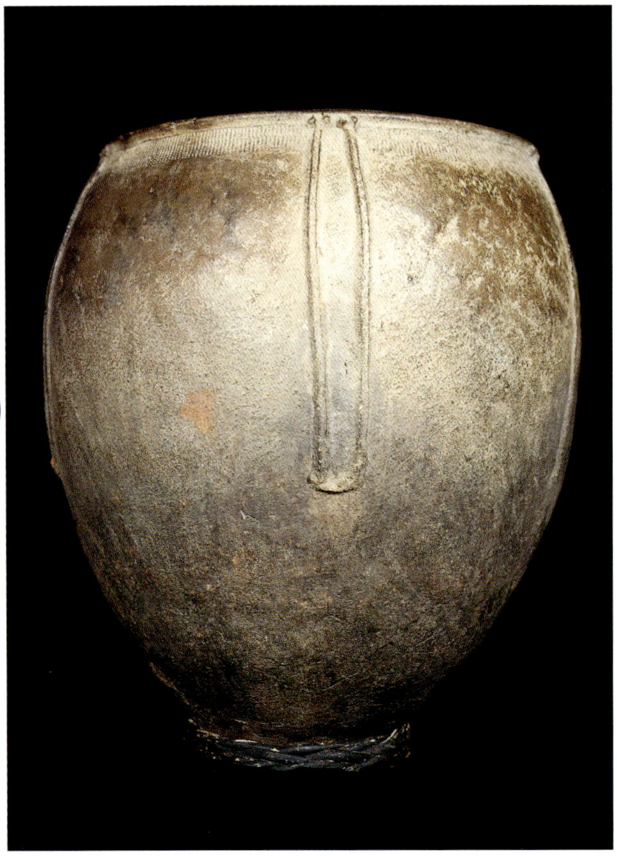

108

## Vessel

Kenya, clay, h: 12 inches
Willis Bing and Audrey Davis Collection

*The form of this vessel is found throughout much of the continent and has been reported as early as Neolithic times.*

109

## Vessel

Kurumba peoples, Burkina Faso
clay, h: 25 1/2 inches
Dianne Komminsk Collection

*The meaning of the abstract figure on this vessel is unknown.*

110

## Vessel

Senufo peoples, Côte d'Ivoire
clay, h: 30 inches
Dianne Komminsk Collection

*Large vessels are for storing water, beer or occasionally, dry foods and even clothing.*

111

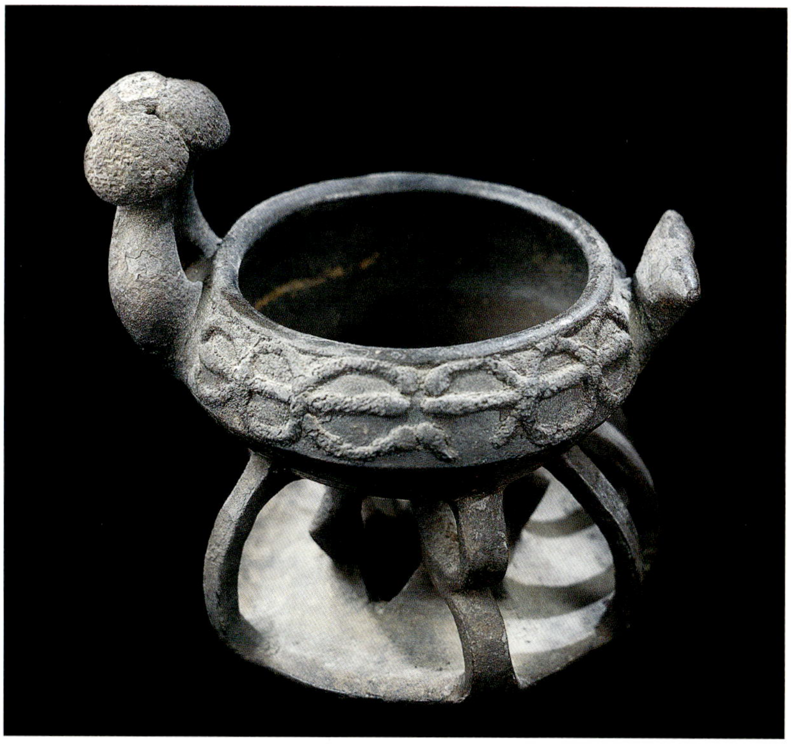

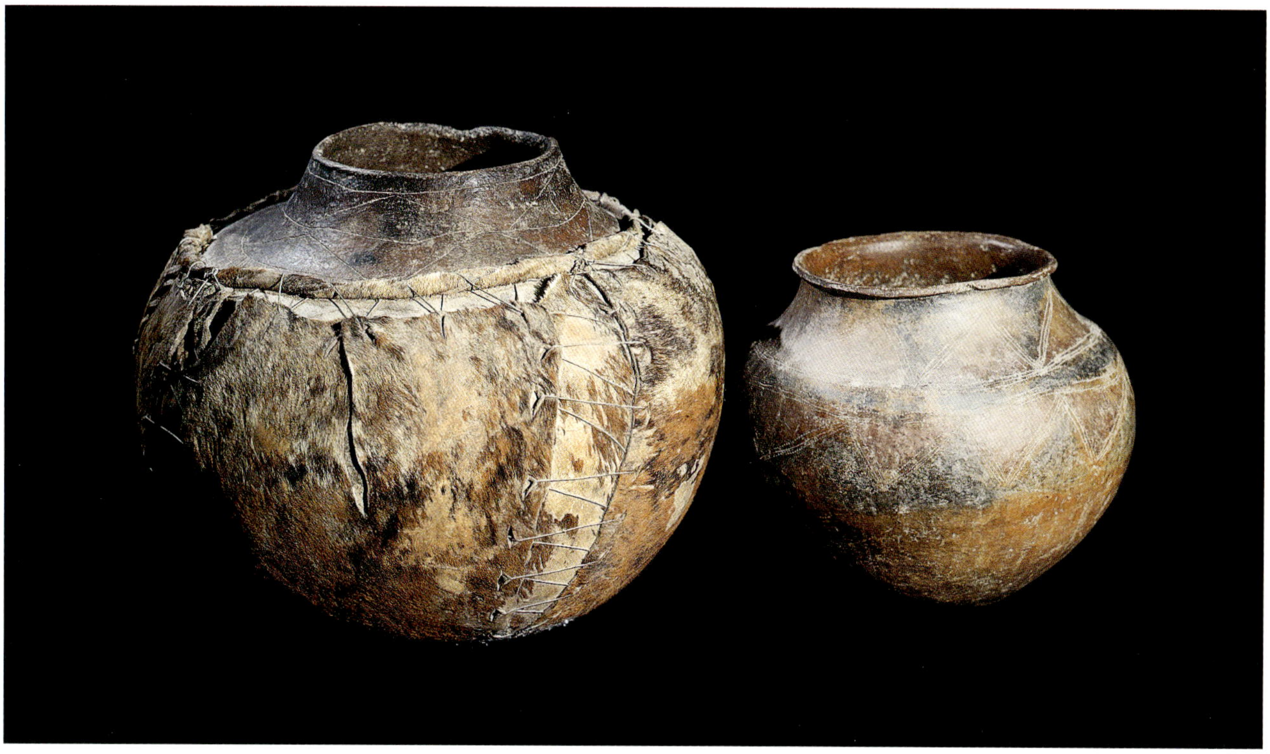

112

111

## Oil pot

Western Grassfields, Cameroon
clay, h: 8 inches
Arthur Shone Collection

*Small containers for condiments accompany larger vessels for serving food.*

112

## Two vessels

Thonga peoples, South Africa
clay, hide, w: 22 inches
Arthur Shone Collection

*The larger, hide-covered vessel most probably was for brewing beer; the smaller served as a water pot. Both are fine examples of utilitarian ware produced over most of the continent by women.*

# BIBLIOGRAPHY


Abiodun, Rowland; Drewal, Henry John and Pemberton, John. ***Yoruba Art and Aesthetics.*** Zurich: The Center for African Art and the Rietberg Museum, 1991.

Anquetil, Jacque (editor). ***L'artisanat creator au Mali.*** Paris: agence de cooperation culturelle technique, 1977.

Barbour, Jane and Simmonds, Doig (editors). ***Adire Cloth in Nigeria.*** Ibadan: Institute of African Studies, University of Ibadan, Nigeria, 1971.

Bastin, M.L. ***Un masque en cuivre martelé des Kongo du Nord-Est de l'Angola.*** African-Tervuren, VII(2): 29-40. 1961.

---. ***Beauté Fatale. Armes D' Afrique Centrale.*** Brussels: Credit Communal, 1992.

Biebuyck, Daniel. ***Lega Culture, Art, Initiation and Moral Philosophy Among a Central African People.*** Los Angeles: University of California Press, 1973.

---. ***The Arts of Zaire.*** Vol. I South Western Zaire; Vol. II Eastern Zaire. Los Angeles: University of California Press, 1985, 1986.

Boone, Sylvia Ardyn. ***Radiance From the Waters: Ideals Feminine Beauty in Mende Art.*** New Haven: Yale University Press, 1986.

Bravmann, Rene. ***African Islam.*** Washington D.C.: Smithsonian Institution Press, 1992.

Brincard, Marie Therese (editor). ***Sounding Forms: African Musical Instruments.*** New York: American Federation of Arts, 1989.

Cornet, Joseph. ***L'art royal Kuba.*** Milan: Sipiel, 1982.

De Mott, Barbara. ***Dogon Masks: A Structural Study of Form and Meaning.*** Ann Arbor: University of Michigan, University Press, 1982.

Drewal, Henry John and Mason, John. ***Beads, Body and Soul: Art and Light in the Yoruba Universe.*** Los Angeles: UCLA Fowler Museum of Cultural History, 1998.

Drewal, Henry John; Pemberton, John and Abiodun, Rowland. ***Yoruba: Nine Centuries of African Art and Thought.*** New York: Harry N. Abrams Inc., 1989.

Ezra, Kate. ***Art of the Dogon: Selections from the Lester Wunderman Collection.*** New York: Harry N. Abrams, Inc., 1988.

Felix, Marc Leo. ***100 Peoples of Zaire and Their Sculpture: The Handbook.*** Brussels: Zaire Basin Art History Foundation, 1987.

Gebauer, Paul. ***Art of Cameroon.*** Portland, Oregon: Portland Art Museum, 1979.

Griaule, Marcel. ***Masques Dogon.*** Paris: Institute d'Ethnologie, 1963.

Hersak, Dunja. ***Songye Masks and Figure Sculpture.*** London: Ethnographica, 1986.

Herreman, Frank and Petridis, Constantijn (editors). ***Face of the Spirits: Masks from the Zaire Basin.*** Antwerp: 1993.

Johannesburg Art Gallery. ***Art and Ambiguity: Perspectives on the Brenthurst Collection of Southern Africa.*** Johannesburg: Johannesburg Art Gallery, 1991.

Kabandika, Kalubudi-a-Lemba. ***Le bugaleengi ou rite d'accomplissement: sa morphologie et sa symbolique chez les Mbaganyi.*** Cahiers de religions africaines, XIX (37): 53-81, 1985.

Maurer, Evan and Batulukisi, Niangi. ***Spirits Embodied: Art of the Congo. Selections from the Helmut F. Stern Collection.*** Minneapolis: The Minneapolis Institute of Arts, 1999.

Meurant, Georges. ***Shoowa Design: African Textiles from the Kingdom of Kuba.*** New York: Thames and Hudson, 1986.

Neyt, Francois. *La Grande Statuaire Hemba du Zaire.* Louvain-la Neuve: Université Catholique de Louvain, Institut Superieur d'Archeologie et d'Histoire de l'Art, 1977.

---, *Traditional Arts and History of Zaire.* Brussels: Société d'Arts Primitifs, 1981.

---. *Luba: Aux sources du Zaire.* Paris: Musée Dapper, 1994.

Northern, Tamara. *The Art of Cameroon.* Washington, D.C.: Smithsonian Institution Traveling Exhibition Service, 1984.

Perani, Judith and Wolff, Norma. *Cloth, Dress and Art Patronage in Africa.* New York: Berg, 1999.

Phillips, Tom (editor). *Africa: The Art of a Continent.* New York: Prestel Publishing, 1995.

Plaschke, Dieter and Zirngibl, Manfred. *African Shields: Graphic Art of the Black Continent.* Munich: Panterra Verlag, 1992.

Ratzel, Friedrich. *Volkerkunde.* Volumes I and II. Leipzig and Vienna: Bibiographifches Intituit, 1894.

Roberts, Allen F. (editor). *Staffs of Life: Rods, Staffs, Scepters and Wands from the Coudron Collection of African Art.* Iowa City: University of Iowa, 1994.

Roberts, Mary Nooter and Allen F. Roberts. *Memory: Luba Art and The Making of History.* New York: The Museum for African Art, Munich: Prestel, 1996.

Ross, Doran (editor). *Elephant. The Animal and Its Ivory in African Culture.* Fowler Museum of Cultural History, Los Angeles: University of California, 1992.

Schaedler, Karl-Ferdinand. *Weaving in Africa South of the Sahara.* Munich: Panterra Verlag, 1987.

---. *Earth and Ore: 2,500 Years of African Art in Terra Cotta and Metal.* Munich: Panterra, Verlag, 1997.

Schwab, George (edited with additional material by George W. Harley). *Tribes of the Liberian Hinterland.* Papers of the Peabody Museum of American Archaeology and Ethnology. Cambridge: Harvard University, 1947.

Sieber, Roy. *African Furniture and Household Objects.* Bloomington: Indiana University Press, 1980.

---. *African Textiles and Decorative Arts.* New York: Museum of Modern Art, 1972.

Sieber, Roy and Herreman, Frank. *Hair in African Art and Culture.* New York: Prestel, 2000.

Sieber, Roy and Walker, Roslyn. *African Art in the Cycle of Life.* Washington, D.C.: National Museum of African Art, 1988.

Strother, Zoe. *Inventing Masks: Agency and History in the Art of the Central Pende.* Chicago and London: The University of Chicago Press, 1998.

Thompson, Robert Farris. *Black Gods and Kings: Yoruba Art at UCLA.* Los Angeles: University of California, 1971.

---. *Paintings from a Single Heart, Preliminary Remarks on Bark-Cloth Designs of the Mbute Women of Haut-Zaire.* Munich: Fred and Jens Jahn, 1983.

Vogel, Susan M. *Baule: African Art Western Eyes.* Boston: Yale University Press, 1997.


TWO RECENT GENERAL TEXTS
ARE RECOMMENDED


Perani, Judith and Smith, Fred T. *The Visual Arts of Africa: Gender, Power and Life Cycle Rituals.* New Jersey: Prentice Hall, 1998.

Visona, Monica Blackmun (editor); Poyner, Robin; Harris, Michael D.; Abiodun, Rowland and Blier, Susan Preston. *A History of Art in Africa.* New York: Abrams, 2000.